THE UPPER HOUSE

THE UPPER HOUSE

A JOURNEY BEHIND THE
CLOSED DOORS OF THE U.S. SENATE

TERENCE SAMUEL

palgrave
macmillan

For Jodi

First published in 2010 by PALGRAVE MACMILLAN® in the U.S.—a division of
St. Martin's Press LLC, 175 Fifth Avenue, New York, NY 10010.

Where this book is distributed in the UK, Europe, and the rest of the world, this is
by Palgrave Macmillan, a division of Macmillan Publishers Limited, registered in
England, company number 785998, of Houndmills, Basingstoke, Hampshire RG21
6XS.

Palgrave Macmillan is the global academic imprint of the above companies and has
companies and representatives throughout the world.

Palgrave® and Macmillan® are registered trademarks in the United States, the
United Kingdom, Europe, and other countries.

ISBN: 978-0-230-62361-3

Library of Congress Cataloging-in-Publication Data
Samuel, Terence.
     The upper house : a journey behind the closed doors of the U.S. Senate / Terence
Samuel.
        p. cm.
     ISBN 978-0-230-62361-3 (hardback)
     1. United States. Congress. Senate.   2. Legislators—United States.
3. Politicians—United States.   I. Title.
JK1170.S36   2010
328.73'071—dc22

                                                                                2010012675

A catalogue record of the book is available from the British Library.

Design by Letra Libre

First edition: June 2010

10 9 8 7 6 5 4 3 2 1

Printed in the United States of America.

CONTENTS

AUTHOR'S NOTE

It is not always easy to determine exactly when any political era begins or ends but we clearly live in an age that began to take shape with the presidential election of 2000. It's another thing still when you personally witness the falling away of the old and the emergence of the new, as I did in 2000 when I covered the election for *U.S. News and World Report*. The 2000 general election season released a certain toxicity into the American political bloodstream, the effects of which continue to linger all these many years later.

George W. Bush emerged from the chaos as the forty-third president of the United States, but that year the intense civic—if not always civil—conversation that every presidential election represents turned into the ugliest kind of bar fight; the pathology of that moment would ripple through American politics for years to come. The thirty-six days before the Supreme Court decided the election, with its ruling in *Bush v. Gore*, stand as a monument to the dysfunction of the time. The ruling itself will likely take a permanent place alongside some of the Court's other great disgraces—Dred Scott, Plessy, Korematsu, the Slaughterhouse cases. The Court's decision made Bush president in what turned out to be a critical time for the country.

On the night that Bush did or did not get elected, depending on your viewpoint, Tom Daschle, the diminutive South Dakotan who was leader of the Democrats in the Senate, watched the election returns in a room at the Hotel George, a half-mile from the U.S. Capitol Building. Democrats were in the minority in the Senate and still feeling the sting of the 1994 Republican

Revolution, in which the country swung radically to the right and the Democrats lost control of the Congress. In that election, Republicans picked up eight seats in the Senate for a total fifty-six. In the House of Representatives, they grabbed fifty-four seats formerly held by Democrats. The 1994 drubbing seemed less a rebuke of the Democratic Party than the wholesale dismissal of all the important ideas and ideology of an era. The New Deal was dead, the Great Society was dead, the welfare state that grew from the legislation of the 1930s through the 1960s was showered with disgrace.

At the time, Democrats did not know what had happened to them, and even on election night in 2000, six years later, as Daschle and his lieutenants sat watching the returns, they still did not understand what the American people wanted. Conservatism was not just ascendant, it had triumphed. In the coming years, political writers would detail how Republicans had put a permanent lock on control of the government, as Tom Hamburger and Peter Wallsten did in *One Party Country: The Republican Plan for Dominance in the Twenty-first Century.*

In the Senate results of 2000, however, another story was being written. The seeds of a more fractious American future were being sowed, and it would be in the Senate that the very difficult issues of the next decade would get their most important hearing. The country would be broken and divided, and the Senate would reflect that almost too perfectly. Reflecting later on that period, Daschle wrote: "We have come to a point in our nation's history where—as individuals and as a society—the spaces that lie between hope and despair, between triumph and disaster, between vision and blindness or between candor and deceit have never been so minuscule."[1]

Even though Democrats were not confident enough to hope for control of the Senate, by the end of the night they had won five Republican seats and lost one of their own, for a net gain of four. It would be days before there was any public certainty about the outcome of the race in Washington State, where Maria Cantwell would survive a tough battle against the incumbent Republican Slade Gorton, but Daschle knew from the numbers that night that Cantwell was the likely winner.

So at the end of a very long November evening, Daschle left the Hotel George and headed to his home in northwest Washington. It was past three in the morning, and before he hopped into his SUV, he looked at his aides in bewilderment: "Fifty-fifty," he said, shaking his head. On the empty sidewalk, with the dark Capitol dome in the background, Daschle's astonishment was at the political serendipity of the moment, but what he was confronting was more evidence of a system badly broken and a people evenly divided—both in the country and in the Senate.

It was that election of 2000 that started me thinking about the odd workings of what some senators like to call the "world's greatest deliberative body." In the next few weeks, while the country was obsessed with the postelection shenanigans in Florida, Daschle and his Republican counterpart, Trent Lott of Mississippi, set about trying to figure out a framework for making the Senate work under these difficult circumstances. In a time of upheaval in the Senate, with one party losing its majority, I watched two men, as personally and politically different as can be, devise a way to get an institution they both loved to work, at least for a while.

"With the start of the 107th Congress, we were facing something the Senate had never faced in modern times, a situation in which neither party had the upper hand," Daschle remembered. "Suddenly—wonderfully for us and nightmarishly for the Republicans—the phrase *power sharing* had entered our lexicon."[2]

The Senate, from its beginnings, was built on the idea of compromise, and it has been compromise, or the willingness to compromise, that has preserved its relevance in the form laid down in the Constitution for the past two centuries. Lott, who would be the majority leader—George W. Bush was in the White House, and Vice President Dick Cheney as the president of the Senate provided the tie-breaking vote that gave the GOP the operating majority—suddenly found himself forced to put more Democrats on committees than he wanted to: Daschle got the even split on committee memberships that he wanted, but Republicans continued to chair those committees.

The first thing Trent Lott had to do, once he got down to the business of running the Senate as majority leader, was concede that his power was diminished. He was forced to bring to the floor a bill that he had avoided for a long time—a campaign finance proposal known as McCain-Feingold. Lott had come to despise the antics of Arizona Republican senator John McCain, believed by many to be the Senate's consummate grandstander and self-promoter. McCain called himself a maverick and seemed to frequently challenge his party in order to preserve that reputation. As the first order of business in 2001, Lott allowed the McCain-sponsored bill on campaign finance reform to come to the floor and to be debated without restrictions for days on end, even though Republicans were stridently opposed to it. Sitting in his office looking over the National Mall, Lott told me: "This is not the way I usually like to see the Senate operate, but it was done by design. Sometimes you design chaos. Sometimes you design order."[3]

This was to be a time of chaos. And none of it was intentional. The Senate had been evenly divided before—in the Great Senate Deadlock of 1881. Although the deadlock lasted eleven weeks, it took place before there was talk radio and twenty-four-hour cable news to poison the atmosphere. It had also lacked the drama of having the Democratic vice president, who had just lost an election in the Supreme Court, act as the tie-breaking vote for the first seventeen days of the session. Between January 2 and January 20, 2001, when George Bush and Dick Cheney took their oaths of office, the president of the Senate was Al Gore, who had just lost the bitter recent election to them, and so for seventeen days Democrats had control of the Senate by virtue of Gore's tie-breaking vote. Alas, they chose to do nothing dramatic or memorable with it.

The great political mood swings that would define the first decade of the new millennium were quickly evident in the Senate. The fifty-fifty split lasted only five months, and it would take a while for the Republican Party and its president to face repudiation equal to the Democratic setback of 1994. This change began quietly in the springtime of the first year of the George W. Bush presidency—in the United States Senate.

In the spring of 2001, Washington was a raw place—and it would set the tone of the venomous politics of the decade. We were not that far removed from the impeachment and acquittal of Bill Clinton, and one sure sign that the battles would be reignited rather than extinguished was that among the new class of Democratic senators in the new Congress was the former first lady, Hillary Clinton, who was making her first move toward running for president.

The new Republican president, despite the closeness of his win, embarked on an ambitious tax-cutting effort—$1.35 trillion over eleven years. The Senate approved a budget that aimed to hold the increase in government spending to 4 percent. The Republican-led Senate cut funds for the hiring of new schoolteachers, at a time when the federal budget surplus was projected to run upward of $5.6 trillion over the next decade.

There was a growing sense that President Bush was playing ideological politics and bullying anyone who did not agree with him. On the night of May 23, 2001, in a flare-up of bipartisanship, Lott and Daschle served as joint hosts for "The Leader's Lecture," a relatively new and quiet Capitol Hill event in which former distinguished members of Congress are invited to speak. It was part nostalgic reminiscence, part roast.

The evening began with a cocktail reception in Lott's office, a sprawling, rambling warren of rooms on the West Front of the Capitol. The hors d'oeuvres were served on heavy china, and the cocktail glasses sat on embossed coasters that announced "Majority Leader."

The speaker that evening was former president Gerald R. Ford, who, having spent most of his political career in the House of Representatives, was duty-bound to poke fun at the Upper House, for its pomp and pretensions. As vice president for seven months in late 1973 and 1974 under Richard M. Nixon, until Nixon resigned in disgrace over the Watergate scandal, Ford had served as president of the Senate. In his lecture, Ford quoted one of his presidential predecessors, Calvin Coolidge. Said Ford:

> I must confess that a lengthy career in the House had not fully prepared me for the byways of the world's greatest deliberative body. In preparing for this lecture, I came across something from another Vice President, Calvin Coolidge. "At first I intended to become a student of the Senate rules," wrote Coolidge, "but I soon found that the Senate had but one fixed rule, which was to the effect that the Senate would do anything it wanted to do whenever it wanted to do it.
>
> "When I had learned that, I did not waste [any more] time . . . ," Coolidge went on, "because they were so seldom applied."

But it was Ford's take of the current situation in Washington that interested me. His lecture, delivered in the august Old Senate Chamber, seemed to be a warning to everyone in Washington, but particularly the new president George W. Bush, that their brand of winner-take-all politics was hurting their cause and the country. Ford went on:

> A few mistake the clash of ideas for a holy war. I never claimed to be a political philosopher. I never claimed to be anything more than a plain-spoken Midwesterner, conservative on money and liberal on human rights. While I never regarded government as an enemy, I was perfectly happy to have politicians of both parties stay out of the people's wallets, out of their classrooms, out of their boardrooms, and out of their bedrooms.
>
> For me, tolerance is more than a virtue, it is the crowning glory of a society whose greatest strength lies in its diversity. I am hardly alone in this. At heart, most Americans are pragmatists. We want to make things work, we want to be self-reliant, but not at the expense of the community. We value authenticity as much as ideology, especially in this age when so much of what passes for public life consists of little more than candidates

without ideas hiring consultants without convictions to stage campaigns
without content.[4]

The next day, May 24, 2001, Senator James Jeffords of Vermont resigned
from the Republican Party, declared himself an independent, and started
voting with the Democrats. Jeffords had been at odds with the Bush administration over the monumental tax cuts and the spending cuts the administration was pursuing on education. But in the end, he said it was the
ideological bullying that had driven him out of the party.

A mere four months into the new administration, the seeds of its even-
tual collapse were sown. In a political decade that would be defined by terrorism, war, and economic upheaval, the United States prepared for the
onslaught with a divided and broken government that reflected a divided
and fractious populace. In the ensuing years, the American psyche was re-
ordered by the September 11, 2001 attacks; we went to war in Afghanistan
and Iraq, and George W. Bush was reelected. A presidential reelection is a
triumph, but the Bush presidency ended in ignominy, and the unraveling
began in that spring of 2001.

INTRODUCTION

Barack Obama took the oath of office as a United States senator on January 4, 2005, and promptly began running for president. Very quickly,
he began using the peculiar kind of celebrity that comes with being a senator to introduce himself to Washington, to a new generation of political
power brokers, and, more broadly, to the American people. "He was running for president even as he was still getting lost in the Capitol's corri-
dors," the *New York Times* noted.[1] Obama pointedly bypassed the
Democratic Party power structure, in defiance of the norms of behavior for
a junior senator. Obama did not worry about getting better committee as-
signments, and he did not defer to more senior members when trying to di-
agnose his party's problems or in offering prescriptions to fix them. By the
fall of 2006, to the surprise of even the most dedicated admirers of his vast
political gifts, he was admitting publicly that he was thinking about the
White House.

"With an eye on his next goal, Obama treated the Senate as a bridge to
be crossed—a place to learn the conventions of Washington, win powerful
friends and shape what advisers referred to as his 'political brand,'" the *Washington Post* reported. "Despite meager legislative accomplishments, Obama
built a reputation among many Democrats as a hard worker, a reformer, an
eager learner, a smart politician."[2]

He came to see the Senate not as a place to do things, but as a place to
be someone.

Four years, two weeks, and a day after that Senate oath, Obama was standing on the West Front of the Capitol being sworn in as president. The brevity of his tenure in the Senate speaks to his exquisite grasp of how the nation's political landscape and its institutions had changed over time. More precisely, his triumph flowed from a deft understanding of the incongruous role the Senate plays in our politics, our governance, and our national mythology. Maybe more than any American politician in the last hundred years, Obama saw the Senate for what it had become: not so much the great anchor of prudent self-government that the framers intended it to be, but a platform, a vehicle, a point of leverage, and, for him, a launch pad to greater glory.

Still, Obama was not the first senator to have imagined the Senate in this way. It is an old joke in Washington that more than half the senators see a future president when they look in the mirror each morning. And since 1960, the last time a sitting senator won the presidency, fifty-two others have tried. Indeed, one of the ways the Senate is least representative of the nation is how thickly it is populated with aspiring presidents; almost always, about 10 percent of the hundred incumbent senators have already run for president. The problem, of course, is that a presidential run from the Senate hardly ever succeeds. History and habit weigh heavily against it. Only twice before Obama—Warren Harding in 1921 and John Kennedy in 1961—have sitting senators become president. And here's why, in the words of Tom Daschle, who came within minutes of announcing a presidential bid in 2004, before deciding against it: "Two things develop the more time you spend here: One is a mind-set that we did it this way before, we should do it this way again, and I think that's a real burden. More importantly— and Hillary and McCain are the perfect examples of this—the longer you are here, you take on enemies. And these enemies don't forget."[3] But it is a measure of the kind of ambition that the Senate attracts in the first place that of the forty-four men who have served as president, sixteen of them had previously served in the Senate, not to mention the many others who kept trying—Henry Clay ran for president four times and lost each time.

△

The Senate remains one of the grandest political stages anywhere in the world, a show ring where the most ambitious and the most able go to display their talents or sharpen their skills, especially if they are eyeing a move to 1600 Pennsylvania Avenue. The high failure rate has on occasion produced great statesmen, politicians who use the Senate for what it was meant to be used—to protect us from ourselves. "Slow" was always the idea in the Senate as James Madison envisioned it. He wanted a check on "the impulse of sudden and violent passions, and to be seduced by factious leaders into intemperate and pernicious resolutions."[4]

In a very basic way, the real value of the United States Senate is its ability to produce failure and frustration in the guise of good and prudent government. It is a place where ambition goes to die, but it dies with grand ceremony, arcane rules, and high prestige, and it remains a venue of real power if a senator knows how to use it. The result is that it continues to attract singular characters of towering intellect, surpassing ambition, and compelling personal and political biographies—men like Henry Clay, who essentially started the Civil War, and Arthur H. Vandenberg, who rewrote American foreign policy after World War II; or others like Everett Dirksen, a conservative (by the standards of the day) Republican who helped write and pass the landmark civil rights legislation in the 1960s, while supporting the disaster that was the Vietnam war.

Pennsylvania senator Arlen Specter—who completely altered the political calculus in Washington in 2009 when he switched parties, abandoning the GOP for the Democrats—is one recent example of a compelling personal story. Specter, the son of a junkyard owner from Russell, Kansas, was single-handedly responsible for more than doubling the funding for cancer and other research to the National Institutes of Health while he chaired the Appropriations Subcommittee on Health. And in his time in the Senate, he has survived open-heart surgery, a brain tumor, and Hodgkin's disease. This, to me, is a classic example of senatorial ambition and determination.

The Senate remains one of the few places on earth where one person can, literally, make a difference: Daniel Webster on preserving the Union; Lyndon Johnson on voting rights; Edward M. Kennedy on lowering the voting age; and lesser-known contemporaries such as Jon Tester, who made his contribution by increasing the mileage reimbursement for veterans, and Amy Klobuchar, who effected a ban on the importation of lead-based toys from China.

And the composition of the Senate—dependent as it is on multimillion-dollar campaigns—still manages, particularly with its newest members, to tell us something about what the country is thinking collectively at the time of any specific election. "There are some thematic similarities running through each new class that tells you something about where the country was at the time," said Senator Jim Webb of Virginia, a freshman in the 2006 class. "There is an unspoken commonality of viewpoint."[5] In this regard, the Senate lives up to what Madison hoped for in Federalist no. 63, when he mused that the Senate would provide a "due sense of national character."[6]

This sense of national character is revealed in the composition of the body. And despite the arcane, sometimes pointless political machinations that go on in the Senate, the important debates that take place in our country genuinely get their fullest hearing in this chamber. From day to day it may look like failure, because this debate often does not lead to immediate action, but the Senate as an institution makes a virtue of legislative inertia. This is the Senate's constitutional role—a counterbalance to the potentially impulsive character of the House and the naturally autocratic tendencies of the executive.

Every senator comes to the Senate with high expectations and grand ambitions. And more often than not, these hopes get ground down by the burden of the democratic process. To succeed, the Senate forces the senator to live up to a high institutional standard—a unique combination of infinite patience, strategic compromise, and political and physical longevity. After a year in the Senate, Jim Webb, the Virginia Democrat, concluded that very few people get to, or remain in, the Senate by accident. "At bottom these are people who have taken risks, exposed themselves to the public eye, and paid a certain price to reach the Senate floor. And one should never underestimate either their determination on matters that are important to them, or their mental toughness."[7]

The Upper House is a story of the people, the institution, and the country as they are revealed in the day-to-day workings of the U.S. Senate. Periods of national crisis have manifested themselves in the results of recent senatorial elections. In 1958, Democrats netted thirteen new seats that laid the groundwork for John F. Kennedy's New Frontier and Lyndon B. Johnson's Great Society programs of the 1960s. Domestically, the country was in the grip of what came to be known as the Eisenhower Recession. Unemployment was skyrocketing, and the administration, through its support of right-to-work laws, seemed to be taking the side of business against the workers. On the international front, the intensifying Cold War left Americans feeling threatened by Moscow's ambitions. On October 4, 1957, the Soviet Union sent *Sputnik 1* into orbit around the Earth, beating the United States into space and severely undermining America's confidence in its technological and military superiority.

Out of that national sense of nervousness came a sixty-five to thirty-five Democratic majority, with Democrats, in 1959, picking up both seats in the new state of Alaska and splitting them in the new state of Hawaii. Johnson returned as majority leader, and in that freshman class were future giants of the Senate—Edmund Muskie, Philip Hart, Robert C. Byrd, Eugene McCarthy, and Vance Hartke. Thomas Dodd, father of Senator Christopher Dodd, was part of the Democrat sweep of 1958, which then led to a series of pivotal and defining events that helped make the sixties.

It was the class of 1958 that gave John F. Kennedy, and then Lyndon Johnson, the votes to pass Medicare, the Civil Rights Acts of 1964, the Voting Rights Act of 1965, and the Fair Housing Act of 1968, along with increasing the minimum wage, expanded federal aid to education, and Johnson's War on Poverty. The class of 1958 voted to establish the Peace Corps in 1961 and for the first nuclear test-ban treaty in 1963. In 1970, *Time* noted, "They provided the votes that enabled Lyndon Johnson to say, with less hyperbole than he regularly employed, that the Congress of 1964 'met more national needs . . . than any other session of this century or the last.'"[8]

Intense disagreement over Vietnam would cause Johnson to lose the support of those "liberals" in the class of 1958, and it would set a dour tone in the country and the Senate for the next decade. In the 1970s, the Senate dealt with the Pentagon Papers and the Watergate scandal. President Nixon resigned in 1974, and in 1975, the Church Committee, investigating wrongdoing by the CIA and FBI, found that the agencies had been involved in a widespread and illegal domestic spying operation against antiwar activists and organizations during the Nixon administration. By 1980, at the height of the Iran hostage crisis, Ronald Reagan was invoking, successfully, Vietnam as the reason for American paralysis and diminished stature in the world. On August 18, 1980, in a speech to the Veterans of Foreign Wars Convention in Chicago titled "Restoring a Margin of Safety," Reagan said, "For too long, we have lived with the 'Vietnam Syndrome.' . . . It is time we recognized that ours was, in truth, a noble cause. . . . We dishonor the memory of 50,000 young Americans who died in that cause when we give way to feelings of guilt as if we were doing something shameful. . . . There is a lesson for all of us in Vietnam. If we are forced to fight, we must have the means and the determination to prevail or we will not have what it takes to secure the peace."[9]

Reagan's campaign theme of restored American dignity, or, rather, reversing the "Vietnam Syndrome," won him forty-four states and a crushing electoral college victory of 489 to 49, and gave Republicans twelve new Senate seats, the largest swing since the liberal class of 1958. For the first time in twenty-six years, since 1954, the Senate was back in Republican hands. It was the beginning of the Reagan Revolution, which would last for the next twenty-five years.

The Senate elections of 2006 and 2008 gave Democrats the largest major-ity enjoyed by any party since 1976, and put them in a position to move a bold and ambitious agenda. But the Senate has changed. The original pur-pose of the Senate was for deliberate, dispassionate discussion, very much at odds with the American mythology of today, when bold, decisive action always seems to be the imperative. But American politics at every level has become too contentious for the Senate to live up to those ideals of pru-dence and equanimity. The last decade, rife with "intemperate and perni-cious resolutions," provides a ready example of what happens when the "anchor against popular fluctuations" gives way.[10]

The Senate has had a Gilded Age and a Golden Age, and now we are liv-ing through what might fairly be described as the Stunted Age. Six years after *Bush v. Gore,* the country had changed its mind, and again the news was manifested in the Senate election to the 110th Congress. The Democratic surge that began in 2006 reached its apex with the election of Al Franken in Minnesota in 2008, which gave the Democrats sixty votes in the Senate and the ability to end Republican filibusters. The idea of robust deliberation fu-eled by unfettered debate is part of Senate lore. The original idea was that any senator should be able to talk as long as he or she would like on any sub-ject. It was a way to equalize the power between small states and big ones.

"Unfettered debate, the right to be heard at length, is the means by which we perpetuate the equality of the States," Robert Byrd, the West Vir-ginian who is the longest-serving senator in history, said on the Senate floor during an intense debate about the future of the filibuster. "In fact it was 1917, before any curtailing of debate was attempted, which means that from 1789 to 1917, there were 129 years [when] the Senate rejected any limits to debate. Democracy flourished along with the filibuster."[11]

In 1917, the Senate imposed its first rules allowing two-thirds of sena-tors present to vote an end to the debate. In 1949, this was amended again to two-thirds of sworn senators. And in 1975, the current arrangement of three-fifths of sworn senators, or sixty, was adopted. With obstruction as the central tactical feature of whichever party finds itself in the minority in the Senate, the ability to stop the filibuster with sixty votes has become the new standard of political control for the majority.

One year into the Obama administration, the country's mood changed again. Unfortunately for the president, the death of Senator Edward Kennedy posed an electoral challenge to the Democrats in Massachusetts, and they failed. The Democrats' filibuster-proof majority was over. The glee Republicans exhibited in obtaining a forty-first seat with the election of Scott Brown revealed their increasingly positive view of obstructionism. It became clear that the Senate is today the best place to stop things, rather than to make things happen.

Scott Brown's election in 2010 served the Republicans as Jon Tester's election had aided the Democrats in 2006. Effectually, his vote allowed them to control the parliamentary processes of the Senate. The Democrats in the past had wanted to use this majority for their own obstructionist purposes— to end the war in Iraq. Now Scott Brown's election was greeted by the Republicans as their opportunity to torpedo the president's comprehensive health care reform. And for a while it looked like that's exactly what would happen. These decisive wins were opposite sides of the same coin. In both cases, the people were screaming "stop."

You could argue, and I do, that this Stunted Age of the Senate was given new life late on election night 2006 in a dark courthouse in Butte, Montana.

CHAPTER ONE
ELECTION NIGHT

The political world was about to shift on its axis, but Jon Tester was tired, so he went to bed. It was the early hours of November 8, 2006. Triumphant Reaganism, as represented by the conservative presidency of George W. Bush and the twelve-year GOP dominance of the United States Congress, was about to meet its Waterloo in Big Sky Country. For eighteen months Tester had campaigned for a Senate seat against the three-term incumbent Republican Conrad Burns, but he did not stay up in hopes of hearing the results. When the polls first closed, Tester waited with his family in a hotel room, his supporters milling about the ballroom downstairs, but now it was the wee hours. What had been a long night was only getting longer, and there was no end of counting in sight. Tester was a farmer; he was used to going to bed early and getting up early. Now, about the time he might ordinarily think of getting up, Tester was going to get some sleep.

Jon Tester grew up on the land that his father and grandfather had farmed in northern Montana for a hundred years. He lived on the land that he learned to farm as a boy—flat, open fields where he grew organic lentils, red and white barley, and quinoa. He was proof that farm life is hard. In the summer of 1966, when he was nine and before he entered the fifth grade, he was slicing steaks with a meat cutter in the family's butcher shop and ran the three middle fingers on his left hand through the machine. The fingers were severed, gone forever. Even with seven fingers, he had five on his right hand, and so he would get his college degree in music, specializing in the trumpet.

He liked to joke that the trumpet was a concession to his injury, because, in fact, he really always wanted to play the saxophone, an instrument that requires a full complement of digits. Tester said he remembered little of the accident. "I must have been in shock," he said. "It did not hurt at the time." He remembers his mother taking him to the hospital in Havre, where he was seen by Dr. Jim Elliott. "Basically, he just filed off the bone and sewed up the skin."[1]

While he was a senior at the University of Great Falls, Tester married his college girlfriend, Sharla, who also descended from several generations of Montana farmers. She grew up in Box Elder, Montana, twenty-five miles from Jon's hometown of Big Sandy.

Sharla said that friends often teased her about being married to Jon. "They would say, 'How's it feel to be married to seven-tenths of a man?'" When the Testers' first baby, Christine, was born, the doctor who delivered her was the same Dr. Elliott who had sewn up Jon's hand almost fifteen years earlier. He looked at the newborn and declared that she "can't be Jon's kid, she's got all ten fingers."[2]

Tester became a high school music teacher and later ran for the Big Sandy school board. From there, his ascent into politics followed a classic model. The school board led to the Montana state senate in 1998. After his reelection to the Senate in 2002, he became the minority leader. And in 2005 he was the Senate president. In 2006, the issue he campaigned on all along was that the Bush administration had turned its back on the "little guy." He pointed to the war in Iraq and to the widespread corruption that had taken over the Republican Party, as evidenced by the resignation of Florida congressman Mark Foley for sending sexually explicit text messages to teenage pages in the House of Representatives and the conviction and imprisonment of congressmen Bob Ney of Ohio and Duke Cunningham of California—Ney for his links with disgraced super-lobbyist Jack Abramoff and Cunningham on charges of bribery, tax evasion, and wire and mail fraud.

Indeed, Tester's race would in some ways turn on the issue of Conrad Burns's relationship with Jack Abramoff, a onetime Republican honcho who

would go to jail for fraud and corruption. Burns had received campaign con-
tributions of more than $150,000 from Abramoff and had a difficult time
explaining away their relationship.

It didn't help Burns that in July 2006, in the middle of the campaign, he
confronted a crew of firefighters from Virginia who were in Montana to
help fight forest fires and told them they had done a "piss-poor job" on the
100,000-acre fire near his home in Billings.[3] Burns had something of a history for headline-making remarks. During his 2000 reelection drive he had
referred to Arabs as "ragheads."[4] He eventually apologized—but only after
the public pressure got very intense.

Then, of course, there is the famous N-word story. In 1994, Burns met
with editors at the local paper in Bozeman and recounted a conversation
he had had with an old rancher who wanted to know about life in Washington, D.C. "Conrad, how can you live back there with all those niggers?"
the man wanted to know, according to Burns. His response? "It's a hell of a
challenge."[5]

△

At about 3:00 A.M. on November 8, 2006, nine hours after the Montana polls
had closed, 565 paper ballots, each the size of a page from a legal pad, disappeared from the tabulation table on the second floor of Butte–Silver Bow
County Courthouse. The county clerk and recorder, Mary McMahon,
scoured the room for them with her two deputies. As they looked in ballot
bags, under tables, and in the tabulator machines, she reached the inevitable
conclusion that the only solution, after counting ten thousand of the sixteen
thousand votes cast, was to count them again.

For McMahon, November 7 had been a day without a beginning or an
end. She had celebrated her fifty-fifth birthday the day before and had slept
only a few hours going into election day. Long before the election, McMahon had decided to consolidate the twenty-five voting precincts within
Butte's city limits into a single location at the civic center downtown—in
place of the long-standing neighborhood polling places—and the decision

had sparked a good bit of controversy. But given her small staff, centralization seemed right: It made it easier to respond to any election-day glitches.

The irony that the first problem with counting—which had never materialized under the old system—was occurring now, under her bespectacled watch, was not lost on McMahon, who had been overseeing Butte–Silver Bow's county elections since 2000. A lot of state officials were waiting for her to complete her count. The constant ringing of the phone was a clear indication of that. But as the minute hand advanced steadily toward four o'clock, McMahon had no choice but to remove the Butte–Silver Bow partial returns from the overall state tally on the secretary of state's website and quickly shift into redo mode.

A few other counties were still out, too. Cascade, Flathead, and Gallatin—all in the western part of the state—had experienced counting troubles of some sort. Irregularities had forced officials in Meagher County (pronounced Marr), a relatively poor area in central Montana with a population of less than two thousand people, to count all its votes over by hand instead of relying on the electronic tabulator machines. And in Yellowstone County, near Billings, where the voting machines were new, election officials had started a recount to make sure that the tallies were correct.

Yellowstone, the largest county in the state, was a Republican stronghold and home to the Republican candidate Conrad Burns. Preliminary numbers showed that Burns had taken the county as expected, albeit by the tissue-thin margin of 1,222 votes. But with the results from most of the state's 563 polling places already in, Democrat Jon Tester, the organic farmer from the little town of Big Sandy, near the Canadian border, was ahead by about 1,700 votes.

The possibility existed, of course, that Burns could cut into Tester's lead. Meagher County, with its nine hundred votes, was expected to go heavily for Burns, though it hadn't enough votes to overtake Tester. In fact, because most of the outstanding counties were so small and because the margins in Yellowstone showed that Burns was not blowing Tester away, it became obvious as the hours wore on that Butte–Silver Bow, the largest

Democratic county in Montana, was going to decide who would represent Montana in the 110th Congress: the three-term, gaffe-prone incumbent, or the farmer with the flattop and the left hand with the three missing fingers.

Together, the two men had spent $12 million trying to win this seat, a relatively small amount compared to races around the country, but still a Montana record. It was the tightest Senate race in the country, and its resolution now lay in McMahon's hands.

By election day 2006, many Americans were angry at what George W. Bush's war on terror had become. Instead of going after the terrorists who had ripped a hole in the American psyche on September 11, 2001, the United States was now bogged down in a seemingly endless conflict in Iraq, where American soldiers were targets of warring factions in a civil insurgency. The electorate's disillusionment was palpable: Poll after poll had shown that Americans were ready to get out of Iraq. But the president and his Republican allies in Congress had retreated to a position of defending the war at all costs while accusing the war's critics of wanting to cut and run. The debate became increasingly frustrating. Even as the violence escalated in Iraq, the president and his administration seemed impervious to any arguments that contradicted their stay-the-course narrative.

It's customary for voters going to the polls in midterm elections to send a message of disapproval to the incumbent in the White House. Over the past seventeen midterm elections, dating back to 1942, the party holding the White House has lost an average of twenty-eight House seats, and an average of four seats in the Senate. November 2006 would be no different. It was almost a foregone conclusion that Democrats were going to take control of the House of Representatives and that some of the Republican incumbents in the Senate had no chance of getting reelected. It had been months since any poll had shown Rick Santorum of Pennsylvania, the Senate's third-ranking Republican, within single digits of his challenger, Robert Casey Jr., the state auditor general and son of a legendary former governor.

Running in Virginia against incumbent George Allen, Jim Webb was easily the most unusual of the 2006 Democratic challengers. A graduate of the U.S. Naval Academy, a marine captain in Vietnam, secretary of the navy under Ronald Reagan, and a successful novelist, he was an unusual political figure—and hardly a Democrat at all. In Vietnam he earned the Navy and Marine Corps' second-highest honor, the Navy Cross, as well as a Silver Star, two Bronze Stars, and two Purple Hearts. He got into the race, he said, after he watched the Bush administration's botched response to Hurricane Katrina in 2005. (Webb's wife, Hong Le Webb, who escaped South Vietnam with her family when she was seven years old after the fall of Saigon in 1975, grew up in New Orleans.)

Webb had to survive a Democratic primary in which he was not the official party choice. He'd had to answer questions about whether he was truly a Democrat and about his controversial writings on the role women have and should play in the U.S. military. His defense of Air Force officers involved in the sexual assault scandal known as Tailhook in 1991 seemed to be especially problematic. Webb was a fierce critic of the administration and the war in Iraq. His grown son, Jimmy, was an army captain serving in Iraq, and Webb wore his son's combat boots throughout the campaign.

After Webb won the March primary, he trailed Allen, widely seen as one of the front-runners for the 2008 Republican presidential nomination, by double digits. On August 11, 2006, the race was closer, but with Allen clearly ahead. That day the senator confronted a Webb campaign volunteer, uttering words that would become infamous. Campaigning in far southwest Virginia, near the Kentucky border, Allen turned the crowd's attention to S. R. Sidarth, a twenty-year-old University of Virginia student of Indian descent who had been trailing him for weeks: "This fellow here, over here with the yellow shirt, macaca, or whatever his name is. He's with my opponent. He's following us around everywhere. And it's just great," Allen said. The crowd laughed. Later he added: "Let's give a welcome to macaca, here. Welcome to America and the real world of Virginia."[6]

Sidarth, born and raised in Virginia, had captured the entire episode on his camcorder, and the moment ended not only Allen's reelection bid, but also his shot at the presidency. "Macaca" quickly became a synonym for political self-destruction. Allen, a former governor and the son of a legendary Washington Redskins football coach, at first claimed that he didn't know what he meant by the word and then refused to apologize for ten days. When it was reported that the word is a common racial epithet used among the French in North Africa, Allen apologized. Allen's mother grew up in Tunisia. Suddenly, Webb was in striking distance—inside the margin of error in many polls.

On the eve of the November 2006 elections in Minnesota, any clear understanding about how fundamentally the country had changed was missing from all the analyses. The prevailing intelligence held that the country was closely divided politically and that President Bush and the Republicans still had an advantage on issues of national security and dealing with international terror.

In Ohio, Republican senator Michael DeWine, a two-term incumbent whose moderate views once made him a perfect fit for his state, trailed and could never seem to get any traction against his challenger, Representative Sherrod Brown. Brown was a liberal U.S. congressman from Cleveland, a man whose strong opposition to free trade (he would renegotiate NAFTA and other trade agreements because he felt that they lacked proper labor and environmental standards and therefore put American workers at a disadvantage) and vocal support of gay rights positioned him on the party's left and had, before 2006, made many Ohioans wonder whether he could get elected statewide.

And in Rhode Island, Lincoln Chafee, the only Republican senator to vote against the Iraq war, found himself in a tight race for reelection, despite the fact his name was political gold in the state where his father had served as governor and been elected to the Senate four times. Chafee went into election day with approval ratings in the high sixties and still lost to former attorney general Sheldon Whitehouse. According to the day's exit polls, about 40 percent of Americans said they had cast their votes in direct opposition to the president.

From the outset of the election season, the Democrats got lucky; not a single one of their incumbents seemed to be really in trouble. Six months before election day, the most imperiled seat looked to be the one in Minnesota being vacated by department store heir Mark Dayton. Jennifer Duffy, an analyst for the nonpartisan *Cook Political Report,* concluded that "the contest to succeed [Dayton] is likely to become a classic open seat struggle in which everything from candidate quality of campaign competence, fundraising and the overall political climate matters." Duffy noted that Republican candidate Mark Kennedy was "battle-tested by difficult reelection campaigns" and predicted that his race against Democrat Amy Klobuchar would be "hotly contested and is the GOP's best shot at picking up a Democratic seat."[7]

In the end, Mark Kennedy lost by more than 20 percentage points, the biggest margin of defeat in any contested race in 2006. He'd run a terrible campaign. Amy Klobuchar was an ambitious politician, methodical and disciplined, and a woman who actually enjoyed raising money. By the time election day came around, it was no surprise that she won. Klobuchar's win also raised Democratic hopes that they might be able to keep Minnesota in the win column in the 2008 presidential contest, after having won it only narrowly in 2004.

Klobuchar, a state prosecutor in Hennepin County, which includes Minneapolis, seemed the perfect candidate for Minnesota. She knew the state well, and its people knew her; she was entirely comfortable with herself, and she was a hard worker. Still, only a few months before the election, her most urgent ambition was to be state attorney general.

In Tennessee, Republican Bob Corker was locked in a close race with Congressman Harold Ford. The Corker-Ford challenge was closely watched as an indicator of how badly damaged the GOP was going into the election and for the historical potential it held to produce in Ford the first African American senator from the South since Blanche Kelso Bruce, the Reconstruction-era Republican from Mississippi who served one full term in the Senate from 1875 to 1881. In 1879, Bruce, a former slave, became the first African American to preside over the Senate.

One particular television advertisement during that election caused a stir. The ad, financed by the Republican National Committee, seemed to intentionally link Ford to white women in an effort to undermine him with voters who might still disapprove of the idea of interracial relationships— particularly the sexually charged idea of black men with white women. Corker denounced the ad immediately, and has insisted ever since that poll numbers show it hurt his campaign more than it did Ford. But the specter of racial politics hung over his victory long after election day.

What was happening in 2006 was the end of the Reagan Revolution as we understood it at the time—the demise of the voting patterns that elected Ronald Reagan. Middle- and working-class Americans who had traditionally voted Democratic but had become more conservative (becoming so-called Reagan Democrats) elected him twice, and the continuation of that pattern in 1994 gave Republicans complete control of the Congress for the first time in fifty years. In 1994, America was not at war and people were arguing about and voting on how to manage prosperity under the Clinton administration. Rather than behaving purely as obstructionists, the opposing parties were promoting different ideas of governance. By 2006, this evenhandedness was clearly no longer the case.

Election night brought even better returns than were expected by Democrats. They began the day with forty-five senators, which meant the party needed to hold on to what they had and add six seats to take control of the Senate. By the time most of the votes were counted, Democrats had not only knocked off the Republican incumbents in Pennsylvania, Ohio, Rhode Island, and Missouri, but also held on to all their seats. The only bright spot for the GOP, in fact, was a close win in Tennessee, where Bob Corker, the former mayor of Chattanooga, narrowly defeated Ford to keep the seat held by the retiring Senate majority leader Bill Frist.

Harry Reid, the Senate's top Democrat, and Charles Schumer, the New York Democrat who headed the Democratic Senatorial Campaign Committee (DSCC), which raises money to finance the campaigns of Senate Democrats, took adjoining suites on the eleventh floor of the Hyatt Regency on Capitol Hill, where they spent election night. Schumer and Reid hoped to be able to make congratulatory calls to winning Democrats across the country, but as the polls closed on the East Coast, they were in the same fix as Jon Tester. There was little they could do except wait. Reid and Schumer spend a considerable portion of their waking hours making hundreds of decisions, small and large, with cell phones pressed to their ears and directing their troops. "Harry Reid uses his cell phone like a weapon," said Jim Manley, a longtime Capitol Hill press secretary who became Reid's communications director.[8] But these election night calls were special.

Just after eleven o'clock, Rebecca Kirzner, a Reid aide who worked in his press office, poked her head into his bedroom to tell him that Claire McCaskill was about to deliver her victory speech in St. Louis. McCaskill, the state auditor, had challenged the incumbent Republican James Talent, who had just called her to concede. As McCaskill took the stage to rousing cheers, Reid walked over to the plasma screen television and kissed her image. Reid is a low-key, soft-spoken Mormon who loves Woody Guthrie and is not given to public displays of emotion. For him, this TV kiss was like dancing naked on a bar.

Reid would be making his calls. His first call earlier that evening had been to Robert Casey in Scranton, Pennsylvania, and Bernie Sanders in Burlington, Vermont, congratulating them on their wins. Another excited call was to Amy Klobuchar, who won by 22 percentage points. The fact that she had won so handily in Minnesota, a swing state, was especially gratifying to Reid.

One and a half miles down Pennsylvania Avenue, at the White House, the mood was considerably more restrained. After a light dinner of corn bisque and tomato salad, the president, who knew by ten thirty that Democrats would take control of the House, made a relatively early night of it.

△

There were no early nights in Montana. Like Virginia and Missouri, Montana had recently been a solidly Republican state. George W. Bush won Montana twice, beating Al Gore by 25 percentage points in 2000 and John Kerry by 20 points in 2004. But as November 8, 2006, dawned, the fact that Montana's Senate race was teetering toward a little-known Democrat was a testament to the GOP's problems as embodied in the incumbent president. Bush had become the best political weapon the Democrats had had in years.

None of this mattered to Mary McMahon. In the months leading up to election day she had set up a system to assure accuracy and transparency, and now, her small staff notwithstanding, Room 208 of the Butte–Silver Bow Courthouse was crowded with lawyers representing both parties from the state and national levels, each one of them there to make sure that the interests of their candidate and his corresponding party were protected. Such on-the-ground presence is also a way for campaigns to gather first-hand information about what's going on in each county courthouse in the state. It is how they know if they are hitting their number projections for each precinct, each county, each congressional district. Democrats were desperate to know if they were going to be able to hold off Burns in Silver Bow. "We need to win that fucker by seven thousand votes," was the raw analysis of one Tester operative.[9]

Word of the missing votes got back to the Tester campaign. The campaign manager, Stephanie Schriock, who was finance director for Vermont governor Howard Dean's thwarted presidential campaign in 2004, had grown up in Butte and knew Montana politics well. When she heard the news, she collapsed, literally dropping to her knees on the floor of the campaign "boiler room," where she had gone to get away from the crowd and in hopes of getting any information that might bring the long night closer to some resolution.

For his part, Tester and his family—Sharla and his mother-in-law, two kids, son-in-law, and his granddaughter, Kilikina—were still in their suite on the second floor of the Best Western Heritage Inn in Great Falls waiting anxiously and watching television. "The thing about election day," Tester said, "is that after months and months of running, there is nothing else to do but wait. We had done everything we could, so I was okay however it turned out."[10] The same could not be said for the thousands of supporters who had congregated downstairs in the hotel ballroom waiting for the celebration to begin; hundreds of balloons were anchored to the ceiling; hundreds of bottles of champagne were chilled and waiting to be popped.[11]

Apart from the fact that Schriock had been working nonstop for sixteen months, some of her stress came from trying to figure out what to do during the uncertainty. The people in the ballroom at the Best Western wanted to see their candidate, but she and others in the campaign worried that any celebration before a concession would be premature and violate the traditions of Montana politics. So Tester stayed out of sight. Later he would call that a mistake. "If I had to do it all over again, I would go downstairs and be with my people."[12]

Among those in the Tester crowd in the ballroom that night was state Senator Steve Gallus, a Democrat who represented Butte–Silver Bow County in the state legislature. He knew the county and Mary McMahon well. Once word of the disappeared votes leaked out, McMahon's phone went crazy, and Gallus was one of the most persistent callers. "Senator Gallus was calling every ten minutes," McMahon said, "to the point where we quit answering the phone because we knew it was him calling." There was nothing to say to him—or to anyone else. "At that point, I had my own crisis to deal with, so I tried not to let other people make their crisis mine too."[13]

But it was getting hectic, and McMahon was at the center of a storm. As the phone kept ringing, she somehow sensed it wasn't some unknown campaign lawyer or even Steve Gallus calling. In fact, it was the Montana chief executive, calling from the Tester suite. Governor Brian Schweitzer, a farmer from Whitefish, in the northwest part of the state, is known for both his size—which is large—and his volcanic personality, which is at its most intense when he brings it to bear on politics.

That night, Schweitzer was wearing his traditional jeans with cowboy boots and a bolo tie. And the political animal in him understood that Silver Bow was the key to the election. "I was looking at what was out—Sheridan County, Dawson, Cascade," he later told me.[14] He did not think Tester needed to win all four counties, but he had to keep it close. The biggest swing district was Silver Bow and its sixteen thousand unreported votes. "So I get on the phone and I call Silver Bow, and I say this is the governor, and whoever answers the phone starts to babble, saying, 'They are still counting.' I say, 'Take it easy, settle down, it's OK. I'll call back when you're done. You'll be done before daylight.'"[15]

Sometime before daylight, Jon Tester, not knowing whether he had won or lost, went to bed in Great Falls. His supporters, not knowing if he had won or lost, drifted out into the night and went home. Not one balloon had been released. For the real political thoroughbreds, however, sleep was the last thing on their minds. Schweitzer, along with Montana's senior senator, Max Baucus, and their staffs, were in another room at the Heritage Inn, poring over numbers.

Political campaigns often take on the rhetoric of war. Candidates attack each other, somebody gets ambushed, someone else is outgunned or overrun. The way in which political and military campaigns most probably resemble each other is that each is contested with the previous one in the forefront of everyone's mind. So the old saw about generals fighting the last war may be equally applicable to politicians and political consultants.

Conrad Burns had won the election in 2000 by a narrow margin, especially narrow considering that President Bush was beating Al Gore in Montana by 25 percentage points. The close race made Democrats frustrated in

2000 but hopeful for 2006. The man who had come so close to topping Burns six years earlier was Schweitzer, the voluble rancher from Whitefish, who, in addition to his dairy business, grew mint and once had a thriving bull semen export business. He came out of that election despising Conrad Burns. There was none of the grudging respect that political opponents often develop for one another. It's possible no one wanted to see Burns lose as much as the governor of Montana did. He was not going to sleep. His staff ordered Big Macs from McDonald's and cans of Red Bull energy drink—not that anybody needed it.

In the meantime, up on the second floor of the courthouse, McMahon's job was to compare numbers on the ESS-M150 electronic tabulator machines with returns from each of the county's sixty-nine voting machines' printed tabs. McMahon's error-prevention system was in place, with three different groups of officials to make sure nothing went wrong. There was the three-person receiving board, which collected the ballot boxes; the precinct register containing the names of every voter; the poll book, which every voter signed; and the numbers of the first and last ballots distributed in each precinct. If that was all in order, the boxes moved to the staging board, another threesome that made sure that only ballots from a particular precinct were counted in that precinct. They would stack the ballots by precinct.

Then it was time for counting. The ballots were moved to the tabulation table where they would be run through the M150s so that those numbers could be compared with the precinct tabs. If they matched, they would move to the wrap and seal table, where they would be preserved for the official statewide count. Somewhere between the staging board and the wrap and seal table, the 565 votes from Precinct 7A disappeared. It took her awhile, but McMahon figured that one stack from the staging table was accidentally stapled to another without being tabulated and had already been wrapped and sealed in a pouch to be sent to the secretary of state, a process which is the official record of the election. "We were dead-on at 1:30 A.M., and that's what was so frustrating about what happened," McMahon says. "It was extremely stressful—and that's putting it mildly."[16] Once the ballots were wrapped and sealed, it was illegal to open them, a deterrent to election fraud. McMahon knew she would need a court order to find the missing votes. She put in a call to county judge Kurt Kruger, who had the authority to have the ballot pouches reopened. But that court order could not be entered until seven o'clock in the morning. It would be nine thirty before Mary McMahon found out whether her hunch was right.

It is difficult to understand all the ways in which the 2000 presidential election, and especially the next thirty-six traumatic days in Florida with its truckloads of hanging chads and butterfly ballots (or something), forever changed the way we do American politics. One measure is the hundreds of people deployed in close proximity to every courthouse, school gymnasium, and church basement where votes are cast. The practitioners of this highly specialized political art form like to refer to it as voter protection. They are mostly volunteers whose chief qualification for the job, it seems, is having been in a place or on a campaign where their candidate or their party came up short or barely won. Their presence is meant as a show of force, a demonstrated willingness to go to war over every single vote. They mill around while the polls are open, apparently doing nothing, making sure that everyone knows they're looking. But they also are the eyes and ears of the campaign on the very front lines of the battle. So when two sets of ballots are mistakenly stapled together, they're the first ones to spread the news.

Some soldiers in this khaki-clad or gray-suited army are lawyers; others are old political operatives who have either won or lost a recount before and know how the fight is waged. With polls indicating that Montana was going to be close, Democrats had deployed 150 lawyers from the Election Day Legal Protection Program. "You just sit there and make sure that certain things don't happen," said Katherine Miller.[17] She was a party operative who cut her recount teeth in 1998 in a legendary Nevada race for the U.S. Senate, in which a second-term senator named Harry Reid beat then-congressman John Ensign. After several recounts, Reid won by 428 votes out of almost 5 million cast.

One of the things that the Tester crowd desperately wanted to avoid was a recount. And it was this idea that kept Schweitzer and others up all night even as the candidate slept. Schweitzer said, "All I could think of was Florida, and I didn't want this to turn into a Florida."[18]

△

The possibility of a recount was also the concern in Virginia, where Jim Webb was slightly ahead of George Allen, the GOP incumbent. It was now clear that if Democrats could win in both Virginia and Montana, they would take control of the Senate, but nobody in Montana or Virginia was thinking of control. They just wanted to win.

It was still difficult for many people to believe that a Democrat could win a Senate seat in Virginia—particularly against Allen. It was Marc Elias's job to believe. As counsel to the DSCC and an expert in recount election law, Elias was in Virginia to watch the returns come in. He watched all night. In the campaign office at the DSCC, he had set up telephone hotlines to each state with a contested race. There were a lot of calls from Maryland that day and some from Virginia. His candidate, Jim Webb, was trailing much of the evening, but big Democratic areas like Tidewater and Richmond, with their large concentrations of black voters, and the more liberal, chiefly urban, northern Virginia had still to report. Virginia was going to be close.

As the night wore on, it became increasingly clear to Elias that Montana—and Butte–Silver Bow in particular—would be the key to Democratic fortunes. He decided to go to Montana himself and was anxious to know whether Republicans had come to the same conclusion he had. He kept checking for signs that the other side was sending resources to Montana, but there were none. No Republican lawyers were flying in, nor was there an uptick in challenges from Republican poll watchers in any of the courthouses. Montana was ripe for a recount fight, but Republicans were battered and bruised from all their losses, and they were slow off the mark.

Elias decided to try to downplay his concerns. Even though Webb declared victory late Tuesday night, the results were not official, and Allen had not conceded. So on Wednesday afternoon, the Webb campaign called a press conference to detail why they were confident they had won. On the phone with national reporters was Elias, who said that he was in Virginia. But just barely. In truth, he was on the General Aviation tarmac at Dulles International Airport, on his way to Great Falls, Montana.

△

At 7:30 A.M. on November 8, County Court Judge Kurt Krueger, who, incidentally, was also on the ballot for reelection, issued an order allowing Mary McMahon to reopen the ballot pouches. There, as she'd suspected, were the two stacks of ballots accidentally stapled together, of which only one had been tabulated. Tester's margin was less than 1,900 votes, but he was ahead. And that was enough for Schweitzer.

The governor, along with Senator Baucus, campaign manager Schriock, and Tester's communications director Matt McKenna decided that victory should be declared. McKenna woke Tester and told him they were going to do all the morning shows and were going to declare him the winner. They tried to buttress this claim by asking the Associated Press to call the race for Tester. There wasn't even a hint of a Burns concession, and the AP bureau chief wanted to wait. Schweitzer, trying not to sound threatening, offered an ultimatum: He said that Tester was holding a press conference at ten thirty to claim victory and that it would then be incumbent on the AP to get a response from Burns's people. At ten fifteen, Tester appeared on the *Today* show to talk about his race with cohost Matt Lauer. The strategy was to declare victory early and often in an effort to forestall any talk about a recount.

During one break, when Tester was off camera, McKenna whispered the latest numbers in his ears; he was still clinging to a lead of fewer than two thousand votes, and there was only one county out. "He asked me what was still out," McKenna said. The next live shot captured a complete swing in Tester's mood. It was if his entire body exhaled. "I've seen that tape since, and it's amazing—the body language," Tester later commented. "That's when I knew I'd won."[19] It was Butte–Silver Bow, a heavily Democratic county.

On the *Today* show, Tester talked about what the new Democratic-controlled Senate would mean to the country. "Now is the time to put politics aside and work together," he began.[20] Lauer interrupted him to say that they had to cut away because President Bush had made an unexpected appearance in the Rose Garden and was speaking. The news: Secretary of Defense Donald Rumsfeld had resigned.

The voters, it seemed, had made their point.

CHAPTER TWO
THE GREAT REVERSES

For two and a quarter centuries, the U.S. Senate has been a consistent, persistent, reliably negative force in American politics and thus in American life. Designed to be the ultimate check in a delicate system of checks and balances, the Senate began as and remains a big "no" factory. The Senate was not conceived so much as an instrument of government as a curb on it. In many ways, the nays, in the Senate, almost always have it. "The Senate, more than any other body in American government, is a place where a very few people, and on occasion even a single member, can stop things from getting done," Jim Webb has observed.[1]

The Senate has lived up to the task since 1789, with 221 years (and counting) of rejections and refusals, denials and delays. It said no to John Rutledge's Supreme Court nomination in 1795; no to an end to the slave trade in 1825; no to the establishment of a national bank in 1841; no to the Treaty of Versailles first in 1919 and then again in 1920; and no, repeatedly no, to the enactment of civil rights laws during most of the nineteenth and twentieth centuries. It also said no, eventually, to the Vietnam war and to the conviction of President William Jefferson Clinton on charges brought by the House of Representatives.

In the fall of 2006, American voters said no to the war in Iraq, and expected that newly elected senators would do the same. But in an ironic twist, saying no to the war meant taking a series of positive actions that put them on the yes, and more difficult, side of the question. Democrats tried to set deadlines for withdrawal of U.S. forces from Iraq; Republicans said no, and prevailed.

△

Even in the most hopeful moments, there was cause to worry that the voters would have their hopes frustrated, that gridlock and pointless contentiousness would persist. History tended to support such concerns. Congress, in general, and the Senate, in particular, had not endeared itself to average Americans. Going into election day 2006, the GOP-led Congress had a 67 percent disapproval rating, according to the Gallup Poll. That was about the same level of satisfaction enjoyed by the Democratic-led Congress going into the 1994 midterms that ended in a Republican rout. Increasingly, Congress was seen as part of a government that simply could not meet even the most modest expectations.

"When George Bush became president, oversight largely disappeared. From homeland security to the conduct of the war in Iraq, from the torture issue uncovered by the Abu Ghraib revelations to the performance of the IRS, Congress has mostly ignored its responsibilities,"[2] observed Thomas E. Mann and Norman J. Ornstein, two prominent Washington scholars, putting into words the widely held opinion that a large part of the systemic failure belonged to the Republican-led Congress for totally abdicating its oversight role over the Bush administration.

In November 2006, they wrote in *Foreign Affairs,* "In the past six years . . . congressional oversight of the executive across a range of policies, but especially on foreign and national security policy, has virtually collapsed." Further,

> The few exceptions, such as the tension-packed Senate hearings on the prison scandal at Abu Ghraib in 2004, only prove the rule. With little or no midcourse corrections in decision-making and implementation, policy has been largely adrift. Occasionally—as during the aftermath of Hurricane Katrina last year—the results have been disastrous.[3]

One week before the 2006 elections, the Brookings Institution convened a meeting in Washington about the future of the United States Congress. The event was dejectedly titled "Will the November Election Help Mend the Broken Branch?" The prognosis was not good.

Longtime *Washington Post* columnist E. J. Dionne, also a senior fellow at the Brookings Institution, was the moderator. He was joined by former Republican congressman Vin Webber of Minnesota, as well as Ornstein, a scholar at the American Enterprise Institute, and Mann, a senior fellow in governance studies at Brookings. The themes to be explored by the panel were taken from the title of a book Ornstein and Mann had recently written called *The Broken Branch: How Congress Is Failing America and How to Get It Back on Track.* They pointed to what they described as a "decline in institutional identity" that resulted in a modern Senate populated by mavericks, party hacks, and ideologues, rather than the statesmen for whom it was intended.

"The rules and procedures of the Senate were a key to its unique role as the world's greatest deliberative body," wrote Mann and Ornstein, "and even those who were frustrated by them and by their application, especially when an intense minority thwarted the will of the majority, were respectful of their centrality to the Senate itself."[4]

It was hard to find that institutional reverence anywhere on Capitol Hill in recent years. Washington had become much like the cable television shoutfests that dominated the television ratings. There seemed to be nothing special about the Senate, and increasingly it seemed as hotheaded as the House had ever been.

During a particularly nasty debate about the future of the filibuster in 2005, I asked Senator Mark Pryor what had happened to the Senate. His father, David Pryor, had been a senator from Arkansas before him, and he had watched the institution change over time. Pryor did not miss a beat: "Too many former House members,"[5] he said, suggesting, as many old-timers in Washington believe, that the Senate had lost some of his storied decorum and gravitas and, as a consequence, some of its effectiveness.

The rules of the House are strict, and they almost always guarantee that the majority wins. The one-minute speeches that house members get to deliver during morning business are among some of the longest they get to give, and that brevity abhors nuance and complex expression of ideas, and often gives rise to shouting. Senators, on the other hand, routinely request fifteen or twenty minutes to make a single point. In March of 2007, when he had been in the Senate for only three months, Ben Cardin of Maryland told me he was having difficulty expanding his one-minute speeches to fill the fifteen or twenty minutes he now had to speak on any issue. "I'm adjusting to having all that time," he said.[6] The leaders of both parties in the Senate at the time, Republican Trent Lott and Tom Daschle, were both former members of the House, but both men had developed an intense regard for the institution. Indeed, it was after Lott was replaced as majority leader by Bill Frist, a man with no congressional institutional history or inclination to acquire one, that the Senate endured some of its worst moments in recent memory.

First was the Terri Schiavo fiasco.

Schiavo was a Florida woman who had been in a coma since 1990; she was being kept alive by an intravenous feeding tube. Her husband, Michael, and her parents, Robert and Mary Schindler, clashed over her care. The parents wanted Schiavo to continue being fed via the tube, while her husband said she would not have wanted to live under these conditions. It was a human tragedy made all the worse because it was so public. It had given rise to a long series of court cases.

When a Florida judge ruled in the husband's favor, allowing the removal of the feeding tube, Republicans—sensing a chance to curry favor with their base politically—decided to make the life and death of Terri Schiavo a political issue by casting it as a choice between the values of those who want to protect life and those who believe in a culture of death. Congress was out for the Easter recess in 2005 when the judge ordered the feeding tube removed. Republican leaders called both houses back into session to deal with the issue. They pushed back the recess, returned to Washington, and, along with the president of the United States, jumped headfirst into the life of Terri Schiavo, including the issuing of subpoenas to Michael and to Terri Schiavo herself to appear before a congressional inquiry of the House Government Reform Committee.

Intervention was a crude miscalculation on their part. Most Americans simply did not see a political component in this personal tragedy and did not line up in regular ideological order. According an ABC News poll taken in March 2005, 69 percent of Americans said they would want the feeding tube removed if they found themselves in circumstances similar to Schiavo's. Seventy-five percent said that Congress should not have intervened, and 70 percent said that President Bush should not have involved himself in the matter.[7] People seemed to intuit that intruding inside a family's private torment is one step too far for the government to go.

Majority Leader Tom DeLay went to the floor of the House and, dabbing tears from his eyes, talked about Terri's—and he always called her Terri—parched mouth and her "throbbing" hunger pangs. But it was Senate majority leader Bill Frist who cut the most embarrassing figure. Frist, a brain surgeon by training, insisted while he was in the Senate that he be addressed as "Doctor Frist." Invoking his medical training, Frist said that, based on a videotape he had seen of Schiavo, he could not be sure that she was in a "persistent vegetative state" as many experts had claimed. The videotape was four years old at the time, and there were five years' worth of legal and medical opinions in the Schiavo case asserting that she had almost no prospect of recovery or rehabilitation.

More than one judge had found the evidence sufficiently reliable to allow the feeding tube to be removed. Frist, who was openly considering a White House bid in 2008, saw this case as a chance to affirm his pro-life bona fides, and tried to use the Senate for this flimsy purpose.

Schiavo's feeding tube was removed on March 18, 2005, and Michael Schiavo would have his dying wife receive the last rites of the Roman Catholic Church on Easter Sunday.

Congress tried to pass a bill mandating that a federal court hear the case to consider a court order that had been issued in Florida. "Congress is continuing to work to pass legislation to give Terri Schiavo another chance at life," Frist said on the Senate floor in a rare Sunday session on March 20, 2005. "The Senate will remain here throughout the afternoon and, if necessary, late into the evening in order to act immediately on this bill once it is ready. Because Terri Schiavo is being denied lifesaving nutrition this very moment, time is of the essence."[8]

The "Senate in session" that day included three senators, and the bill passed the Senate unanimously by 3–0, and was then approved by the House after a long debate that ran on past midnight. The president, who had flown back to Washington from his vacation home in Crawford, Texas, signed the bill at 1:11 A.M. on Monday. But the case never went to federal court, and Terri Schiavo died on March 31, 2005. Michael Schiavo said that Terri had wanted to be cremated and that he planned to bury her in his family plot in Pennsylvania in defiance of her parents' wishes; they wanted a wake, an open-casket Roman Catholic funeral, and for her to be buried near their home in Florida where they could easily visit the grave. In the end, she was cremated and her remains buried at the Sylvan Abbey Memorial Park in Clearwater, Florida. Her parents were not invited to the funeral.

One Florida judge, Pinellas Circuit Court Judge George W. Greer, who more than once issued rulings that Schiavo's feeding tube could be removed, was willing to defy the entire GOP government in Florida and Washington. The Florida legislature even passed a law to give then-governor Jeb Bush, a Republican, the right to overrule Greer's ruling that the feeding tube could be removed. That law was found unconstitutional. Greer's defiance was a reminder to the GOP of why having more conservative judges at the state and federal bar was so important to their cause. Those judges are often the final arbiters in the culture wars, and the GOP was still determined to wage and win those wars.

△

In the spring of 2005, President Bush sent a slate of judges to the Senate for confirmation, a usual process in the continual renewal of the federal courts. Democrats pilloried each of them as out of the political mainstream, cast them as hostile to civil rights and workers' rights, and filibustered the nominations. In a deal, the Democrats agreed not to filibuster three of the judges on the list—Priscilla Owen, Janice Rogers Brown, and William Pryor—in exchange for making the other four go away.

The deal rendered both sides vulnerable to charges of political capitulation and hypocrisy, and there was a clear sense that Frist and the GOP Senate leadership (which had the deal foisted on them) seemed determined to blow it up at the earliest opportunity. Frist reminded everyone that he was not a part of the deal, and he reserved the right to pursue the elimination of the filibuster altogether, an expedient labeled the "nuclear option" by Democrats and the "constitutional option" by Frist.

"I do not want to use the constitutional option," he said, "but bad faith and bad behavior during my tenure as majority leader will bring the Senate back to the point where all one hundred members will be asked to decide whether judicial nominees deserve a fair up-or-down vote."[9] This was in some ways payback for what the Republicans had done to Clinton nominees a decade earlier, which in turn had been payback for what Democrats had done to Reagan nominees a decade before that. But Frist's words did not seem an idle threat, and, as befits a nuclear solution, it profoundly shook the Senate's foundations. The nuclear threat was finally allayed by the formation of the bipartisan "Gang of Fourteen" that preserved the filibuster and facilitated the nomination of a total of five of the controversial judges.[10]

Democrats, happy that they had preserved the filibuster, tried to move on. That was hard when the GOP was bent on making sure that they had the judges in place to win more moral victories when the opportunities presented themselves.

In the end, the fight over the filibuster and the nuclear option had less to do with judges and filibustering than it had to do with opposition to abortion rights, gay marriage, and contraception and with being in favor of school prayer—values that so consumed the GOP establishment that for someone like Frist, who wanted to be president, they were hard to resist. Evangelicals and other Christian conservatives, who had been working to seat a more conservative federal judiciary, had little interest in talking about anything else.

The Republican senators who supported the deal came under attack. "It is senators like [Mike] DeWine and [John] Warner and [Lindsey] Graham who have snatched defeat from the jaws of victory," said Tony Perkins of the Family Research Council.[11] He issued a threat to those senators whose actions he considered a betrayal, saying that religious activists would be alerted to them. "And it won't take long for them [the congregations] to take action on their own," Perkins promised.

Against that backdrop, Thomas Mann of Brookings concluded: "Congress is indeed broken. It is evident if you look at its essential characteristics—to represent, to legislate, to check and balance—in each of these dimensions Congress has become very disappointing indeed."[12]

The ten senators newly elected to the 110th Congress in November 2006, nine Democrats and one Republican, were not part of an unusually large class. It's just that they were mostly all from one party. More interesting perhaps, along with the midterm elections of 1918 and 1986, it was only the third time in the last century that control of the Senate had switched hands during a president's second term, suggesting the voters had responded to the election as if it were a recall. Midterm elections are the only mechanism voters have to go after a president they are no longer happy with, even one they have just reelected. In all three of these midterm turnarounds, the reversal resulted from the diminished popularity of the president.

The first turnaround occurred in the 1918 congressional elections, held days before the armistice that ended the fighting of the First World War, when Democrats lost seven seats in the ninety-six-seat Senate. Woodrow Wilson, having been reelected in November 1916 on his record of having kept the United States out of the war, then decided in 1917, a month after his second inaugural, that the United States could no longer stand aside and let Europe crumble. Wilson went before a joint session of Congress to ask for a declaration of war against Germany. "The world must be made safe for democracy," he famously declared. "Its peace must be planted upon the tested foundations of political liberty. We have no selfish ends to serve. We desire no conquest, no dominion. We seek no indemnities for ourselves, no material compensation for the sacrifices we shall freely make. We are but one of the champions of the rights of mankind. We shall be satisfied when those rights have been made as secure as the faith and the freedom of nations can make them."[13]

It took Congress four days to accede to Wilson's request, and on April 6, 1917, they declared war on Germany. What followed was a kind of wartime hysteria fueled by anti-German sentiment followed by the "Red Scare" of anti-Communist anxiety in the wake of the Bolshevik Revolution in Russia. New wartime regulations left the American people deeply disenchanted with the president and his party: First, an involuntary military draft for young men between twenty-one and thirty was enacted, followed by the Espionage Act of 1917, which outlawed almost any kind of antiwar protest on the ground that it gave, in the words of the law, "aid and comfort to the enemy."[14] The Espionage Act was amended in 1918 to include the very restrictive provisions of the Sedition Act of 1918, a series of anti-free-speech provisions that prohibited the use of "disloyal, profane, scurrilous, or abusive language" directed toward the government, the American flag, or the U.S. military. Violations of the Sedition Act were punishable by fines of up to $10,000 or prison terms of up to twenty years.[15]

Wilson, who had been narrowly reelected, saw his popularity go into free fall.

That November, Democrats lost five seats in the Senate and twenty-five in the House, and when Congress reconvened the following year, Republicans were in control of the Senate. Germany signed the armistice agreement less than a week after the general election of November 5, but despite that victory, Wilson had very little political capital left. When, in 1919, he sought ratification of the Treaty of Versailles—intended, he said, to "build a lasting peace"—he understood the problems he would have in the Senate, where the election had changed everything.[16]

The new majority leader was Wilson's old nemesis, Massachusetts senator Henry Cabot Lodge, who also chaired the Foreign Relations Committee. Lodge had established himself as an alternative authority to Wilson on international affairs, and had no interest in seeing the establishment of the League of Nations, the idealistic international organization Wilson was championing as part of the Versailles Treaty. When the president presented the treaty to the chamber, he struck an alarmist tone intended to pressure the Senate and the American people to follow his ambitions for the League of Nations: "Dare we reject it and break the heart of the world?" he asked.[17]

In the end, of course, the answer was yes. Wilson's troubles in many ways boiled down to the fact that he no longer controlled the Senate, and that the Senate was actively thwarting his plans. His old animus against Lodge, augmented by these new frustrations, turned to rage one day and pushed him to denounce his Senate detractors as "contemptible, narrow, selfish, poor little minds that never get anywhere but run around in a circle and think they are going somewhere."[18]

Wilson, bent on getting around opposition in the Senate, went on an aggressive speaking tour across the country to boost public support for the treaty, but when it finally reached the Senate floor in the fall of 1919—

freighted with amendments and revisions that reflected the Senate's opposition to Wilson's plan—it had almost no chance of passage. Wilson suffered a debilitating stroke that October, and in November, Majority Leader
Lodge put the treaty on the Senate calendar.

Even in his illness, Wilson was unwilling to concede anything to the
Senate, and so, in late November 1919, the Senate rejected the peace treaty
that officially ended the First World War, the first time in history that they
had ever voted against such a document. But, in many ways, that is what the
Senate was intended to do—obstruct, forestall, prevent, forbid—as the giant
constitutional no machine. After Wilson's two terms were up, it would take
Democrats twelve years to win the White House again, with Franklin D.
Roosevelt in 1932.

△

Ronald Reagan was the second president to lose control of the Senate in
the midterm elections after his reelection. What happened in 1986 was a
monumental defeat. His party had controlled the Senate for the first six
years of his term, and Reagan decided that this one remaining election of
his presidency was to be his last hurrah, his final chance to show his wiz-
ardry at moving voters. In a flurry of campaigning across the country,
Reagan put his personal popularity on the line to try to retain Republican control of the Senate. But unemployment was above 7 percent, and
news of the Iran-contra scandal had begun to leak out. In late October,
on a campaign swing through Missouri on behalf of then-governor Kit
Bond, he told an adoring crowd in Springfield, "If you want to vote for
me, vote for Kit Bond."[19] All the 1980 freshmen who had ridden Reagan's
coattails into the Senate were now up for reelection, and he tried to cast
1986 as a rerun of 1980, asking voters to keep in place the team they had
elected then.

"It almost feels like 1980 all over again," Reagan said. "There's never
been a race where the choices are so clear and the difference so distinct."
And he continued, "For if we lose the Senate, the liberal Democrats will

march us back to the grim days of the '70s."[20] The opposition party generally has an advantage going into the midterms, but Reagan had been elected
with a forty-nine-state win over Walter Mondale, and it was an open question whether Democrats could effectively counter his personal popularity.

What they had going for them was that Reagan was presiding over an
economy in which the unemployment rate had stubbornly hovered around
7 percent nationally for more than two years, and was much higher than
that in some key states. And five days before the elections, press reports revealed that the president had approved the selling of arms to Iran to secure
the release of the Americans held hostage in Lebanon by terrorists believed
to be closely associated with the Iranian regime. It had been a hostage crisis in Iran that had weakened the presidency of Jimmy Carter leading up to
the 1980 election, and that helped bring Reagan to power. Now the tide was
flowing the opposite way.

The arms story leaked in November 1986, five days before the midterm
elections, when a Lebanese newspaper revealed that the members of the
president's National Security Council (NSC), including Robert McFarlane,
who was National Security Advisor from 1983 to 1985, had been involved
in the sale of weapons (for a profit, via Israel) to Iran. After the initial story
broke, U.S. Attorney General Edwin Meese revealed that proceeds from the
secret arms transfers had been diverted to help the rebel forces in
Nicaragua, whom Reagan had been supporting actively and publicly. This
news opened up the possibility that the president may have known about
and sanctioned the diversion of funds. That was never established, but the
Tower Commission, set up to look into the scandal, concluded that the president had failed in his official responsibilities.

"The N.S.C. system will not work unless the President makes it work.
After all, this system was created to serve the President of the United States
in ways of his choosing. By his actions, by his leadership, the President
therefore determines the quality of its performance," the commission wrote
in it final report. "The President's management style is to put the principal
responsibility for policy review and implementation on the shoulders of his

advisors. Nevertheless, with such a complex, high-risk operation and so much at stake, the President should have insured that the N.S.C. system did not fail him."[21]

The president's detached style had become a point of discussion in Washington, and at seventy-five, there were people questioning whether his faculties were slipping. In their 1988 book, *Landslide,* journalists Doyle Mc-Manus and Jane Mayer quoted one senior White House official who told them that the president's aides were signing his initials to important documents, and that there was a plan in place to invoke the Twenty-fifth Amendment to the U.S. Constitution, allowing the transfer of power to the vice president if the president were to be incapacitated.

It is hard to gauge how much the Iran-contra disclosures affected the outcome of the election; the scandal would balloon after the election was held. But Reagan and the Republicans were not able to hold on to the Senate. Seven of nine freshmen who had been part of the Reagan win in 1980 were defeated, and Democrats picked up open seats in Nevada and Maryland to take control of the Senate, fifty-five to forty-five, for the first time since Reagan was elected. This was widely heralded, mostly by Democrats, as the end of the Reagan Revolution.

Some of the notable members of the 1986 class were Democrats Bob Graham of Florida, John Breaux of Louisiana, and Barbara Mikulski of Maryland, along with South Dakota's Tom Daschle and Nevada's Harry Reid, both of whom would go on to serve as majority leader. Among the new Republican senators was a restless, cocky, two-term congressman from Arizona named John McCain.

Desperate to salvage his personal reputation and repair what may have been his most important political relationship—with the Senate—Reagan fired his chief of staff, Donald T. Regan, and replaced him with onetime majority leader Howard Baker, a former Tennessee senator known for his skills at peacemaking and diplomacy who had not sought reelection in 1984 after eighteen years in the Senate. Baker was well known for his role as the highest-ranking Republican member of the Senate committee that investigated the Watergate scandal.

Reagan is perceived to have recovered in large part because of Baker's skill, but in many ways that election of 1986 set the rancorous tone that would become the hallmark of Washington over the next ten years, when things got worse. Under Reagan, both parties started adopting a scorched-earth policy—they didn't just want to win an argument, they wanted to obliterate the other side. In the eighties and nineties it was easier to debate what you were fighting for. In the mid-2000s and beyond it was about what you were against, as well as discrediting the other side. Reagan's great political talent was that he was able to be positive and uplifting and offer attractive ideas while at the same time completely undermining the other side.

In the spring of 1987, Reagan got his chance to nominate a third justice to the Supreme Court after Lewis Powell, a moderate, said in April that he would retire. Reagan announced, on July 1, just before the recess for Independence Day, that he would nominate Robert H. Bork to replace Powell. The conservative legal scholar was famous for being the man who carried out Richard Nixon's order to fire Watergate special prosecutor Archibald Cox in what became known as the Saturday Night Massacre.

Democrats struck back immediately. The Senate's most reliable liberal voice, Ted Kennedy, was on the floor of the Senate within what seemed like minutes. And what he had to say echoed like battle trumpets; they heralded the start of a tactical approach to politics that both sides employ to this day:

> Robert Bork's America is a land in which women would be forced into back-alley abortions, blacks would sit at segregated lunch counters, rogue police could break down citizens' doors in midnight raids, schoolchildren could not be taught about evolution, writers and artists could be censored at the whim of the Government, and the doors of the Federal courts would be shut on the fingers of millions of citizens.[22]

That salvo set the tone, not just for that nomination but for most nominations in the next twenty years. Bork later said he had made a calculated decision not to respond, because he did not want to sanction this process as the way to choose Supreme Court nominees. "Naturally, when people heard these things and believed them, they were quite right to be worried," Bork later told the *Washington Post.* "If I'd gone on the talk shows and straightened out the record . . . if I had started campaigning, I might have made it. But I think that would have ratified that way of choosing a judge. And I wasn't going to do it."[23]

The Bork battle raged all summer, and the Senate finally voted on confirmation in late October, after the new Court session had begun. The vote was fifty-eight to forty-two against the nomination, easily the widest margin by which the Senate ever rejected a nominee. Bork later said he could never forget the Kennedy quote or the impact it had on derailing his nomination.[24]

Even as Democrats began to show their strength by shooting down Bork, there were signs that the Reagan Revolution was far from over. In fact, after the 1986 midterm election, two Democratic strategists admitted that Reagan had so fundamentally changed the frame of American politics that even in victory Democrats were playing on his terms. He had made conservatism kind of the default position in American politics, a force with which nonconservatives had to reckon.

"With a Democratic gain of eight seats, commentators have widely hailed these victories as a rejection of the President's policies and a demonstration that his coattails have gotten considerably shorter. But most of us who advise Democratic candidates for state and national office know that this is not really the case," Mark Penn and Doug Schoen wrote in the *New York Times.* "In fact, this election represents a much more complicated result. It marks the institutionalization of the Reagan agenda in United States politics." Penn and Schoen went on to make the point that the Democrats who had been victorious in 1986 had in fact embraced Reagan's message—

lower taxes, small government, tough-guy diplomacy—in order to win. "In campaign after campaign, Democratic candidates and their strategists recognized at the outset that they had to demonstrate that they accepted the basic outlines of the President's policies before they could begin differentiating themselves from their opponents. Failure to do this, Democrats understood, would lead to defeats similar to the one suffered by Walter F. Mondale in 1984."[25]

The conservative ideal of lower taxes, smaller government, and less regulation became the dominant paradigm in American politics. This notion of having to play on Republican, or at least conservative, terms has been a hallmark of Democratic politics for much of the last thirty years, and it explains the difficulty they often have winning elections. Republicans have controlled the White House for twenty of the last thirty years and have done only slightly worse in the Congress, controlling the Senate for thirteen of the last thirty years.

The most recent period of control began in 2006, the third time a sitting president's party lost control of the Senate after being reelected. On November 8, President George W. Bush woke up and confirmed what he knew when he went to bed: The GOP had lost control of the House—and the Senate was not looking promising. Virginia and Montana were still out. Harry Reid had hardly slept. Democratic lawyers, still fearful of a recount in Montana, were making plans to bring in lawyers with recount experience from neighboring states—meaning Washington State, which had had an unending gubernatorial recount in 2004. Republicans, however, seemed stunned by the blows inflicted and, in essence, walked away from the election.

Just before 1:00 P.M. Eastern Time, the president went to the East Room of the White House and delivered a concession speech on behalf of the GOP:

I'm obviously disappointed with the outcome of the election, and as the head of the Republican Party, I share a large part of the responsibility. I told my party's leaders that it is now our duty to put the elections behind us and work together with the Democrats and independents on the great issues facing this country.

Bush seemed oddly jocular: referring to the losses as "a thumping."[26] Defense Secretary Donald Rumsfeld had submitted his resignation the day before, and now Bush, in some measure acknowledging the fact that the disastrous war in Iraq had caused his party's undoing, was accepting the resignation of the war's chief architect:

> The election has changed many things in Washington, but it has not changed my fundamental responsibility, and that is to protect the American people from attack. As the Commander-in-Chief, I take these responsibilities seriously. And so does the man who served this nation honorably for almost six years as our Secretary of Defense, Donald Rumsfeld. Now, after a series of thoughtful conversations, Secretary Rumsfeld and I agreed that the timing is right for new leadership at the Pentagon.[27]

The election was lost largely because the war was being lost; the country had elected to do something about it. In this respect the 2006 election was a classic recall reaction: The voters would have recalled the president had they been able to, so the electorate sought instead to put a roadblock in the way of his carrying out his program—in the form of a new Democratic majority in the House and Senate.

The success of the Democrats in 2006 was in part due to the deep antipathy that voters felt toward President Bush and his Republican foot soldiers in the Congress. But it also was due in part to the fact that most of the candidates no longer felt they needed to apologize for being Democrats or that they somehow had to "demonstrate that they accepted the basic outlines" of Reagan's conservative principles before they could make a case to the voters. One prominent lobbyist who had given money to Democratic candidates for many years saw there was something different about the

Democratic class of 2006. "They wanted to do important things and they were comfortable with who they are," she told me, requesting that she remain anonymous. "That was different and refreshing."[28]

The voters who had put Democrats in this new Senate expected them to go into action politically against the president. It is the institution in the government that has the most immediate check on a president's ambitions, as represented in his programs. "The United States Senate is a venerable institution," Jim Webb wrote later. "It is also an odd kingdom of 100 fiercely protected fiefdoms. . . . In terms of volatility, behind all of its courtesies the United States Senate is composed of 100 scorpions in a jar. And one should be very careful in deciding how and when to shake that jar."[29]

The American voters in 2006 had shaken the jar, and they expected results. The House has the power of the purse, but any one senator can frustrate the president with two simple words—"I object." This ability to obstruct and delay is not how new senators coming to Washington understand their power. They come thinking they have a constructive mandate to act; they believe they will truly represent the interests of their constituents and help create a more perfect union. What they find is something entirely different.

CHAPTER THREE
ORIENTATION

On the Monday after the 2006 elections, November 13, 2006, Montana's junior senator-elect, Jon Tester, would enter the U.S. Capitol for the first time since he was a child. According to the strict seniority system of the Senate, Tester was ranked one hundredth—dead last in the world's most important deliberative body. Having won the closest race in the country a few days earlier, he was on top of the world, but decidedly at the bottom of the class. "I'm lower than the mayor of Chattanooga," he observed. "No, the former mayor of Chattanooga."[1] He was referring to Republican Bob Corker, who was ranked up at ninety-seventh, ahead of the new senators from Rhode Island and Minnesota, too.

The system by which seniority is determined for new members is a complex one that assigns credit for public service. As a former president of the Montana Senate, Tester might have expected to be placed higher than Corker, who was a two-term mayor of Tennessee's fourth-largest city. Former senators who have returned get the most seniority credit, followed by members of the House, followed by former governors. Beyond that, a state's population is the deciding factor. Tennessee, with 6.1 million people, is more than six times the size of Montana, which is one of seven states (and the District of Columbia) having fewer than a million residents. (Not that it was any consolation to Tester, Montana was the largest of these.) "We're number one hundred" would become a frequent cry among Tester staffers during everything from softball games to negotiations (failed) on the energy bill. The challenge for Tester, and his fellow lowly freshmen, was how to transcend their ranking and make the Senate work for them. "The key to this job," Senator Bernie Sanders of Vermont would say later, "is learning how to use power. That's it."[2]

As Senator No. 100 entered the Capitol, a police officer asked him to empty his pockets so as not to set off the magnometers that were now part of everyday life on the Hill and much of official Washington. "Just like at the airport, you put it all through?"[3] Tester smiled broadly. Just then, the officer recognized the new senator-elect and waved him through without subjecting him to the security check. This was Tester's first taste of the privileges of office.

What had been caution before September 11, 2001, was, by the fall of 2006, a familiar simmering anxiety. There were constant reminders that this building was a natural target for those who wanted to do harm in the most conspicuous way: The plane brought down in a field in central Pennsylvania on 9/11 was headed for the Capitol. That was a fact lost on no one. After the anthrax contamination scares in 2001, emergency gas masks began appearing above people's desks in the Capitol. When freshman senator Ben Cardin of Maryland got his new office on the fifth floor of the Hart Senate Office Building, he often made a point of telling visitors that it used to be Tom Daschle's office, where the anthrax spores were received in 2001.

The anxiety generated by the attacks of 2001 obviously changed the way Americans lived, and the fallout was both small and large, even in the U.S. Senate. Amy Klobuchar quickly figured out that one of the best ways to work the Senate was to buttonhole other senators on the floor of the chamber for information and to talk about possible deals. In her eagerness, she sometimes left her purse hanging around the cloakroom or some of the other anterooms to the Senate chamber. But fear of terrorism meant that unattended purses, even in the Senate, were no longer casually regarded, and were seen as a possible threat. It never took the Capitol Police long to make sure she retrieved it.

On occasion, the simmer would rise to a boil and the anxiety would turn to panic. In June 2004, the nation prepared for a lavish state funeral for the late president Ronald Reagan. The occasion provided one of the best examples of how the terrorist attacks of September 11, 2001, had changed America. George W. Bush's presidency was seen by many as the final blossoming of the Reagan Revolution, so when Reagan died on June 5, 2004, what followed was something approximating a canonization: a six-day state funeral that would involve flying the president's body from his home in Los Angeles to the Capitol, where he would lie in state for a day and a half before being flown back to California for burial.

Reagan's body arrived in Washington on June 7. The Capitol was abuzz with the sense of occasion. In the late afternoon, at about 4:25 P.M., an alarm sounded in the Capitol. It was a weak, tinkling alarm, without even the urgency of the bells that ring in senators' offices to alert them it is time to vote. But Capitol Police officers began moving through the building insisting the alarm was real and that people should get out. Most began walking, then upgraded to a slow, rolling jog.

When it was clear the evacuation was not happening fast enough, officers articulated the specifics of the threat. "We have an inbound aircraft," said one of them on the north side of the building. Suddenly everyone was moving faster, for a few moments literally running for their lives. Majority Leader Bill Frist raced from the building. A Capitol Police officer trying to help Nancy Pelosi out of the building ended up lifting her out of her shoes. The plane in question turned out to be a small private jet piloted by the governor of Kentucky, Ernie Fletcher, who had gone slightly off course in the very hypersensitive Washington airspace. A Blackhawk helicopter and two F-15 fighter jets were dispatched from Andrews Air Force Base to intercept the plane. In a few minutes, Fletcher began speaking with the control towers again, and the crisis was over.

Only nine of the ten soon-to-be senators had arrived in Washington for freshman orientation. Claire McCaskill of Missouri—whose campaign was marked by tough talk, much like her predecessor Harry Truman—one of the marvels of the election season, set Washington abuzz by skipping the customary event to vacation in Bali. It was one of McCaskill's first displays of an independence that would come to characterize her early tenure in the Senate and in some ways the tenure of the whole freshman class, who quickly established that they were not all that eager to play by the rules. At a time when the political choristers would have advised against doing anything that might be construed as arrogance, McCaskill blew off the first requirements of her win. In doing so, however, McCaskill was keeping a promise she'd made to her family to take a vacation after the election—win or lose—and she had Harry Reid's blessing to do it. So Bali it was, though in secret. For days, no one in the press knew where McCaskill was.

The other hard-to-find senator-elect was Bob Corker, the Tennessee Republican. Corker is a small man; he says he's five foot, seven inches tall, but he comes across much shorter. He had no new Republican colleagues to bond with, and he did not share in the sense of celebration that attached to the new Democratic class, so he was often out of sight. He had made millions of dollars, first in construction and then as the largest private real estate owner in Hamilton County, which includes Chattanooga. Corker is not a natural politician, but he has personal warmth and a talent for ingratiating himself that does not seem contrived.

Faced with eight new senators from the opposite party during orientation, Corker decided to resort to humor. On a bus ride to a dinner one night, Corker reminded a few of the Democrats, including Bob Casey, of all the attention that Harold Ford had attracted during the campaign because of the historic implications if he won. "You guys should be glad I won," Corker said. "If I hadn't won, no one would know who you guys were." Laughter all around. "I thought it was funny," said Casey, whose sense of humor is notoriously dry.[4]

At 4:30 P.M. on November 13, the freshmen gathered in the President's Room—a room just off the Senate floor built as an addition to the Capitol in the 1850s to accommodate the president of the United States when he had business, bill signings for example, with the Senate—to have their pictures taken for identification cards. Spouses get ID cards as well. Then they met in a second-floor room for a more relaxed introduction. Dinner had originally been planned for the LBJ Room with Senators Ted Stevens and Daniel K. Inouye, Senate legends from Alaska and Hawaii respectively, as the featured guests, but that event had been canceled because the freshmen were invited to the White House for dinner with the president.

At the White House, freshman senator Jim Webb avoided the receiving line. Bush eventually found him and tried to make small talk. "How's your boy?" the president asked, referring to Webb's son, Jimmy, who was serving in Iraq. "I'd like to get them out of Iraq, Mr. President," said Webb, resorting to one of the themes of his campaign. The president's temper flared. "That's not what I asked you," he said, and repeated: "How's your boy?" Webb was unflinching: "That's between me and my boy, Mr. President," he said, and that is where the conversation ended.

Someone leaked word of the exchange to the *Washington Post,* and Webb confirmed it two weeks later.[5] When news of this exchange became public, Webb was roundly criticized for disrespecting not just Bush but the presidency. He later told me that he was very focused on ending the war in Iraq and bringing the troops home and was in no mood to make small talk about his son with the commander in chief. This was a pretty spectacular display of independence for a senator on his first day, and a testament to his belief that one should never—even on your first day on a new job—shy away from a fight. Even with the most powerful man in the free world.

△

That first Monday, the new members did their work behind closed doors—learning how to get their offices up and running, prepare their budgets, use franking privileges, and keep abreast of complicated ethics rules. There are two different computer operating systems available to Senate offices. The entire process had to be handled with two staff members, because that is all the rules will allow before the senator is actually sworn in. Trying to deal with the hundreds of résumés with only two people, or trying to interview potential staff members while you're not in Washington but back in Big

Sandy, or Minneapolis or Scranton or Burlington, is difficult, to say the least. And all of it happens between Thanksgiving and Christmas.

Once inside the building, Jon Tester and his new colleagues did a lot of smiling and posing for pictures. Advice about how to be a senator poured in from all corners. Ted Stevens, approaching his eighty-third birthday, had been in the Senate for thirty-eight years, making him then the longest-serving Republican in the Senate. He teamed up with Democrat Daniel Inouye, who had represented Hawaii since it became a state in 1959, first for four years in the House and then since 1963 in the Senate. When Stevens was elected, Alaska had been a state for only a decade. Stevens and Inouye talked about how they worked together on defense issues. The differences in their party, their politics, their home states, and their ability to work together was an attempt to show the new senators how the Senate should work.

The members of the Senate who had been through this process most recently, notably Barack Obama, had dispensed their brief wisdom about how to be successful in the Senate. As did the ones for whom freshman orientation was a distant memory: "I told them what I tell all new senators," said Robert C. Byrd, the longest-serving senator in the entire 220-plus-year history of the institution. "Keep your head down and work hard."[6]

While the "work hard" component of the advice remained important, nobody in the television age gets anywhere keeping his head down. The thing a senator most wants to do with his head is get it filmed talking on network television on Sunday mornings. The ways of leveraging power in the Senate has changed from the days of Daniel Webster, Henry Clay, and Robert C. Byrd, and the freshmen knew it.

Harry Reid was ecstatic, and it was easy to tell: He was smiling. Reid, a resolutely dour personage around the Capitol, has openly confessed to not being a fun guy. In 2006, at age sixty-seven, he was tireless and driven, rising early each morning to run or do sit-ups or yoga. That first day, Reid gathered the new members in his new conference room on the second floor of the Capitol for a meeting with the press. The room is small but lavish, with a massive gold-plated mirror on the north wall and portraits of JFK and

FDR on the others. A few years prior, the Democratic and Republican leaders had decided that when there was a change in the majority, the parties would keep the same offices in order to prevent constant moving and redecorating. So the Democratic heroes on Reid's wall had been there since Tom Daschle's time as both majority and minority leader.

Charles Schumer, the New York senator who headed the campaign committee that helped get all of the Democrats elected, sat in their midst, beaming like a proud parent. "Chuck does have a mother-hen quality when it comes to this group," said J. B. Poersch, executive director of the Democratic Senatorial Campaign Committee (DSCC).[7] This committee is essentially set up by Senate Democrats to help them win elections, by either protecting incumbents, winning the seats of retiring members, or knocking off Republican candidates. The Republican version is called the Republican Senatorial Campaign Committee. In 2006, the DSCC raised and spent more than $100 million on senatorial races, money above and beyond the $250 million spent by individual campaigns for the thirty-three contested seats.

Harry Reid's conference room was packed with reporters. So many, in fact, that they were asked to enter in waves. The photographers went first. The pencils next. Schumer was bragging about the group. Over his left shoulder he pointed at Bob Casey: "Casey was never ahead by less than double digits," Schumer began. "Not like Webb here . . ."

"I'm here, aren't I?" Webb grumbled out of the corner of his mouth.[8] And for that, both Webb and Schumer were grateful.

Tester remembers the first time he met Schumer, at an event in New York. Tester was still in the primary fight with State Auditor John Morrison, which meant that Schumer technically could not take sides, but Tester recalls being a little put off by the New Yorker. "He did not give me the warm and fuzzies," Tester later said.[9] Well, Schumer could not have been warmer and fuzzier now that Democrats had retaken control of the Senate on the strength of Tester's and Jim Webb's narrow wins. And no matter how close the election was, Webb was now a U.S. senator and part of the majority, and Schumer was beaming.

Later, outside the conference room, Jim Webb was surrounded by a crush of reporters, answering questions about the closeness of his win, the war, and the oddities of the sudden attention. The early rap on Webb was that he was insufficiently political for the rigors of the Hill, that he wouldn't be attentive enough to the ugly practicalities of Washington to assure his survival.

Much of that concern was sparked during the election, a race that had involved none of the usual cult-of-personality elements so common in today's political campaigns and where, early on, Webb proved to be an underwhelming fund-raiser and poor glad-hander. When Webb explained that his most important formative experiences as an adult were commanding marines in battle and enjoying the solitude of being a writer, it's not hard to understand why he sometimes seemed to be having so little fun during the campaign.

Webb allowed to the throng of reporters that he couldn't stay long because he was finishing an op-ed for the *Wall Street Journal*. Two days later, the piece appeared, and it was not about the war in Iraq, but instead about the evolving class disparities in the country. "The most important—and unfortunately the least debated—issue in politics today is our society's steady drift toward a class-based system, the likes of which we have not seen since the nineteenth century," Webb began his article.[10] This was the second indication that very first day that the last thing Jim Webb was going to be as a senator was predictable.

Amy Klobuchar spent her first night in Washington in a friend's basement. In an interview with her hometown newspaper, she referred to that evening sarcastically as "my glamorous 'beginning.'"[11] But Klobuchar was clear in her head about what the election meant, and believed that the people elected to the Senate with her represented a deep desire among the American people for something different. People wanted action, she said: "When you look at our candidates and their backgrounds . . . they mostly came from jobs where you actually had to get some things done—when you go back to

what Webb did before he was a novelist. You had people who were very focused on results and conveyed that confidence that they were able to get
things done. We all have made clear that we came here to do something,
not just be a senator."[12]

Klobuchar would have time to be a senator if she was able to pull off
what she envisioned. She was forty-six years old, the youngest member of
the new class, but not the youngest person in the Senate; that distinction
belonged to the first-term Republican from New Hampshire, John Sununu,
who was forty-two. There were seven others younger than she, including
Blanche Lincoln of Arkansas, John Thune of South Dakota, David Vitter
of Louisiana, and Mark Pryor also of Arkansas. Whatever difficulties
Klobuchar and others may have had adjusting to the Senate was presaged
by the fact that the average age of a U.S. senator at the opening of the 110th
Congress was seventy.

After the new members and their staffs had been laden with briefing
books, lectures, and presentations on everything from the Italian art in the
Capitol to whom to hire to run their office, on Tuesday, November 14, Democrats gathered in the Old Senate Chamber to elect their leaders. Harry
Reid, the converted Mormon from Searchlight, Nevada, was chosen majority leader. His chief lieutenant, the Democratic whip, was Richard Durbin,
the senior senator from Illinois, who had recently embarked on a second
career, promoting the presidential candidacy of his junior senator, Barack
Obama. Patty Murray, a former preschool teacher and citizen activist now
in her third term, was elected secretary of the Democratic Conference,
making her the third-ranking Democrat in the Senate and one of the most
powerful women in the country.

The Old Senate Chamber sits off a mini-rotunda, just north of the main
rotunda under the Capitol Dome. It is a museum to a more glorious time.
In this small room, with a second-floor balcony hemmed in by a wooden
railing, the Senate met for nearly half a century, after the nation's capital
moved from Philadelphia, from 1810 until 1859, the period known as the
Golden Age of the Senate, which ended in the run-up to the Civil War. It

is in this chamber that the reputation of the Senate was essentially established. This was the realm of John C. Calhoun and Henry Clay. It was here that the Missouri Compromise was crafted in 1820; it was in this room in 1845 that the Senate sat its first Jewish senator; it was here in this room that the issues of slavery, territorial expansion, and economic policy affecting the new nation were debated, leading to the Compromise of 1850. And it was here on March 7, 1850, that Daniel Webster secured the Senate's reputation as the world's greatest debating society with his three-hour soliloquy in defense of the Union.

"Mr. President, in the excited times in which we live, there is found to exist a state of crimination and recrimination between the North and South," Webster said. "There are lists of grievances produced by each; and those grievances, real or supposed, alienate the minds of one portion of the country from the other, exasperate the feelings, and subdue the sense of fraternal affection, patriotic love, and mutual regard. I shall bestow a little attention, Sir, upon these various grievances existing on the one side and on the other."[13]

In his speech, Webster dismissed the idea that secession could be achieved by peaceful means. At the same time he denounced abolitionist societies as having done nothing to help end slavery and urged non–slave states to return fugitive slaves to their owners as a constitutional show of goodwill to the South. Webster's speech, morally compromised as it seems today, is credited with preventing an imminent war and preserving the Union for ten more years, making it stronger, and strong enough, to survive the conflict that eventually came.

On that day Webster had begun his speech by declaring: "I wish to speak to-day, not as a Massachusetts man, nor as a Northern man, but as an American, and a member of the Senate of the United States. It is fortunate that there is a Senate of the United States; a body not yet moved from its propriety, not lost to a just sense of its own dignity and its own high responsibilities, and a body to which the country looks, with confidence, for wise, moderate, patriotic, and healing counsels."[14]

That Tuesday, the day after the freshmen settled in, Reid, with the help of his nine new members, was elected not just leader of the Democratic Caucus, but majority leader of the United States Senate—a job that gave him the right to talk first in the Senate each day.

Much had happened in the century and a half to diminish, in many minds, the lofty reputation of the Senate as the model of legislative prudence and effective self-government. But in the bright fall of 2006, there was, at least among its newest members—on the implicit promise to the country that they were going to fix the mess in Iraq—the hope that the Senate could live up to Webster's aspiration for it. "Despite having to get used to all these rules and this kind of glorious setting," Klobuchar said, "I just kept thinking about how we have to get things done."[15] She later hung a poster in her office that said: "If we fail this time, it is a failure of imagination."

Harry Reid emerged from the meeting that morning with a somewhat contradictory strategy. The Democrats had decided that they would forcefully confront President Bush on Iraq, but that they would forgo the use of the most potent weapon in that battle—the option to use congressional power to cut off funding for the war. The strategy seemed a sad confection mixed by the recognition that Americans wanted the war to be over with a lingering fear that Democrats would be painted as unpatriotic, weak-kneed, and naïve about the complexities of the world. The tepid and layered opposition to the war on the Democratic side was a concession to those fears, and when Democrats talked about "changing course in Iraq," rather than ending the war, it was a measure of exactly how intimidated they were by years and years of losses to the GOP.

Then it was time for lunch. The Democrat senators, old and new, walked past the soon-to-be minority leader's office that Bill Frist would relinquish to Mitch McConnell, the Kentucky Republican, past the Ohio Clock, a grand eight-foot-tall wooden grandfather clock crowned with an eagle that was a gift from the people of Ohio, past the busts of vice presidents, past the marble stairs above which hangs a grand painting of the Battle of Saratoga. They entered the LBJ Room for a buffet lunch of chicken and fish. Amy Klobuchar began at the salad bar.

"I went to the buffet table and I got a salad and a soup and brought it back," she remembered later, "and I'm ready to dive in and Patty Murray grabbed my arm and said, 'Amy: You are about to eat the bowl of Thousand Island dressing.' Turned out I had taken—I thought it was wild rice soup—the entire bowl of Thousand Island dressing. Someone told me later that I should have said, 'That's what we do in Minnesota: We eat the Thousand Island dressing.'"[16]

△

From very early on, Klobuchar had lived a public life. Not that she chose it. Her father, Jim Klobuchar, was a columnist for the Minneapolis *Star Tribune*, and he would regularly chronicle her doings, including details of her marriage, in his column.

Klobuchar likes to joke that her political career started the summer she was eleven. She formed a babysitting club with two friends. Every day that summer they spent the afternoon rounding up neighborhood kids and taking them to one of their three houses. A few weeks into their new enterprise, and with enough money raised to have some fun, Klobuchar decided that the young entrepreneurs should go on a road trip to Kansas City. But that required convincing their mothers to let them take a Greyhound Bus almost 450 miles all by themselves. Klobuchar would lead the lobbying effort. According to the *Star Tribune*, the girls successfully pleaded their case, over a formal lunch with typed menus and a main course of chicken salad in cantaloupe.

"That was the precursor of all my organized activities to try to convince people," Klobuchar told the reporter.[17] "I liked to organize things," she said. "I got people together to do things, sometimes for fun, but always for a purpose."[18]

Klobuchar's parents divorced when she was a high school freshman. Like everything else in his life, Amy's father wrote a column about the divorce, which was painful to her.

Klobuchar excelled in high school and went happily off to Yale, where she was glad that no one knew who she was. "I wanted to go to a place where people couldn't spell my name," she said.[19] She majored in political science. Her college internships—first with the state attorney general's office and then in the office of vice president, and former Minnesota senator, Walter Mondale—would set the course for the rest of her life. Her college senior thesis was on the construction and political history of the Hubert H. Humphrey Metrodome, home of the Minnesota Twins and the Minnesota Vikings, and one of the first in a long list of professional sports stadiums built in the country using a huge pot of public money. The thesis became a book which she dedicated to her parents, and at one point she quoted her father as "one *Minneapolis Star* columnist" who, reacting to the myriad plans for the stadium, "jested that the state had 'finally reached that utopian plane of the democratic dream: one man, one stadium.'"

The reference was a joke, of course, and a clear illustration of where the senator's sense of humor comes from. But the book would also signal the beginning of her serious thoughts about the political process. She wrote: "Although ideological differences enter into local disputes, they do not produce the philosophical or moral clashes which characterized the country's struggle over civil rights legislation or the debate over the nation's involvement in the Vietnam War."[20]

Writing in 1982, she referenced those struggles and moral conflicts as part of the recent American past, but similar ideological clashes would come to define her public future as well.

After Yale, Klobuchar went to law school at the University of Chicago and then went home to Minneapolis to take a job at a law firm and to begin her political career. She quickly got involved in Democratic Party politics, which in Minnesota meant the Democratic-Farmer-Labor Party. She joined a group of other young DFLers who regularly got together to drink beer and talk politics. She became the classic activist, volunteering on campaigns and donating money when she could.

Klobouchar wanted to get engaged during Bill Clinton's inauguration in 1992. Her future husband refused, saying that he would not be overshadowed during that big moment by the new Democratic president. Amy is seven and a half years older than her husband, John Bessler, who, she likes to point out, qualified for a Eurailpass student discount on their honeymoon because he was twenty-six and she was thirty-three. Bessler grew up in Mankato, Minnesota, and on their first date, a blind double date at a bowling alley in Minneapolis, Klobuchar became convinced that John was not interested in her, and that he was in fact keen on the other woman. Halfway through the evening, no longer trying to impress him with how she looked, she went to the bathroom, took out her contacts, and put on her glasses. "My eyes hurt," she later recalled.[21] It took Bessler less than twenty-four hours to ask her out again.

The importance of politics in their relationship was established early. John, who has written books on lynching and capital punishment, is also a lover of all things Lincoln. So when he finally decided to ask Amy to marry him, he chose to propose not during the Clinton inaugural but on Lincoln's birthday, February 12. The salesman at the jewelry store, however, reasonably believed that he was looking at another romantic who was going to propose on Valentine's Day, a banality that infuriated John.

When they did get married, in July 1993, the reception was not held in one of the fancy hotels in downtown Minneapolis or outdoors on one of the state's ten thousand lakes. Instead, it was held at the Humphrey Institute at the University of Minnesota, where the guests could commune with the spirit of one of the great Democrats of the twentieth century, and Walter Mondale, the other Minnesota vice president, was in the front row.

Klobuchar's daughter, Abigail, was born in 1995. Her health insurance plan at the time allowed new mothers only a twenty-four-hour hospital stay, a practice that became known pejoratively as "drive-by delivery." In this case, the baby had problems that would not allow her to go home in twenty-four hours. Milk bubbled through her nose during feedings. She could not swallow. But Klobuchar had to leave the hospital; the baby stayed behind.[22] The couple got a room nearby and went back and forth to the hospital. Eventually, doctors put a tube in the infant's stomach and sent her home. For months, Abigail's parents took turns going to work and being the primary caregiver.

In the end Abigail turned out fine, but when the Minnesota legislation took up a proposal the following year to require health plans to allow new mothers to stay in the hospital for forty-eight hours, Klobuchar was the star witness. She packed the hearing with women and their children. The bill passed.

In 1997, with little experience, she entered the race for Hennepin County attorney, facing former judge and assistant U.S. attorney Sheryl Ramstad. The race was nasty, and Ramstad sought to make it about experience, frequently reminding potential voters that she was already prosecuting cases when Klobuchar was still a high school student.[23]

During one memorable campaign exchange, reported in the *Star Tribune*, Ramstad charged that Klobuchar was like Klobuchar's relatives—a street fighter from the Iron Range—referring to the part of the state where iron ore was once mined by tough, hardworking men, the children of immigrants from Eastern Europe. Klobuchar burst out laughing and thanked Ramstad. She narrowly won the election, by less than 1 percent of the vote, and established herself as a candidate with a big future.

Jeff Blodgett, a Democratic activist who worked on her first campaign, told the *Star Tribune*, "She will do what it takes to be successful."[24] But it was not just her drive that impressed people. Klobuchar also had to walk the fine line required of female candidates: smart but nurturing, tough but warm, strong but reassuring. "In our society it's still a problem for women to come across on both those dimensions," said Steven Smith, a political science professor at Washington University in St. Louis who follows Minnesota politics. "She's overcome that better than most."[25]

Senator Mark Dayton, who had had trouble adjusting to Washington, announced in 2005 that he would not seek reelection. In April 2006, *Time* named Dayton one of the Senate's five worst members, citing his "erratic behavior" as evidenced by his decision to shut down his office in 2004 because of a terrorist threat. "The 99 other Senators had access to the same intelligence and kept their offices open, even while Dayton went on television to tell his constituents not to visit the Capitol," *Time* noted.[26]

In the wake of Dayton's announcement, Klobuchar was definitely interested in pursuing the Senate seat, but it was not something she had given a lot of thought to up to this point. The Senate was something off in the future, and she worried that it might seem like she was getting ahead of herself. And there were people actively discouraging her from running. One skeptical adviser told her she would have to raise $3 million right off the bat to be seen as a credible candidate. She also understood that she had a firmer claim to the DFL endorsement for attorney general. But she could not shake the sense that she was being presented a unique opportunity.

It all crystallized, finally, on an ice-covered lake in central Minnesota. In February 2007, Klobuchar and Bessler went ice fishing with Earl Maus, the Cass County attorney, and his wife. Klobuchar had made the fishing date for the previous December, but there had not been enough ice on the lakes, and so the trip was rescheduled. "Another effect of global warming," Klobuchar joked later.[27] The new date was during the Eelpout Days, a local fishing festival. Every winter, Minnesotans go fishing for eelpout, an ugly lake fish that hunts at night and in the depth of winter when no other fish are swimming in the frozen lakes. "The whole way up I'm on the phone talking to people, telling them I'm thinking of running for the Senate,"[28] she said. She talked to everyone she knew. Most of her political friends did not think well of her chances to win the DFL Senate nomination.

But it was increasingly clear to her that this is what she wanted to do. She and John and the Mauses sat on the lake in their fish house, their rods baited and hanging deep in the water. Klobuchar could think of nothing else. She knew the obstacles, money being the biggest one: She would have to raise maybe $10 million for a Senate race. After several hours of conversation, Maus asked what became a bottom-line question: Did she think she could do a good job in the Senate?

The answer was yes. "And he said, 'Then I think you should go for it,'" she told me later. "And I said 'OK Earl.' And that was it, it was settled. From then on I was running for the Senate."[29]

Klobuchar joined the other new senators in Harry Reid's conference room on November 14, 2006. Then she took part in the leadership elections and attended a "power coffee" with other female senators hosted by Democratic senator Barbara Mikulski of Maryland. Klobuchar enjoyed the perceived sense that somehow the roles were reversed with her husband: She said that John discovered, to her dismay, that there was an official Senate china pattern available to new senators who wanted a new set of dishes. He was not the only male spouse in the new class—though McCaskill's husband had stayed in Missouri—while Bessler made a point early on that he would attend all the spouses' events. He said that he came to understand the value of those activities: "I sometimes actually pick up information that is useful to her."[30]

One day during an event for the spouses of new senators, all the women went to the bathroom together, leaving Bessler alone in the room. Noting his plight, Terese Casey, wife of Pennsylvania senator Bob Casey, came back to chat with him. Her husband took his role in the Senate pretty seriously, Klobuchar pointed out. "He keeps asking me where his transition memos are," she said jokingly.[31]

Klobuchar was pleasantly surprised by the bipartisan tone in Washington right after the election. She told the *Star Tribune*, "The president's reaching out—[Defense Secretary Donald] Rumsfeld's already gone. [Republican senators] Olympia Snowe and Norm Coleman both called me. And I'm very hopeful that we're ushering in an era where we're actually going to be getting things done for the people of our state, which they haven't been doing for six years."[32] Amy Klobuchar and the other victorious Democrats had campaigned on the proposition that the Republicans during the Bush era had been serving only their ideology and their own narrow self-interest. She and her freshman class of senators had been elected to change that.

This is typical of the hope and optimism of the first days—new senators think they are going to be the ones to make a difference, that this time things are really going to change.

CHAPTER FOUR
SWEARING IN

Section 1 of the Twentieth Amendment to the U.S. Constitution established that the terms of members of Congress will begin and end on January 3, unless Congress moves the date, which it now routinely does to accommodate the holidays. In 2007, the date was moved, if only by one day. So two months after their election, and eight weeks after beginning orientation, the freshmen senators were ready to take their seats.

The 110th Congress convened on January 4, 2007, a Thursday morning that dawned kindly on the national capital—clear blue skies, light breezes, temperatures in the midsixties. Not your typical early January day in Washington, and for that reason the kind of day people remember. Providence, it seemed, approved of the shift in power taking place and decided to match the weather to the drama of the moment.

From the outside, the Capitol gleamed in the brightness of midwinter sunshine. Inside, history was on tap. Most conspicuously in the House chamber, where a sixty-seven-year-old grandmother named Nancy Pelosi was about to become the first female Speaker of the House of Representatives. The daughter of a Baltimore political family, Pelosi rose to power as a notoriously liberal congresswoman from San Francisco. With her swearing-in she would be third in the line of succession to the presidency and the most powerful elected woman official in the history of the American government. The world took note.

Pelosi appeared on the front page of nearly every newspaper in America. True to the sentimentality common in the American print media, the favorite photograph was one of Pelosi surrounded by her five children and six grandchildren. The grandchildren had followed their famous grandmother onto the House floor, along with Pelosi's adult daughter, Alexandra, even though House rules bar people who are under twelve from the chamber without explicit permission. The appropriate loophole in this situation was that each new Congress establishes the rules by which it will govern itself, and since those rules had not been established, they did not yet apply.

△

Change was in the air across the Rotunda on the Senate side of the Capitol as well. Thirty-three newly elected or reelected senators were taking the oath of office, beginning new six-year terms. Americans still like to think of their government as simple, revolutionary, and devoid of the high ceremony associated with monarchies. Ours, after all, is a government of, by, and for the people, designed to venerate the individual and eschew high ceremony. But anyone who has ever watched a presidential inauguration or attended a state funeral understands the conceit involved in those beliefs, and the opening day of any new Congress is rife with pageantry.

The senators take their oath of office in groups of four. Every two years, one-third of the Senate seats are up for reelection, so at the start of each Congress, thirty-three or thirty-four senators get sworn in. Freshman classes tend to average about a dozen, but they are often a mix of members of the same party replacing retiring members or some balance of Democrats and Republicans that preserve the status quo. The ten members of the freshman class of 2007 represented a huge change: nine new Democrats, six new Democratic seats, and a shift in power. In this way, it resembled the freshman class of the 1958 election, which was made up of fifteen Democrats and three Republicans, or the class of 1980, which had eighteen Republicans and two Democrats. In both cases, the country made a decisive political statement.

The Democratic sweep of 1958 returned Lyndon Johnson as majority leader of the Senate and laid the groundwork for the Great Society programs of the 1960s. Democrats picked up thirteen Republican seats, and when Hawaii and Alaska later joined the Union, they sent four Democrats to Washington. The '58 class included men who would later become icons of American liberalism like Eugene McCarthy of Minnesota, Philip Hart of Michigan, and Edmund Muskie of Maine.

In 1980, the elections were dominated by bad economic times and the sense of helplessness evoked by the seizure and ongoing occupation of the U.S. embassy in Tehran. Reagan promised Americans that he would restore the country's stature in the world and waged a remarkably successful campaign against "big government," making conservatism the dominant political force in the country for a generation. The freshman class that year included Dan Quayle of Indiana, Charles Grassley of Iowa, and Warren Rudman of New Hampshire. Even if none of them turned out to be a political powerhouse, their collective success marked the beginning of the Reagan Revolution.

In 2006, before the election, Jim Webb anticipated a big class and predicted that it would be "an important one" as well. Time and the 2012 elections will tell.

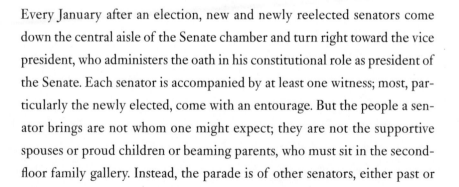

Every January after an election, new and newly reelected senators come down the central aisle of the Senate chamber and turn right toward the vice president, who administers the oath in his constitutional role as president of the Senate. Each senator is accompanied by at least one witness; most, particularly the newly elected, come with an entourage. But the people a senator brings are not whom one might expect; they are not the supportive spouses or proud children or beaming parents, who must sit in the second-floor family gallery. Instead, the parade is of other senators, either past or present. Often, but not always, among the escorts is the other senator from the same state. For others, it is a political hero or personal mentor who serves in the Senate or who once did.

That Thursday in January 2007, the alphabetical roll call began with the junior senator from Hawaii, who was beginning his fourth term; the junior senator from New Mexico; a freshman from Ohio; and the longest-serving senator ever. The clerk began.

"Mr. Akaka, Mr. Bingaman, Mr. Brown, and Mr. Byrd."

Democratic majority leader Harry Reid stood up for Daniel Akaka of Hawaii; Pete Domenici, the senior senator from New Mexico, escorted the junior senator, Jeff Bingaman. Sherrod Brown, the new Ohio senator, had former Ohio senator John Glenn, his political mentor, at his side. And in a reversal of the junior-senior pairing, Jay Rockefeller, the great-grandson of industrialist John D. Rockefeller, a giant of a man at six feet, seven inches, escorted the ailing Robert C. Byrd down the aisle. Rockefeller had been elected to four terms in the Senate by West Virginia voters, but he remained the state's junior senator because of Byrd's record-setting tenure. Byrd, a member of the 1958 freshman class, during the 110th Congress would become the longest-serving senator in American history.

Richard Cheney administered the oath:

> I do solemnly swear that I will support and defend the Constitution of the United States against all enemies, foreign and domestic; that I will bear true faith and allegiance to the same; that I take this obligation freely, without any mental reservation or purpose of evasion; and that I will well and faithfully discharge the duties of the office on which I am about to enter: So help me God.[1]

The oath, in somewhat variegated forms, has been uttered by every person who has served in the Senate since it first convened in 1789. Initially it was just a simple pledge to support the Constitution. But during the Civil War, Northern Republicans wanted to make sure that secessionists were not using the Senate to advance a breakup of the Union. And since 1864, the overt reference to enemies "foreign and domestic" has been part of the oath.

After the oath is administered, the new senator signs the Oath Book, putting the pledge in writing, and moves on. The next group takes center stage.

Ms. Cantwell, Mr. Cardin, Mr. Carper, and Mr. Casey.

Mrs. Clinton, Mr. Conrad, Mr. Corker, and Mr. Ensign.

Mrs. Feinstein, Mr. Hatch, Mrs. Hutchison, and Mr. Kennedy.

Ms. Klobuchar, Mr. Kohl, Mr. Kyl, and Mr. Lieberman.

Mr. Lott, Mr. Lugar, Mrs. McCaskill, and Mr. Menendez.

Mr. Nelson of Florida, Mr. Nelson of Nebraska, Mr. Sanders, and Ms. Snowe.

Ms. Stabenow, Mr. Tester, Mr. Thomas, and Mr. Webb.

After the eight groups of four, remaining was the thirty-third senator, the freshman from Rhode Island, Sheldon Whitehouse, who was in a group all by himself. Among the newly sworn-in senators was the reelected junior senator from New York, Hillary Rodham Clinton, whose husband, the forty-second president of the United States, Bill Clinton, sat in the front row of the public gallery looking like an excited child. He fidgeted; he waved to friends on the floor; he whispered in his daughter Chelsea's ear. As one of the most recognizable people on the planet, his presence created a definable buzz in the visitors' galleries. With Democrats taking control of the Senate, with six new faces, it was clear that most of the visitors were Democrats or supporters of Democrats who would be excited to see Bill Clinton.

Photographers are not allowed in the Senate chamber, so there was no way to record the historic moment. To partially address the problem, the swearing-in process is re-created in the Old Senate Chamber. There the freshmen are surrounded by relatives and friends, instead of other senators, for a photo op that often ends up on the senators' holiday greeting cards.

The ten new freshmen in 2007 represented the 1,886th through the 1,895th persons to serve in the United States Senate. Amy Klobuchar was listed as the 1,893rd senator in American history. She, along with her husband, John Bessler, and her daughter, Abigail, took one picture with Cheney, then added her mother, Rose, who was in a wheelchair, for a second shot. Jim Webb was number 1,890. He was photographed with the vice president alongside his wife and infant daughter.

While the junior senator from New York waited her turn for the Cheney picture, her husband decided to use the bathroom in the press gallery and startled the press corps: "They told me the nearest bathroom was in the press gallery. . . . I figured I've had enough barbs that I can handle it," Clinton said as he slipped away.[2]

The first-floor hallways were jammed with people. Friends and relatives of the new senators were all around, snapping photographs, and gawking at some of the famous faces walking the halls. Ted Kennedy and Hillary Clinton caused instant backups. Bill Clinton generated almost complete gridlock. Even for some new senators, the day seemed overwhelming. Bob Corker, the lone freshman Republican, got caught in the crush as the Clinton family—along with the secret service agents, aides, admirers, and reporters—came barreling toward the Old Senate Chamber. Corker, who had been chatting with two reporters from Tennessee newspapers, seemed stunned into retreat as the Clinton gaggle went by.

△

Later, the entire Senate, old members and new, gathered in the Old Senate Chamber to talk about how wonderful it would be to work together. The new majority leader, Harry Reid of Nevada, and his Republican counterpart, Minority Leader Mitch McConnell of Kentucky, addressed the gathering, along with Alaskan Ted Stevens, the longest-serving Republican in the Senate and a man with a reputation for extreme grouchiness. The talk was about cooperation and courtesy and how they wanted to work across party lines for the good of the country. But there was palpable skepticism among the freshmen.

As she arrived, Klobuchar announced, "I'm here for the civility meeting."[3] Two months after the election Klobuchar was clearly learning the ropes.

In public, others maintained a more hopeful stance. "It was a great forum. I believe we would have a much better debate if we didn't have cameras," said John E. Sununu, a New Hampshire Republican. He added, "This is always a time of optimism because legislative proposals have yet to be debated."[4]

Later that day, when the new Senate got down to business, Harry Reid tried to inspire a little optimism. He began by quoting Franklin Roosevelt: "The future lies with those wise political leaders who realize that the great public is interested more in Government than in politics."

> I have chosen this line to open this new session of the Senate because the wisdom it imparts is as relevant today as it was 67 years ago. The American people are expecting positive results from this 110th Congress, not more partisan rancor. Today we are not candidates; we are U.S. Senators. We 100 are from different States, we 100 represent different people, we 100 represent different political parties, but we share the same mission: keeping our country safe and providing a Government that allows people to enjoy the fruits and prosperity and, of course, our economic freedom.

It was a valiant attempt at positive thinking, but Reid knew even then that there was very little reason to be hopeful—he told me in private later that week that he didn't think the Republicans would be willing to compromise—but he continued laying out what was ahead:

> As the new Congress begins, the challenges facing America are complex. They range from a protracted war in Iraq to a health care crisis right here at home, from a middle class that is squeezed to an energy policy that is warming our globe, from a higher education system that has exploded in costs to jobs where benefits have all but disappeared. We Senators can make a difference in each of these areas if we remember we are here to fight for our country, not with each other.[5]

The Republican leader, Mitch McConnell, followed Reid onto the high ground:

> [The Senate] is the legislative embodiment of individual and minority rights, a place where the careful design, crafted by our Founding Fathers, pretty much operates today the way they planned it 220 years ago. We saw this 43 years ago with the Civil Rights Act of 1964, when the two parties forged a difficult alliance to reach a great goal. Segregated buses and lunch counters are difficult to fathom now, but their end only came about through the kind of cooperative resolution that has marked this body from the start. At its best, the Senate is a workshop where difficult challenges, such as civil rights, are faced squarely—and addressed—with good will and careful, principled agreement. At a time such as our own, when so many issues of consequence press upon us, it must be nothing less.[6]

Reid, McConnell, and anyone else paying attention knew that cooperation was going to be a low priority in the upcoming Congress. Republicans had staked their entire future on a close alliance with the president and had chosen to defend him and his policies to the death. The voters had punished them by turning over control of the Congress to Democrats, who now felt the need to deliver on their promise of ending the war in Iraq. For their part, Republicans seemed to understand that the revolution that had begun in 1980 was over.

By 2007, all the Republican generals and most of the foot soldiers from the 1994 uprising were gone: former speaker Newt Gingrich, former majority leaders Tom DeLay and Dick Armey, and Rick Santorum, who lost his seat in 2006. Now Republicans were dealing with sex scandals involving congressional pages and allegations of corruption surrounding lobbyist Jack Abramoff. As a consequence, Dennis Hastert, the longest-serving Republican Speaker of the House, had decided to resign.

In 1994, the Republicans' election-time policy statement, the Contract with America, was aimed at finishing what Ronald Reagan had started. It was centered in a conservatism defined by fiscal responsibility, national security, and moral values. It had been a tough doctrine to live by, and they often faltered, but they believed passionately and people were persuaded. But after controlling both houses of Congress and the White House for most of George W. Bush's six years in office, the Republican Party had drifted. They began spending money in ways they once decried and produced record deficits in the federal budget. And then, of course, there was Iraq, a strategic and political blunder so monumental that it might doom the party for a generation. "The Republican Party of 2006 is a tired, cranky shell of the aggressive, reformist movement that was swept into office in 1994 on a wave of positive change," GOP strategist Frank Luntz wrote in *Time* magazine a month before election day in 2006. "I worked for them. They were friends of mine. These Republicans are not those Republicans."[7]

Many blamed Iraq for the Republican defeats, but in truth it was Bush's plan to partially privatize Social Security that began the great unraveling. In the summer of 2005, Rick Santorum, the third-ranking Republican in the Senate, was thinking about his upcoming reelection campaign, then just over a year away. The president had been reelected and had boasted about his intention to spend his newly earned political capital. Santorum, a two-term incumbent, hitched his wagon to that star and went on the road to sell and defend Bush's Social Security reform plan. But at one event at Drexel University in Philadelphia, he got hammered and, for all his certainty and bluster, came away looking like a loser. He simply could not convince anyone that Social Security was a broken government program that needed fixing in the way that he was proposing.

The depth of the hostility that ensued was the first sign that Santorum might not get reelected, that the president might lose out on his plan to allow Americans to invest some of their Social Security savings in the equity markets, that the president might be in over his head, and that the whole gig might be up. The arrogance of the Social Security reform effort and the inability of the administration to move the proposal through Congress provided the first outlines of how the administration and its allies in Congress would eventually collapse under the weight of their own folly. They lost the vote of senior citizens, who liked the way Social Security works and are the most engaged and dependable of all demographic voting blocs. Santorum, of course, became one of the most conspicuous Republican casualties when he lost his reelection bid by 18 percentage points, the largest loss margin for a Senate incumbent since George McGovern of South Dakota lost to James Abdnor by 19 points in the Reagan rout of 1980.

It was in 2005 that Democrats began acting like the official opposition, first on Social Security, then on ethics. Many of them had spent the ten years since 1994 expecting to have an effect on legislation. Except, of course, they couldn't, because Republicans controlled the agenda. In 2005, the Democrats began to vigorously oppose (with minimal hand-wringing) the GOP agenda. They even threatened to shut down the Senate if Republicans tried to change the filibuster rules for judicial nominations. "We are just going to beat the crap out of them," said one Democratic aide, talking about Social Security.[8] The Democrats' rapid response in the mid-2000s to anything that came out of the White House made them seem resolute and determined.

Finally, Democrats appeared to believe in something they were willing to fight for—Social Security. But it was the other, nastier fight where they seemed to be going for the knockout. Republicans had been battling a series of accusations of corruption, and Democrats were using it to the best advantage. Famed GOP lobbyist Jack Abramoff was under indictment for corruption for gifts made to members of Congress, mostly Republicans. The majority leader was indicted in his home state of Texas for election irregularities. But ethics debates are always a touchy subject on Capitol Hill. There is a "mutually assured destruction" quality to them that can scare even the most reckless and partisan of members; ethics complaints are a readily available weapon that can be turned against those who bring them.

Still, the first thing the Senate would vote on that January day in 2007 was as uncontroversial as the weather outside. Senate Resolution 19 honoring the late President Gerald R. Ford, who had died a week earlier, passed unanimously.

△

With the minimal business out of the way, the evening was time for the new senators to celebrate. New Virginia senator Jim Webb was carrying his three-week-old daughter, Georgia LeAnh, around the Capitol, pledging cooperation, insisting that it was possible to get past the vitriol. "We need to be more civil to each other," Webb told a group of supporters. "We have a lot of work to do."[9] Minutes after he was sworn in, Webb introduced a bill, soon known as the "new G.I. Bill," that would provide educational benefits for veterans of the conflicts in Iraq and Afghanistan. The Senate would not pass it for a year and a half.

From that very first day, it was Jim Webb who began to lay out a coherent scheme about how Democrats could rebuild their credibility with the American people. He said he believed that it was time for Reagan Democrats, people like himself, "to return to their Jacksonian roots." Webb later told me:

> It is a message that I believe should be a continuing part of the national debate, and in fact should become the core message of a revitalized Democratic Party. I've said many times that this nation is going through a sea-change in terms of party politics, and that the old labels simply don't work anymore. The political cards are being reshuffled, all across this country. Good, well-meaning people have watched their government flub things up, from Iraq to the aftermath of Hurricane Katrina. They want better leadership, and they want new approaches.[10]

From the beginning, Webb emerged as the star of the freshman class. That first day, Harry Reid found his way to a Webb reception to praise the freshman senator. "To be able to stand by a real American hero says it all," Reid said. "He has physical courage and a lot of brains. We look forward to him being one of the great senators of all time."[11]

The debate on a new ethics bill to govern the behavior of members of Congress began that first week of the session, Monday, January 8, 2007, and would go on for a week and a half. During the debate, Reid walked over to Jim Webb on the floor as asked him if he would be willing to deliver the Democratic response to the president's State of the Union address on January 23. "I was a little surprised, but I said yes," Webb recalled.[12]

Reid's intentions seemed clear. Webb was emphatically pro-military but was against the conduct of the war in Iraq, and because of his December confrontation with the president, he had quickly established himself as a willing bulldog on the war and against the administration.

Reid understood that a tough election struggle can enable a candidate by clarifying his thinking on the issues, but he also understood the value of Webb's history as someone willing to cross party lines. "He represents to me what the new America is all about," Reid said. "He is someone who understands what it means to go to war, what it means to have peace, what it means to work on a bipartisan basis, someone who understands Reagan Democrats and the non-Reagan Democrats and independents and Republicans out there."[13]

The Democratic leadership, its communications staff, and its media consultants sent Webb a draft of what they imagined the speech would look like. "I took one look at it and thought, no way am I delivering that speech," he said. Webb's famous independence was showing almost at once. "There are a lot of things I need to learn up here, but writing a speech is not one of them."[14]

Reid's communications staff expected to have a copy of Webb's speech returned to them by the Thursday before he was due to give it. It is not certain whether Webb promised to deliver it then, but no speech was forthcoming that day. Friday came and went, and still there was nothing. Jim Manley, Harry Reid's communication director, is a frenetic Minnesotan who had worked for Ted Kennedy for eleven years before joining Reid's leadership staff. He is a man prone to anxiety in a job that tends to provoke exactly that. Webb's delays were painful for Manley. "It almost killed me," he said. "I kept asking if I could see what they had, and they kept saying no."[15]

Meanwhile, the Senate continued to debate the ethics bill, known officially as the Honest Leadership and Open Government Act of 2007, for those first two weeks of the session. The nine Democratic freshmen who had made this bill their first priority were heavily involved in the debate. It passed by a vote of ninety-six to two just after nine o'clock on a Thursday night. It was only then, on Friday night, in fact, that Jim Webb sat down to write his response to President Bush's State of the Union report, ignoring completely the draft suggestions that had been offered him by the Democratic leadership. "I think for a long time, Democrats have been talking to the American people about programs, rather than about themes," Webb said, describing what he wanted to address. "I want to talk about themes."[16] He wanted to talk about issues the way people process them in their own lives, or the way a novelist might approach them—not as a government program, or a piece of legislation, or a line item in the federal budget.

By Saturday, Jim Manley was a wreck. Jessica Smith, a bright-eyed redhead who runs Webb's press operation, told Manley that Webb was still rehearsing the speech. Rehearsing? That meant there was a speech, Manley thought, relieved. "Can we see it?" he wanted to know. The answer was no, not until it was done, and Webb wasn't done. The speech showed up on Sunday. "It was beautiful," Manley said, "worth the wait, but it almost killed me."[17]

△

The State of the Union address is an odd midwinter ritual in Washington; it is premised on a time when the chief executive would have more information about the country and the world than the average citizen. It began, with George Washington, as a report to the people as represented by their representatives in Congress. It would have been read and digested over the following weeks and months. Today, in the information age, it has become the president's chance to reset the table, adjust direction, defend sagging policy choices, and bargain with or threaten the Congress, by talking to the whole country.

Democrats, and Reid in particular, were feeling pummeled by the extreme forces of right-wing talk radio. They decided to try to counter the Republican media advantage by cultivating a stable of grassroots media activists to carry their side of the story to the voters. On the day of the State of the Union, they invited a few dozen liberal talk show hosts and bloggers to the Capitol. The big question on the table concerned cutting off funds for the war. It seemed clear to everyone in attendance that this was not going to happen. Senators walked off the Senate floor and wandered into the room of sympathetic media to take questions on everything from Iraq to the State of the Union.

In his slightly awkward way, Jim Webb drifted through the crowd. I walked over and asked if delivering the response to the president was causing him any anxiety. He shrugged his shoulders, the right one seeming to rise higher. "When people have tried to kill you twenty times, you don't worry about a speech." It took me a minute to realize he was talking about Vietnam. I chuckled. I repeated that story to Webb later in the year, and his response was "Twenty? That's probably a little low."[18]

As the members of Congress began gathering for the president's speech, Webb stood apart, the only senator who would not be present for it. In the bathroom off the Senate floor, he ran into two Republican senators. "They were trying to psych me out," he later said. He raised his voice to mimic the first: "The president is going to have this big audience; you're going to be in a little room all by yourself" (meaning the television studio where the response was recorded). The second: "When was the last time a senator had to respond to the president after being in the Senate for what—a month?"[19]

President Bush spoke for fifty-one minutes. He began by acknowledging the historic backdrop against which his speech was to be delivered:

Tonight, I have a high privilege and distinct honor of my own—as the first President to begin the State of the Union message with these words:

Madam Speaker. In his day, the late Congressman Thomas D'Alesandro, Jr. from Baltimore, Maryland, saw Presidents Roosevelt and Truman at this rostrum. But nothing could compare with the sight of his only daughter, Nancy, presiding tonight as Speaker of the House of Representatives. Congratulations, Madam Speaker.[20]

President Bush admitted that the world had changed: "We're not the first to come here with a government divided and uncertainty in the air. Like many before us, we can work through our differences, and achieve big things for the American people." More than half the speech was about the economy, and when he turned to the war in Iraq, it was to reiterate his standing policy of seeing the war through. Not what Democrats or the country was waiting to hear.

Our success in this war is often measured by the things that did not happen. We cannot know the full extent of the attacks that we and our allies have prevented, but here is some of what we do know: We stopped an al Qaeda plot to fly a hijacked airplane into the tallest building on the West Coast. We broke up a Southeast Asian terror cell grooming operatives for attacks inside the United States. We uncovered an al Qaeda cell developing anthrax to be used in attacks against America. And just last August, British authorities uncovered a plot to blow up passenger planes bound for America over the Atlantic Ocean. For each life saved, we owe a debt of gratitude to the brave public servants who devote their lives to finding the terrorists and stopping them. Every success against the terrorists is a reminder of the shoreless ambitions of this enemy. The evil that inspired and rejoiced in 9/11 is still at work in the world. And so long as that's the case, America is still a nation at war.

Bush knew America had been traumatized by the terrorists' acts. He had played that fear for political advantage at every opportunity. This speech was no exception.

Jim Webb sat in a studio in the other side of the Capitol and waited. When the president finished his speech, Webb launched into his rebuttal:

> It would not be possible in this short amount of time to actually rebut the president's message, nor would it be useful. Let me simply say that we in the Democratic Party hope that this administration is serious about improving education and health care for all Americans, and addressing such domestic priorities as restoring the vitality of New Orleans.

Webb was determined to lay out a vision for Democrats on this night, and it may have been the first time that Democrats got to see how much of a Democrat Webb really had become. He continued:

> There are two areas where our respective parties have largely stood in contradiction, and I want to take a few minutes to address them tonight. The first relates to how we see the health of our economy—how we measure it, and how we ensure that its benefits are properly shared among all Americans. The second regards our foreign policy, how we might bring the war in Iraq to a proper conclusion that will also allow us to continue to fight the war against international terrorism, and to address other strategic concerns that our country faces around the world.

On Iraq, he said:

> The president took us into this war recklessly. He disregarded warnings from the national security adviser during the first Gulf War, the chief of staff of the army, two former commanding generals of the Central Command, whose jurisdiction includes Iraq, the director of operations on the Joint Chiefs of Staff, and many, many others with great integrity and long experience in national security affairs. We are now, as a nation, held hostage to the predictable—and predicted—disarray that has followed.[21]

Jim Webb's speech was a huge hit among Democrats in particular and liberals in general. He knew how to construct an argument. Many Democrats felt that they had finally found a credible spokesman to challenge Bush on his war claims.

Clearly, Webb was not following Robert Byrd's edict that new senators should keep their heads down. It was not long before people were mentioning Webb's name as a possibility for the national ticket in 2008. One excited Democratic operative, Brent Budowsky, captured the sense of the moment when he wrote on the *Huffington Post:* "His speech will project the Democratic Party into powerful national leadership on foreign policy, defense and security. He will appeal throughout the nation, and rally Democrats everywhere, with a commanding and strong voice based on experience and judgment."[22]

CHAPTER FIVE
DEBATE AND RESOLUTION

On February 1, 2007, Barack Obama, the junior senator from Illinois, gaveled the Senate into session. He was standing at a podium that rises about three feet above the floor of the chamber and facing a semicircular array of desks. Most of the desks were empty. The desk before him had a box containing two gavels, a microphone, a penholder, and reading material that Obama had brought with him to catch up on. Barry C. Black, the Senate chaplain, stood beside Senator Obama and led the opening prayer.

> Let us pray. Sovereign Lord, permit us to feel your nearness and to know the inspiration of your presence. May our closeness to you help us to choose light over darkness, love over hate, and good over evil. Today, provide for the needs of the Members of this body. Move among them, instructing, lifting, and guiding them, so that whatever they do in word or deed, they will do it to glorify you. Give them the confidence, security, and peace that comes from developing a friendship with You as they open their hearts to the inflow of Your spirit. Show them what needs to be changed, and give them the courage and wisdom to do Your will. We pray in Your glorious Name. Amen.[1]

This was the day, finally, when the new Democratic Senate would cast its first vote on ending the war in Iraq, which had been going on for almost four years. Already more than 3,100 Americans had been killed in Iraq, and the death toll among Iraqi civilians, which was widely debated, was put at more than 54,000.

△

Soon after the invasion of Iraq began, the most compelling reason for it—that Saddam Hussein had or was developing weapons of mass destruction, whatever those were—had become discredited and was uniformly acknowledged to have been false. To make matters worse, in 2004, a devastating series of pictures detailing detainee abuse at the American-controlled prison at Abu Ghraib undermined the moral authority of the United States to conduct the war. As the death toll mounted, the flow of bad news out of Iraq seemed relentless.

The day before the new Congress convened, President Bush, in an extraordinary move for him, wrote an opinion piece in the *Wall Street Journal* in which he seemed to be pledging to work with the triumphant Democrats on everything, including the war: "We now have the opportunity to build a bipartisan consensus to fight and win the war," he wrote.

On close reading, however, the signs of the coming stalemate should have been obvious. President Bush ruled out any possibility of raising taxes and then issued this threat: "If Congress chooses to pass bills that are simply political statements, they will have chosen stalemate. If a different approach is taken, the next two years can be fruitful ones for our nation."[2]

Bush had in some way frozen the Iraq debate by announcing that he would have a new plan for Iraq in mid-January. The White House had leaked that he was going to replace the top military commanders in Iraq, and would ask for the deployment of more troops in the spring and summer. The rumors were that Army Lieutenant General David Petraeus, who had burnished his reputation by securing a measure of calm in the northern Iraqi province of Diyala, was going to replace General George Casey as commander of the multinational forces in Iraq. After Rumsfeld, Casey, it appeared, was to be the second high-profile political casualty of the war.

Casey had been pushing a plan that would have turned over security responsibilities to the Iraqis while reducing the number of American bases and personnel in Iraq. The intensity of the fighting, the rising levels of violence, and the aggressiveness of the insurgency made that plan impossible. As a result, the administration was moving to a new plan that would call for more troops, at the same time that the American people seemed to be begging for a withdrawal. The war seemed a clear issue on which newly empowered Democrats could oppose the president. But still, the party was unclear about how forceful to be in opposition.

Majority Leader Harry Reid said that he would consider the president's proposal if the deployments were temporary, and the chairman of the Senate Armed Services Committee, Michigan's Carl Levin, said that he, too, despite the clear opposition of the American people, was open to hearing the White House's proposal. "The American people are skeptical about getting in deeper," he told the *New York Times* on January 4, 2007. "But if it's truly conditional upon the Iraqis actually meeting milestones and if it's part of an overall program of troop reduction that would begin in the next four to six months, it's something that would be worth considering."[3]

Where was the outrage?

Joe Biden was one of the clearest voices on the matter, decrying troop increases as the wrong strategy and invoking images of the collapse of Saigon as a foreshadowing of the disaster in Iraq. The question of what to do remained elusive, but Democrats were able at least to frame the argument.

In a resolution on military force in Iraq in the Senate on January 8, 2007, Dick Durbin, the senior senator from Illinois and the second-ranking Democrat in the Senate, said, "This war began with deception—a deception of the American people about the threat of weapons of mass destruction. It then moved into a phase of denial." Durbin is a short, compact man from southern Illinois who rose to power by being tenacious, and tenaciously courteous. Durbin continued:

As violence ramped up dramatically, as more and more people died, including American soldiers, it went from deception to denial, and now we are in delusion, a delusion that somehow sending more American troops into the field of battle, putting them in the midst of a civil war that finds its roots in history 14 centuries old, that somehow placing our best and bravest soldiers, marines, airmen, and sailors in this crossfire of sectarian violence, putting more of them there, as the President is likely to suggest, is going to bring this to an end sooner.[4]

Now, on February 1, Senator Biden was introducing a nonbinding measure that had passed through the Foreign Relations Committee the week before. The resolution expressed "the sense of Congress . . . that it is not in the U.S. national interest to deepen its military involvement in Iraq, particularly by increasing the U.S. military presence in Iraq."[5] It was an effort to short-circuit the president's "surge" proposals by which he planned to add tens of thousands of combat troops to pursue a new counterinsurgency strategy.

In his State of the Union address a week earlier, the president had announced that he wanted to send more combat troops to Iraq to contain the violence that had erupted all over the country, killing civilians and military personnel by the hundreds every week. Most of the new troops would go to Baghdad to clear neighborhoods of insurgents, and the rest would go to Anbar Province to fight al Qaeda terrorists. This "surge" in troop strength was intended to take the pressure off the Iraqi government and give it some time and breathing room to create a political solution to a military problem.

"Our goal is a democratic Iraq that upholds the rule of law, respects the rights of its people, provides them security, and is an ally in the war on terror," the president had said.[6] That rationale seemed very far removed from the threat of nuclear or chemical obliteration that had been the initial reasons for attacking Iraq. The changing justifications and the burgeoning disaster that had taken over the execution of the war had left the president largely discredited on the issue.

But in the strange political wind tunnel that is Washington, Bush's surge proposal created a new dynamic. It turned the subject of the discussion away from the propriety of the war itself to the willingness to win it. Bush and the Republicans on Capitol Hill argued, essentially, that even if you were against the war, that discussion was now over and the question had become where you come down on winning it. "Many in this chamber understand that America must not fail in Iraq," Bush warned the Congress, "because you understand that the consequences of failure would be grievous and far-reaching."[7]

As a political strategy, this move was shrewd, if predictable, and surprisingly effective. The debate shifted, and Democrats were now forced to confront a different question: not whether the war was being won or lost but whether the surge would work.

President Bush kept adding to his ever-evolving complex of rationales for the war. In an interview with National Public Radio at the end of January he said: "I understand it's controversial and I understand people are skeptical and I understand there's pessimism here. I also want your listeners to know that a lot of people here in Washington also understand that failure in Iraq would be a disaster for the Iraqi people and for the American people."[8]

Bush could see that the situation might deteriorate: "I'm hopeful that the decision I have made is going to yield enough results so that the Iraqi government is able to take more of the—more of the responsibility,"[9] he told NPR.

Perhaps the president couldn't permit himself to sound anything other than hopeful. If he admitted anything else, he might have to admit that the war itself had been a mistake. George Bush was one of the few people in the world who couldn't do that.

In late January and early February the Senate voted on raising the national minimum wage, and had to pass a continuing resolution to allow the government to spend money, but there was nothing else to debate except Iraq. Senators used whatever time they had on the floor to talk about the situation there, even when it was not the measure to be voted on next. This went on for days, with one side or the other attacking or defending the president's surge proposal.

The Iraqi question was in some ways the main reason the new freshman class was there. Democratic success in 2006 was largely a rebuke of the president's policies in Iraq. And now there was some expectation that these triumphant Democrats would change those policies. "This vote is about being fair to the American people and the millions of voters who chose a new direction last November," said Harry Reid.[10]

The key proponents of the measure were Biden, the six-term senator from Delaware who also chaired the Foreign Relations Committee along with Chuck Hagel, the Nebraska Republican, and Carl Levin. The Biden amendment, as it was known, was to be the first gauge of Democratic strength in confronting President Bush on the war. While the resolution itself had no power to force the president's hand, the hope was that it would demonstrate the gathering strength of the forces against him.

It promised to be a long day.

△

Elected as one of only two new Democrats in the Senate in 2004, when his party lost five seats to the Republicans, Barack Obama was still a freshman, but he was now a second-tier freshman, meaning there were newer senators than he. As such, he was not called upon to do as much of the grunt work of presiding over the Senate as those in the newest class of the majority. This day in February, it was his turn to do the thankless job of presiding, which requires a senator to sit in the chair and listen to speeches on often arcane subjects. Senators may talk about worthy individuals or institutions from their home state in order to have them immortalized in the *Congressional Record.*

Presiding over the modern Senate is a classic case of delegating. Constitutionally, the job belongs to the vice president of the United States, and it was performed by the veep until the Eisenhower administration, when incumbent vice president Richard M. Nixon began spending more time at the White House than at the Capitol. In the vice president's absence, it was determined that the longest-serving member of the majority party would be designated the president pro tempore, and that the presiding duties would fall to him. In the 100th Congress, Robert C. Byrd of West Virginia was the president pro tem, again. Every day that the Senate was in session, it was Byrd's job to appoint an acting president pro tem to perform the duties of the chair.

Those duties are so tedious and time consuming that they have become a form of hazing for freshmen members. The two-hour shifts rotate mostly among freshmen senators from the majority party, and the number of shifts varies per week depending on the size of the freshman class. The nine new Democrats were each on the hook for six hours of presiding time per week. In fact, in advance of the 2006 election, the Democratic secretary of the Senate, Martin Paone, said that the one Democrat in Washington who would be unhappy if Democrats won would be the staff member responsible for scheduling the shifts of the presiding officer.[11]

On this particular day, February 1, 2007, Senator Byrd's—the president pro tem's—designation was read by the clerk: "Under the provisions of rule I, paragraph 3, of the Standing Rules of the Senate, I hereby appoint the Honorable Barack Obama, a Senator from the State of Illinois, to perform the duties of the Chair."[12]

The 2004 Democratic class, which included only Obama and Ken Salazar of Colorado, were required to give only two hours a week, and others more senior gave fewer still. Members of the leadership are exempt, but when the Senate works late into the night or on weekends, presiding is the unhappiest of chores, because there simply must always be someone sitting in the chair pretending to be the vice president of the

United States. To make the job more interesting, in the 1960s Majority Leader Mike Mansfield introduced an award called the Golden Gavel for members who had spent more than a hundred hours presiding in a session. In its current incarnation, the Golden Gavel goes to the freshman who gets to one hundred hours first.

Early on in the session, two favorites in the Golden Gavel race emerged, Sherrod Brown and Amy Klobuchar; Brown because his scheduler was so agreeable to taking extra shifts; Klobuchar because she likes to win. Jon Tester dismissed the competition as rigged in favor of East Coast senators whose travel times to and from home allow them more opportunity to be in the Capitol.

But by late spring, Sheldon Whitehouse of Rhode Island came out of nowhere to win. "I love being in that chair," Whitehouse said. "At worst, you get to just sit quietly and think, but sometimes somebody gives a really interesting speech, and other times there are just soaring moments when you just want to pinch yourself. I just had one of those when I heard Ted Kennedy roaring on about the minimum wage. To see him in his full bore and glory is something special." And it is hard to escape the sense of power and history that surrounds you. "Sometimes you look up and there is Kennedy and Clinton and Obama and Trent Lott and Robert Byrd, and you think, Wow!"[13]

To the Senate on February 1, Senator Biden introduced his amendment:

> Three weeks ago, before the Senate Foreign Relations Committee, Secretary [of State Condoleezza] Rice presented the President's plan for Iraq. Its main feature was to send more American troops into Baghdad, in the middle of a sectarian war, in the middle of a city of over 6 million people. The reaction of the Senate Foreign Relations Committee, from Republicans and Democrats alike, ranged from profound skepticism to outright opposition. That pretty much reflected the reaction across the country.

Senator Biden outlined a plan: "We believe we can redeploy most, if not all, of America's troops from Iraq within 18 months under this plan, leaving behind a small force in Iraq or in the region to strike at terrorists, the jihadists, the al-Qaidaists, keeping the neighbors honest, and training Iraqi forces."

Biden warned the administration to heed the congressional debate. "Time is running out," he said. The resolutions in the Senate would mean that there would be a full-blown debate in the Senate. "I hope the administration will be listening. I suggest we are coequal—Congress, along with the President—in deciding when, if, how long, and under what circumstances to send Americans to war, for shedding America's treasure and blood."[14]

By the time Biden finished talking, a true freshman, Sherrod Brown of Ohio, was presiding. Just before 3:30 P.M., Klobuchar took over the presiding officer's chair, and by the time the Biden amendment came to the floor, just after 5:30 P.M., Jim Webb was sitting in the chair.

The other freshmen appreciated Webb's willingness to accept the tedium of presiding over the Senate. Because he lived close, less than an hour away, Webb was willing to take some of the late shifts so that the others could begin their longer commutes earlier. The advantage to some of those shifts, however, was that sometimes the Senate would adjourn before it was necessary to fill them.

△

The Biden amendment lost ninety-seven to nothing, because, while the floor debate on Iraq continued, a series of backstage negotiations had produced an agreement that would transfer the debate on Iraq to another piece of legislation. In fact, the vote on the Biden amendment was simply a vote on whether the Senate should actually begin debating the president's plan for 21,500 new combat troops in Iraq.

What emerged was a compromise resolution authored by Republican senator John Warner of Virginia and Levin that watered down some of the Biden language, too much so for some Democrats like Chris Dodd of Connecticut and Russ Feingold of Wisconsin, who said they wouldn't support the new measure.[15] In one of the most clarifying moments of the debate, Senator Dodd dismissed the effort by the Senate to send Bush a "nonbinding" resolution. Nonbinding was almost offensive when people were dying, and Dodd rejected the idea and asked why the Senate was not acting like the Senate.

"Why not force them to pay attention to what we say up here?" he said. "This is the United States Senate; this is not a city council somewhere." Dodd would spend the next few months apologizing to city council members all over the country, but he was unapologetic about where he had arrived on the war. "I cannot in good conscience continue to go along with a failed policy that will lead to loss of life. My position on the war is very straightforward: I'm strongly opposed to sending additional troops to a civil war that can't be won militarily."[16]

Rather than voting on the Warner-Levin resolution itself, the following Monday, the Senate voted whether or not to debate the resolution—the vote was 49–47, but it needed sixty votes to pass, and nearly all Republicans, Warner included, toed the party line, supporting efforts by Minority Leader McConnell to bring up alternative resolutions supporting the president's plan and mandating that funds would not be cut for troops in the field, one a McCain-Lieberman measure, the other written by Senator Judd Gregg.

"You can run but you can't hide," declared Harry Reid. "We are going to debate Iraq. They may have gotten all their folks over there to vote against a motion to proceed, they may stop us temporarily from debating the escalation, but they are not going to stop us from debating Iraq. We have lost 3,100 soldiers, sailors, and marines. They are dead."[17]

Within two weeks, Reid dropped the 1,600-word Warner-Levin measure with its twenty-two "whereases" in favor of a House resolution that noted congressional support of the U.S. armed forces but disapproved of the president's decision to send more troops to Iraq. It ran to exactly ninety-seven words.

On February 16, that resolution—House Concurrent Resolution 63—passed the House by a vote of 246 to 182.[18] In a Saturday session next day,

Democrats failed to bring an identical resolution to a vote, as the Senate vote (at 56 to 34) fell four short of ending the Republican filibuster. Senate majority leader Mitch McConnell issued a filibuster threat, even though no one filibusters in the Senate anymore. The actual filibuster, during which a senator or group of senators take the floor and talk at length in order to prevent the body from moving to a vote on a measure they find objectionable, never happens anymore. The sixty-vote threshold is simply a cut-to-the-chase maneuver that recognizes that a controversial proposal can be filibustered if the opponents so choose and that proponents have the votes to end that filibuster if it came to that. Even though the resolution "passed" with majority support, McConnell's threat of a filibuster meant the resolution was doomed to failure.

For everything that happens in the Senate there needs to be a motion to proceed. This happens in two ways—unanimous consent, meaning no senator objects, or a roll call vote on the motion to proceed, which gives a sense of how much support or opposition exists for the proposed resolution. All these procedural votes are effectively testing the ability of the resolution to pass. With each vote, the senators are changing the language of the resolution until the wording is just right and they know it will have enough support to pass.

This is what senators do. To many observers, it looks like a lot of wasted time, but the horse trading and deal making were woven into the fabric of the institution to guard against whimsical lawmaking. The procedure was bound to test the patience of Democratic voters who felt a sense of urgency about the war.

△

Iraq was only one of the areas of confrontation between the president and the new Democratic senators. Sheldon Whitehouse, a square-jawed, patrician-looking former attorney general of Rhode Island, came to the Senate with much less fanfare than Webb or Tester, whose close wins made them heroes in the takeover drama. Nor did he represent a pickup in a huge red state that would be crucial in the presidential election the way Sherrod Brown and Claire McCaskill were in Ohio and Missouri. But White-house's big win in tiny Rhode Island may have said more about what the American people were thinking than any other race in the country: that President Bush and the Republicans needed to be stopped. Whitehouse beat a moderate, well-liked Republican, who had disagreed with and often voted against President Bush and with the Democrats—Lincoln Chafee.

"I think people got frightened that their government had left them and was going in directions that they did not approve of, and they wanted that connection back. They wanted to be heard," said Whitehouse.[19]

While he was not one of the new celebrity senators, Whitehouse quickly developed a reputation as one of the most serious minds in the class. He gained a seat on the Judiciary Committee, which became one of the vessels of genuine Democratic outrage over allegations that the White House had been hiring and firing federal prosecutors for political reasons. Seven federal prosecutors were dismissed by the Justice Department in December 2006 and replaced with interim appointees. It was alleged that the attorneys who lost their jobs were either involved in investigations of Republicans or not investigating Democrats. Attorney General Alberto Gonzales was first questioned at the hearings at a Judiciary Committee oversight hearing on January 18, 2007, two weeks into the new session of Congress.

Though he was the most junior member of the Judiciary panel and was a freshman barely over the threshold of the building, Whitehouse was clearly the most effective questioner on the panel—having been a practicing courtroom attorney much more recently than all the other Democratic members. He had also been, from 1994 to 1998, a federal prosecutor himself. He tangled with Gonzales, who gave testimony to the committee in January, April, and July, and Gonzales's former chief of staff, Kyle Sampson, who appeared in March. Both Gonzales and Sampson claimed that the fired prosecutors were victims of routine turnover at the Justice Department. On occasion, Whitehouse, bouncing out of his chair, could barely contain his rage at the administration.

"You are expected to make a certain transition, when you work for the Justice Department," he said sitting in his office in the Hart Building. He was wearing a blue suit and a blue shirt, and his signature Puma running shoes. "Whatever your politics are, you leave it at the door. That was the code, and that these guys would break that code told me that they would be willing to do anything."[20]

In May, Whitehouse was one of the sponsors of a Senate resolution calling on Gonzales to resign. The resolution passed 53 to 38 but fell short of a filibuster-proof sixty votes. However, with the Gonzales hearings, the Democrats could point to tangible success: In August, the attorney general resigned.

△

Where the Senate is able to exert real pressure on a president's plan to prosecute a war is when it comes time to pay for it. Early in the first session of 2007, President Bush requested funds to continue the war efforts in Iraq and Afghanistan, and Senate Democrats worked to tie continued funding to a withdrawal timetable. The White House promised it would veto any attempt to mandate a timetable, and in the wake of that threat, Democrats acquired a certain swagger. "We're not going to back down on what we think is right for the country," promised Harry Reid in April.[21]

All the time, Senate Democrats tried to reassure Americans that they were opposing the war but not the troops. In March 2007, Amy Klobuchar went to Baghdad and Fallujah, visiting soldiers from her home state of Minnesota. At a press conference of freshmen senators, she said: "They didn't complain about their equipment, they didn't complain about their tour extensions, they didn't complain about the conditions that they were operating in. And the only thing that they asked me to do was to call their moms when I got home to tell them that they were safe. These are brave soldiers, and they deserve the best. And I think the best thing that we can do for these soldiers is to get this policy right."[22]

The new Democrats made a specific linkage between their electoral success in 2006 and the president's determination to stay in Iraq and Afghanistan. "In my state of Pennsylvania, people didn't elect me to come down here and to endorse a stay-the-course, the-president-is-always-right policy. They elected me to lead," said Senator Bob Casey at a press conference with other freshmen Democrats near the hundred-day mark of their terms. "I think it's about time that this president listened to the will of the American people."[23]

At the same press conference, Bernie Sanders, inclined to be more blustery than the average senator, was plain hot. "It's incredible, it is beyond comprehension that this president would veto funds for the troops because Congress chose to acknowledge the will of the American people. Once again, this is a demonstration of a president way out of touch with reality."[24]

On March 27, 2007, a bright Thursday morning in Washington, the Senate approved a bill that would authorize more than $97.5 billion for the war in Afghanistan and Iraq. It was the seventh vote on Iraq-related measures since this session of Congress began. The previous two weeks had been spent feuding with the White House and with congressional Republicans, but, at long last, fifty-one senators were willing to put their names to a call to end the war and bring the troops home, beginning in three months. The aim was to have most forces out in a year. The bill said that three months after he signed the bill, the president would be mandated to start a redeployment of troops out of Iraq, and it anticipated that most troops would be home by March 31, 2008.

The White House, though, was standing firm and threatening to veto the bill as soon as it reached the president's desk. From her podium at the White House, Press Secretary Dana Perino said the president couldn't wait:

"This, again, underscores the need to get the show on the road. Get the bill to the president; he will veto it and then we'll take it from there."[25]

Democrats knew they did not have the votes to override a presidential veto—the bill barely passed in the first place—but their great hope was they'd be able to bring public and political pressure to bear on the president. "If the president vetoes this bill, it is an asterisk in history," Harry Reid said on March 28, 2007, the date the bill passed. "He sets the record for undermining the troops more than any president we have ever had."[26]

The following day, Bush held a ceremony at the White House with Republican leaders. "We stand united in saying loud and clear that when we've got a troop in harm's way, we expect that troop to be fully funded," he said.[27] This was the atmosphere as the Senate left Washington for a two-week Easter break in the spring of 2007.

It had been a frustrating session, but now at least, the Iraq supplemental, an emergency measure that would fund the war between annual budget allocations to the Pentagon, felt like something of a victory for Democrats. Finally someone had said to the president, in a way that seemed to matter, that Iraq was a catastrophe and to the American people that someone in the government meant to do something about it.

Russ Feingold was confident that Democrats had finally found the courage to seriously challenge the president. "The Democratic caucus did not hold together on a timeline at first, it was just me," he said. "I think what you're seeing with this bill are the outlines of what is likely to happen. Maybe not the same words, not the exact language, but the general outline."[28]

The withdrawal timetable would have required the president to begin redeploying troops 120 days after the law was enacted and—other than exceptions for fighting al Qaeda—regarding force and infrastructure protection and for training home armies, no money could be used to fund the continued deployment of troops in Iraq after March 31, 2008.

"When Americans voted in November, they didn't just want us to oppose the surge. They wanted us to end the war," said Bernie Sanders, a cosponsor of the Feingold-Reid proposal. "And that's what some of us intend to do."[29]

▲

As he had promised, President Bush vetoed the bill and asked congressional leaders to talk about a measure without a timetable. On May 1, Harry Reid said, "If the president thinks [that] by vetoing this bill he'll stop us from working to change the direction of the war in Iraq, he is mistaken."[30]

And yet, on May 24, both houses of Congress passed a $120 billion spending bill with no timetable. Instead, the Iraqi government was given a list of eighteen benchmarks it was supposed to achieve to demonstrate it was making progress. Russ Feingold called the measure a "failure" and "a big mistake." It was, he said, "the first real turn in the wrong direction in several months."[31] Among those who agreed with Feingold and voted against the funding bill were Senators Obama, Clinton, and Whitehouse. The final tally of dissenters was fourteen.

Harry Reid, who voted for it, preferred to point to the fact that Democrats had brought the president to the debating chamber—"We have repeatedly forced our Republican colleagues in the Senate and in the House to debate and vote on where people stand with respect to the president's failed Iraq policy."[32] To Harry Reid, in public at least, the fact that the Senate had got to discuss the future of the war was in itself a victory. The Senate's voice had been heard. In the chamber, where senators could talk about withdrawal timetables that were never voted on, and in committee rooms, where senators like Sheldon Whitehouse could engage Bush appointees like Alberto Gonzales, Democrats could take on the president. In the Senate, Republicans could object, and in the end the president would get the money he needed to continue the war.

Legislatively, the president was dealing with a hostile Congress, and on some level that was progress in the right direction, but this was not a debate over the naming of a post office; this was war and people were dying. So the traditions of incrementalism that can so often look like success in the Senate looked liked failure to almost everyone else.

Many of the people who voted for Democrats to end the war were very unhappy with their elected representatives and said so very soon. By the summer of 2007, there would be threats of primary challenges against Democrats, and the lack of popularity of the Congress began to rival that of the president. Harry Reid himself came under intense attack for poorly managing his caucus in the Senate. Had he managed his power properly, he would have achieved more than a symbolic victory.

The most prominent dissenter was famous casualty mom and antiwar activist Cindy Sheehan. She had lost her son in Iraq, and since the president refused to meet with her, she had pitched a tent in protest outside his home in Crawford, Texas. In May, she quit the antiwar movement, deciding that she had waged as good a fight as she was able to and could no longer abide the frustration. What put her over the top was the retreat by Democrats on the withdrawal component of the Iraq supplemental spending bill.

Sheehan denounced Democrats for complicity with Bush and for spineless political expediency. "You think giving [Bush] more money is politically expedient, but it is a moral abomination and every second the occupation of Iraq endures, you all have more blood on your hands," she wrote in an open letter on May 26, resigning from the movement.[33] She ended the letter to the Democrats thus: "We gave you a chance, you betrayed us." The sense of betrayal was real among many Democrats, and Sheehan gave it voice. In July that year she announced that she would run against Speaker Nancy Pelosi for Congress.

Sheehan represented a lot of people who believed that big Democratic wins in the midterm elections had signaled there would be an end to the war. But as the frustrated antiwar activists' disappointment ballooned into outrage and then into disdain and then disgust, it would have been worthwhile to stop and rethink how the Democrats could have prevented the activists' reaction from becoming an overreaction. Overkill is the natural curse of new majorities.

△

It was easy to understand the skepticism about Democratic motives. After all, too many of them voted for the war, and for the Bush tax cuts, and for No Child Left Behind, and for the flawed prescription drug benefit in Medicare—all of which struck the Democratic base as hideously expedient capitulations, the typical Democratic cave-ins. It was lucky that the next thing the president wanted to tackle was Social Security, or we might never have seen Democrats walking upright again.

The war was obviously unpopular, and President Bush's job approval rating continued to drop to historic lows. It would have been tempting for the Democrats to just play the strongest available hand every time, to force him to keep vetoing bill after bill, and to force unpopular votes on the GOP in Congress. That would have been easy, but it wouldn't have ended the war, in large part because the Senate grants the advantage to those who say no. Democrats say end the war, Republicans say no, and the rules accrue to their advantage. The Democrats never would have been able to pass a bill attached to a timetable, nor would they have been able to cut off funds, because they had agreed to stand by the troops on the ground. Renouncing this promise would have given Bush a tremendous political advantage.

In fact, when you consider the public mood at the time, and the president's approval numbers, the vote for the supplemental, while in practice it achieved nothing, may have been the actual gutsy move. It was gutsy because the Democrats were clearly acting against what their base wanted. The war did not end, but the repeated attempts at these small changes painted the Republicans over and over as pro-war—and the taint cost them in 2008.

CHAPTER SIX
MEANWHILE, BACK IN THE STATE

Jon Tester could not wait to get home. It was time for spring planting, and before he left Washington, he was already thinking about the peace he'd find on his tractor. "When you're running a tractor, you can clear your mind," he said. "If you just turn off the radio and relax, you can go amazing places."[1] But first he had to get home.

Shortly after the Senate voted on the supplemental funding bill that called for troop withdrawals from Iraq, on March 29, 2007, Tester and Sharla headed out for their eighteen hundred sprawling acres near the Canadian border. It takes a long time to get from Washington, D.C., to Big Sandy: a three-and-a-half-hour flight from Washington Reagan National Airport or Dulles International to Denver, with a two-hour layover there, followed by another almost two-hour flight to Great Falls. After eight hours of flying, the Testers then jump in a truck and drive almost ninety miles to their house. Big Sandy is tiny, and the Testers live on the outskirts of the little town, down twelve hardy miles of dirt road. When the Senate is in session on Friday, they are at home for two days, then they turn around and do the journey in reverse. "You have to have three days to get anything done back [in Washington]," he said. "That is the biggest challenge for me."

For Tester, frustration with the Senate had come in waves, but all of it fell under the general umbrella of "Too Much Talk, Not Enough Action." That was an essential truth about the Senate that was beginning to sink in.

Tester, who managed to charm people simply by describing himself as a "dirt farmer," was anxious to get back to the farm, and turn over some dirt on the land that his family has owned for more than ninety years, his grandfather having settled it in 1916.

Even with the somewhat triumphant vote on the supplemental funding package, there was no real sense that the war would be ending anytime soon. The immediate fight on the Hill would be about what to do when the president vetoed the bill, as he had threatened. Also on the horizon was a debate about lifting the ban on stem-cell research, which held some promise of a win for the Democrats. But the basic truth about Washington—that nothing ever really happens except very, very slowly—was beginning to dawn on Tester and his freshmen colleagues.

Back in Montana, Tester knew what to do and how to do it. This was a place where action was the imperative, and in which the quality of the decision making was directly borne out in the outcome. It doesn't take much to get Tester into a conversation about the farm. It had been by most standards an awful winter in Montana, cold, damp, snowy, and generally miserable, but everyone who knew Tester understood the wisdom of not complaining about the weather to him. Farmers have an entirely different view than the ordinary person of what constitutes bad weather. For Tester, there is no such thing as too much rain or too much snow. "Water is always good, unless it's during harvest," he said. "This moisture sets you up. It's like money in the bank."

One day in early March, in the Senate recording studio in the basement of the Capitol, Tester had held a conference call with reporters back in Montana. Much of the discussion had focused on the weather, but nearly as much was spent on the situation in Iraq. Tester walked into the studio wearing a smart gray suit that marked a clear wardrobe transition from his early American khakis and chinos, finished with a tweed coat and skinny tie. It was not yet a senator's suit by any means—which is traditional, conservative, and expensive—but surely in the acceptable zone. Some Senate staff have a description for new senators who begin to exhibit signs that the power and the position are going to their heads: they are referred to as "going purple," as in royal purple. Tester, who did not own a suit when he began running for the Senate, would be among the last people to go purple, but a nice gray suit was a necessary concession. The ugliness of his ties would even eventually become a topic of discussion on the Senate floor. Jim Webb made a regular practice of making fun of Tester's ties. "Tester wears glow-in-the-dark ties. If the lights ever go out around here, he'd be easy to find."[2]

That day, the senator seemed a little bored by the discussion of new Bureau of Land Management regulations, and one could almost hear the whirring in his head as he repeated lines from the campaign about "securing the northern border" and "sustainable renewables" and "cellulosic ethanol," all of which were, of course, good for Montana and good for the country. Not so with the weather. This is always an urgent topic if you're worried about farming conditions in the high northern plains.

"It's been a better winter in Montana, than in Washington," Tester said into one of the three microphones rising like skinny cobra heads out of the studio desk. "I've left Montana several weekends where it is forty or forty-five degrees to come back to Washington, where it is fifteen or twenty degrees."[3]

There were twelve inches of snow on the ground back in southern Montana. And while the "better" Montana weather had been easier for travel and better for living, it was not good for farming. There had not been enough moisture—there never is, really—for the dry-land farmers in the high plains, who are entirely dependent on rainfall and snow for irrigation. "After the last few years, we have learned not to complain about moisture," he told the reporters back home, and they grunted their approval. "Moisture" seems an insufficient description of the weather-related cataclysms that were being discussed. After all, there was deep concern that there was so much snow that Beartooth Highway in southern Montana and northern Wyoming might not be able to open on time for the tourist travel season. Reporters were asking about the economic impact of a prolonged closing and wondering what the new senator was thinking and doing about it.

Asked eventually about the war, Tester voiced the mounting frustration that Democrats were beginning to feel. "This war needs to go in a different direction," he said. "It's costing us two billion dollars a week."

△

To get from Great Falls to Big Sandy, Montana, one must head due north and east toward the Canadian border. You go through Black Eagle and Floweree and Carter Fort Benton and Loma before the mountains of the Bears Paw range come into view. The route goes past the confluence of the Missouri and Marias rivers, which stumped Lewis and Clark for ten days in 1805, since they could not initially tell which river would lead them to the Northwest Passage. The Missouri, flowing south and west, has created a beautiful gorge bounded by sheer cliffs of seventy-five-million-year-old white kaolinite.

Tester said he uses the drive to complete what he calls "the mindshift," the psychological change of clothes from senator to dirt farmer. "That's the best part of the trip." Waiting for the Testers at home were their daughter Christine, her husband James Schultz, and the two Tester grandchildren: Kilikina, who is two, and four-month-old Braden, born just after Tester's election.

Inside the Testers' house, the warmth seemed like some kind of special gift. Dinner was pasta—penne made from durum wheat—with a plain red sauce and beer. The Testers were happy to be home. Jon pointed to a big bay window that opened out to the west. There was a wooden deck, a picnic table, and then a limitless expanse of prairie rendered a rosy pink by the disappearing sun. "The sunset out that window is what you miss most," he said.

For Tester, the two-week Easter recess was going to be a mix of a little farming and a little "senatoring," in the words of Kevin O'Brien, Tester's press secretary. Tester had been pegged as the fish out of water in the Senate, an image he promoted by constantly referring to his farming pedigree. These two weeks would be the first extended period back home since Tester was sworn in in January. The plan was to plant some red and white lentils, a little purple barley, and a little black barley. In addition, he was going to plant forty acres of peas for fertilizer, meaning that when the plants are fully grown and producing peas, Tester would simply get on his tractors and plow them back into the ground.

In Washington they missed the quiet and control of their lives here. The campaign had been tough on the Testers. "We talked about whether our relationship was strong enough to survive it," Sharla said of the campaign. "There were times we wanted to quit because it was so nasty," said Jon. "I did not fully understand the kind of machine I was up against or I might have quit. A lot of times politics is just being naïve." Had he understood exactly how tough and nasty the campaign was going to be, he may never have gotten into the race, or may have packed it in early in the game.

Washington was equally difficult to deal with. House hunting, for example, was a shock to the system. "We were looking at condos that cost more than the farm was worth," Sharla said. The Testers' Montana house is an open, rambling split-level they built with the profit from a single organic lentil crop in 1989, shortly after they decided to stop using fertilizer on the farm. Back in Washington they rented an apartment near the Capitol from the friend of a staffer, and kept looking. They looked for months before deciding to keep renting for a while, reinforcing Sharla's notion: "We're visitors in Washington, this is our home." And on a cold spring night, under the northern sky, it was not hard to see the difference. "In Washington it never gets quiet," said Sharla, "and it never gets dark."

△

That April day, the Tester farm was beset with a damp, osmotic cold that seemed to find the deepest part of your being. Tester stumbled into organic farming when someone suggested he plant one small crop of lentils and not use fertilizer or herbicide. They had already been concerned about Sharla's health because of the chemicals. "We would spray all the fields with herbicide and you'd get sick," he said to his wife. "And you could deny it all you want, but you knew it wasn't good for you." The first yield was good, and they stopped using chemicals.

The seeding plans for Friday went as scheduled. Late Saturday, with Tester's son-in-law James at the wheel, the tractor broke down when the clutch went out. "I feel so bad for James," said Sharla, explaining that her son-in-law is a city kid—from Butte—who knows little about farming. He was only trying to impress his father-in-law. On Sunday, Tester drove his pickup truck to Great Falls to pick up a replacement. Three hours later, he returned with his new clutch; a huge box containing a gigantic piece of machinery. In order to install the new clutch, Tester had to remove a small circular bearing. His first attempts did not work. James tried and did not succeed either. "The lock washer goes next to your nut or it doesn't work," Tester said. He was dressed in black jeans and heavy work boots and a jacket to guard against the chill. Morning turned to midday, midday to afternoon, afternoon to evening, and still, the little bearing remained locked in place. At one point, trying to read a set of directions without his reading glasses, Tester gave up: "Sharla, can you come read for me," he said. She did.

It was hard, dirty work, and before long the frustration started to build. "This little bearing right here is what you're trying to get out," Tester said to James. "What the hell are you talking about?" came the disembodied reply from under the ten-foot-tall International Loadstar, which remained immobile in the Quonset hut, while the day's three hundred acres went unplowed and unseeded.

In the end, Tester did what farmers do—he called another farmer for help. Verlin Reichelt, the Testers' closest neighbor, showed up in a few minutes with something called a spinner, and the bearing was out in less than thirty seconds. It was near nightfall, but at 7:30 P.M. the tractor rumbled to life, and the senator took it for a spin.

Later, inside the house, the warmth seemed like some kind of special gift. The day had been lost, so tomorrow would have to serve as a makeup day. What no one knew at that point was that there would be moisture.

At about ten o'clock the next morning, Tester was not feeling well—the hint of a chill that had first appeared in Denver had turned into a full-blown cold, and a forecast for snow made any planting unlikely. I was there, along with a reporter from the *Missoulian*. The sick senator (and frustrated farmer) sat around talking politics, marveling at his own success. In many ways, the tough, gun-loving, down-to-earth, unapologetic Democrat that Tester is stood as the prototype for the party. The sense was that it would be Democrats of the interior West and border South that would bring white and male working-class voters back to the party. He said his net income was never more than $30,000 while he worked the farm. Now one of his best friends in the Senate was Jay Rockefeller, whose net worth was listed in the Senate records as upward of $125 million. Tester's $165,000 salary was the most money he had ever made.

"Rockefeller and I make the same money," he laughed. Rockefeller took an immediate shine to Tester. They would sit next to each other in meetings and crack each other up. Rockefeller gave Tester a tie as a present. "He went out and spent thirty-five dollars or something on a tie," Tester said, incredulous at the amount of money his new friend had laid out. "And it was ugly," Tester said of the gift. "Rockefeller may have money, but he's got no taste."

After three hours, it was time to let Tester rest. I walked out to my car only to find it buried in snow. I began to shovel, and Tester's press secretary, Aaron Murphy, whose car was next to mine, helped. A half-hour effort to drive the car out only served to leave it about six inches deeper in the mud. Eventually, Murphy knocked on the door, and Tester came out. He looked at the cars, headed for the garage, and returned with a chain.

The senator headed for his pickup and pulled up next to my car. He got out of the truck and flopped on his back in the snow, hooking the chain to the axle of my car. With his pickup he pulled me out of the mud. Pointed down the half-mile-long driveway, I headed out in the deep snow. At the end of the driveway, to Tester's dismay, I turned toward a shortcut that I had used on my way in. I reasoned that it would be easier to drive on dirt roads, which were not slick, than on the highway, which was. "I would not do that if I were him," Tester said to Murphy. "You're going to have to follow him to make sure he gets out."

The snow was impressive, heavy, white, endless. The shortcut was a twelve-mile run of road. I had gone seven when the car simply stopped moving. I couldn't see more than a few feet ahead of me, and, of course, my cell phone did not work. The Tester farm is isolated, and cell-phone service is almost nonexistent, except for a few defined spots on the farm, and even then it is erratic and spotty. My text messaging function worked, however, and I sent a text back to Tester's office in Washington. But he already knew I'd likely get in trouble, and in short order I saw Murphy's headlights in the distance coming along the road I had just driven.

He pulled in behind me. "I was just about to turn off, because I thought you'd made it," Murphy said.

"So this is how people die in blizzards," I replied. The snow was coming down hard. We tried to push my car forward and then back. Very briefly, we considered using his car to push mine out of trouble. But it wasn't long before we realized that we were both stuck and, without any cell-phone service, had no recourse. The nearest house, the only visible home, looked to be about a half mile away. Murphy set off to go get some help. But by the time he walked a short distance back up the road, he had a phone signal and called Tester. I huddled in my car, contemplating what it would be like to die cold and alone in Montana.

The senator came to our rescue. Since Murphy was behind me, Tester pulled him out first. Murphy got into the car; Sharla drove the pickup and pulled the car back to the paved road about four hundred yards away. "Don't stop until you get to the highway, and then wait for him," she said, as Murphy pulled away. Now it was time for my car. By now Tester was running a fever, but there he was, under my car, belly hanging out, attaching the chain to the undercarriage. He got in my car, and I hopped in the pickup with Sharla. We began moving toward the road, when Sharla suddenly muttered: "Jon, oh, honey, Jon, Jon." I turned around to see my car in the ditch at the left side of the road with the senator inside. When he unfolded his large frame from the Mercury Mirage, he was furious, and a short burst of profanities ensued. At least he's fine, I thought, as he stepped into the three feet of snow.

Frankly, though, I was a little scared. Rage was radiating off of Tester. Sharla, trying to calm him down, suggested that we call a tow truck. "No, we'll just go get the tractor and pull him out," Tester said. He offered me the chance to ride back to the house with them, which I declined. "I'll just wait here," I said.

Twenty minutes later, I saw the lights on the big tractor coming through the snow. And once again, Tester got under the car and hooked up the chain. As he got out from under the car, he tilted a little to the right and shook my hand; he thanked me for coming. The little tilt I would later come to recognize as evidence of his frustration. The tractor easily pulled the car out of the ditch, and very quickly I was on the highway.

△

The next morning, Tester had a town hall meeting with veterans in Billings, 140 miles away as the crow flies. The drive from Fort Benton to Billings was 220 miles of snowy mountain passes. Tester hopped into an SUV with Sharla and a couple of members of his staff. Bill Lombardi, a former reporter and communications director for Montana's other senator, Democrat Max Baucus, was at the wheel. Lombardi had been the state bureau chief for Lee Newspapers, which owned fifty-four newspapers in twenty-three states, including the dominant papers in the Montana cities of Butte, Billings, Helena, Missoula, and Hamilton.

The other staff member was Jed Fitch, newly hired as Tester's veterans affairs coordinator. For a Democrat from a conservative red state like Montana, Tester's vote against the president's Iraq supplemental bill might be expected to draw criticism back home. Tester's staff set up a series of veterans' events to confront the issue. This was Tester's first trip home since the vote, and the staff was keen to gauge how much trouble they might be in for when he opposed the president. Fitch was the new point man on veterans' issues, but he was also a cover. Fitch, a former Republican activist in college, was an Iraq war veteran who opposed the war and was especially vocal about how the administration had destroyed the effort.

Lombardi clearly knew these mountain roads. It was also clear he did not intend to be late, and he established an eighty-mile-an-hour pace right away. About two hours later the city of Billings appeared below, spreading like a quiet lake at the bottom of the Yellowstone Valley. Off in the distance were the jagged snowcapped peaks of the Beartooth Mountain Range. Cutting across the valley northwest to southwest was the Yellowstone River, a tributary of the Missouri River that branches off in western North Dakota near the Montana border and runs nearly seven hundred miles across Montana into Wyoming to its rise in Yellowstone National Park.

The first stop for Tester was the College of Technology campus of the Montana State University at Billings. The senator wore a tweed jacket with an Oxford shirt with the collar buttons undone. The aim was to be casual, and he succeeded, but there was nothing casual about the reception he received. The best parking spots were made available to him and anyone with him. The cafeteria kitchen staff had prepared a lavish buffet spread, and everyone from the college president to the local school superintendent had scrubbed all other plans in order to be there. The focus that morning was on programs to create practical jobs, the value of one of which—tractor repair—was obvious to anyone who had spent time with the Testers that weekend. The senator wandered through the lab and the workshops. He seemed interested, asked the right questions, and moved on.

The next stop was lunch, and Tester was eager to return to a place that had been a campaign stop favorite. "Let's go to Grains of Montana," he said. So far, the vote for a withdrawal timetable that Tester had cast as he left Washington wasn't proving as big a problem as might have been imagined—but he had yet to meet the veterans. George Bush had won Montana twice. But it was now clear that out in the Mountain West, where sudden springtime blizzards can quickly expose the failings of human calculation, the administration's blunders on Iraq would be shown to be costly political follies.

Tester had been firmly against the war—and had campaigned against it—but conventional wisdom still held that the freshman Democrat would need to be attentive to the larger political realities of red-state America. He would have to be at least a little deferential to the president's approach to the war, to be careful not to appear too loyal to the official Democratic line, and to make sure he never put himself in a position where he could be accused of not supporting the troops. Public apprehension about the war, however, was now so deeply felt that the caution proved unnecessary, and Tester had voted with every other Democrat in the Senate.

That afternoon, the Clark Room (as in Lewis and Clark) on the lower level of the student union building at Montana State University at Billings was not packed, but it was a fair enough crowd—about thirty people. Tester took questions for an hour. And not a single one challenged his vote on the supplemental funding or his position on the war. The most prolonged discussion was about a proposal Tester was advancing to raise the mileage reimbursement for veterans who had to travel long distances to get health care. Because nothing is close in Montana, Tester was proposing to raise the per-mile rate to 48.50 cents (the rate that federal government employees receive) up from 11 cents, a rate set in 1977. His audience seemed supportive. Tester gradually got the veterans' mileage reimbursement rate increased, first to 28.5 cents, then to 41.5 cents per mile. Two years later, Tester, working with Claire McCaskill on the issue, found a way to make sure the mileage reimbursement package was sustained long-term by attaching an amendment to the 2010 budget. Both senators pledged to keep pushing for veterans to receive the same rate as government employees.

One Korean War veteran wanted to know if the senator could intervene with the Veterans Administration to get him a set of teeth. "I had my teeth pulled over in Korea and I've been trying to get a new set of them since then," he said, "and that was in fifty-four." Tester didn't even blink. "That's only fifty-three years," he said. One vet wanted to know the extent of the problems at Walter Reed Hospital in Washington and if and how far they extended to VA facilities throughout the country. Another Iraq veteran complained that he was not eligible for the G.I. Bill and did not understand the bureaucratic reasons why.

Joe Cobos, a retired marine, said he thought the Congress should stay out of the war—but that's not what he wanted to talk to Tester about. He wanted the senator to support funding for math and science courses for his Veterans Upward Bound program. Cobos expressed his gratitude for Tester showing concern for veterans.

The only direct mention of the vote came from a young army wife. Twenty-eight-year-old Heather Scharre, the wife of twenty-seven-year-old sergeant Paul Scharre, who served three tours in Afghanistan, thanked Tester for "supporting the troops by voting for deadlines to bring them home." Paul Scharre had left the army, only to find himself involuntarily recalled in September 2006, and was now on his way to Iraq. "We've been told to expect fourteen to sixteen months," Heather said of her husband's deployment. "We were used to four-month deployments," she said. The adjustments after those tours were difficult enough; she could only imagine what reentry into everyday life would be like after a tour of fourteen or sixteen months. Scharre asked Tester to make sure that returning Iraq veterans had access to counseling, including couples and marriage counseling.

"I think we've been hearing from some people, like the president and the vice president, that if you don't support the war, you don't support the troops," said Scharre, "and I feel very strongly that that is not the case."[4] This was precisely the very fine line Democrats were trying to walk going forward, trying to figure out how to separate the war from the warriors as a matter of political necessity.

Tester did several town hall meetings that week—including some on the Crow Indian Reservation—and said he came away reminded of how people at home have different concerns than those that often dominate the discussion in Washington. He had returned home concerned that his position on the war would be criticized; that hadn't turned out to be the case. People's concerns are more likely to be about their immediate needs, which are mostly things that do not come up in congressional hearing rooms—except as a way to put individual faces on broader policy issues. In response to one audience member at the medical center in Billings, as part of a general discussion about brain injury among Iraq War veterans, he said, gesturing to his flattop, "You have a bad knee, I am missing three fingers, some people have it up here in the head." That expresses the difference between national politics and local politics right there.

Senators are liable to be concerned, upon returning home from Washington, that their image has been somehow tarnished by their work there. As Tester can relate, this apprehension might not be realized. Back at the Capitol, the real work of senators is to somehow translate the concerns of their constituents into broader policy in a place where nothing is ever concrete.

The adjustment was slow for the Testers; initially they were bringing their own steaks—self-slaughtered and frozen—from Montana back to Washington, so that at least some of the time they were eating like they were back home. But Jon Tester said that the important work before the Senate made the transition easier, even when it was contentious and sometimes frustrating.

"The whole debate on Iraq, it's a matter of perspective," he told me. "I don't think that people get up and say things they don't believe in themselves. I just think they have totally different perspectives. I'm not sure that everybody is just as concerned about global warming as I am. It may be down on the list, so that gives you a different perspective." This observation came after passage on an energy bill which did not include an amendment that would have "provide[d] Government grants for engineering and design of coal-to-liquid and coal gasification facilities."[5] Tester, along with other Democratic senators from coal-producing states, could not convince some of his Republican colleagues that it was cost efficient or some of his Democratic colleagues that it was good for the environment.

Despite the setback, Tester remained convinced that on big issues facing the country and the world, the U.S. Senate could still be an arena in which to devise solutions, and he believed that most of his colleagues wanted to be part of those solutions.

"This is absolutely the place to fix it. I think it is," he said. "Why—if you weren't serious about getting something done—would you be here?"[6]

CHAPTER SEVEN
WHAT A SENATOR LOOKS LIKE

Every Thursday morning when the Senate was in session, Amy Klobuchar hosted a breakfast meeting in her office for any Minnesotan who wanted to come see her. It was an easy way to get access to the senator while avoiding the incredibly burdensome process of trying to set up an appointment. It was obviously not a good time for someone to plead a long case, but more often than not, people just wanted to put something in the senator's ear. This was the perfect venue for that.

Klobuchar called these events "Minnesota Mornings," and each week she arrived early on Thursday, excited to meet her visitors. Early in her term, most of the encounters had a victory lap feel to them—people who had met Klobuchar on the campaign trail or who had seen her speak at a rally would drop by to offer their congratulations.

The senator loved these gatherings. "She draws energy from other people," her husband, John Bessler, told me.[1] Klobuchar is especially engaging in situations like this; she remembers small details, details that reveal she knows Minnesota, reassuring her visitors that she was there and that it is important to her.

Among those gathered in Klobuchar's office in the Hart Senate Office Building one Thursday morning was Ron Nierhausen, a reserve police officer in Elk River, Minnesota, who had met Klobuchar at a campaign stop during the 2006 race. Nierhausen recalled his excitement at meeting the aspiring senator. He had used his cell phone to call the police chief back home so he could talk to Klobuchar. Not believing that she was who they claimed, the chief hung up. In Washington, many months later, they shared a laugh about it. She was used to having to overcome skepticism about who she was.

At one "Minnesota Morning" in early 2007, Klobuchar introduced her new chief of staff, Lee Sheehy. He was a longtime Minnesotan who wore bow ties, and was very close to the local Minnesota Democratic-Farmer-Labor power structure in Minneapolis. Sheehy had been director of community planning and development for the city of Minneapolis and before that had been the chief deputy state attorney general under Hubert (Skip) Humphrey III. Sheehy's credentials were important because he was replacing Klobuchar's first chief of staff, Sean Richardson, who lasted only about four months in the job—in part because he did not have Minnesota roots. Freshmen senators always face a balancing act in hiring a staff. They need people who understand them and the state they represent, but they also need old Washington hands to help deal with the capital's power structure, which, obviously, can be hard to navigate.

That day, some of the people visiting were farmers. "There are some barley people here," Klobuchar said to the crowd that had gathered that morning, "and some sugar people." She touted her position on the Agriculture Committee and how beneficial that could be for Minnesota farmers. She noted that the chair of the Agriculture Committee was Tom Harkin, a fellow Midwesterner, from neighboring Iowa. All of this was good for Minnesota, she insisted. And then she introduced the staff: Hillary Bolea, the "agriculture person, and Linden Zakula. Zakula is a good Hibbing name," citing the small city in the north of the state where the press secretary was from. The new chief of staff got a chance to speak and began: "My name is Lee Sheehy, and I'm from Minnesota, too."[2] The crowd applauded, laughing.

One member of the Klobuchar staff was tapped each week to come up with trivia questions for "Minnesota Morning"—either about the Senate or about Minnesota. The breakfast was Minnesota cuisine, for lack of a better word. Today, the featured snack was potica, pronounced *paw-tee-tsa*, a delicacy of Slovenian origin native to the Iron Range in northern Minnesota. It is essentially a sweet roll full of walnuts, butter, and cream, baked in a thin-rolled pastry dough. A batch of potica had been shipped in directly from the Iron Range for this event.

Klobuchar invited her guests to stay and chat as long as they liked with her staff or with one another. She also invited them to visit the Senate chamber later that day, when she would be the designated presiding officer. "I'll be presiding today from three to five, and I get to gavel Ted Kennedy to order," she announced. "You haven't lived until you've done that, and I've not only gotten to do that once, but twice."[3] The Kennedy reference was an easy way to connect her home folk to the Senate with a figure they recognized. But the Senate Ted Kennedy entered in 1962—when Klobuchar was less than two years old—and the one of which she was now a part were obviously very different bodies.

In 1962 there were two women in the Senate; in the spring of 2007 there were sixteen. Klobuchar hoped for more: "We now have sixteen women in the Senate and it is quite a group. I missed the time when they didn't even have their own bathroom," she later said in an online chat with *Washington Post* readers. "Claire McCaskill and I were the two women elected this year, and we are good friends. I'd love to see even more women in the Senate. Someone once asked me when we will have achieved equality in the Senate, and I told them I will know it has happened when our women senators' bathroom is as big as theirs."[4]

Women in the Senate, especially young ones, defy the original meaning of the word "senator," which derives from the Latin *senatus*, which means "council of old men," and is in turn derived from the word *senex*, meaning "old man." "I am constantly being taken for a staffer," Amy Klobuchar complained. "It happens about ten times a day. I guess I just don't look like a senator."[5]

After she was elected, one of Klobuchar's earliest calls was to Barbara Mikulski, the Maryland Democrat who is the most senior woman senator.

Elected in 1986, Mikulski, a brash, bold, sometimes overbearing politician from Baltimore, stands barely five feet tall. She talks like she just got off the bus from East Baltimore, and better than anyone else, she understands what it means not to look like a senator. Mikulski's advice to Klobuchar was classic Barbara, as she later repeated it to me: "What is a senator supposed to look like? When they ask you that, tell them they are looking at it." Pointing to herself, she added, "This is what a senator looks like."[6]

On March 16, 2007, Emily's List, the largest political action committee in the country—which raises money to help elect pro-choice Democratic women—held its annual luncheon in a sprawling ballroom on the seventh floor of the new convention center in Washington. It was, as always, a happy gathering of women in politics—elected officials, activists, operatives, donors. It was also a celebration of the successes of 2006. Pro-choice Democratic women had picked up eleven seats in the House, and the two new women in the U.S. Senate were both pro-choice. Another woman senator, Hillary Clinton, had announced that she would seek the Democratic nomination for president in 2008, and she was at that point the runaway favorite to win.

The excitement in the room was largely generated by the fact that, for the first time, a woman was going to be a viable candidate for president, and given the damage that President Bush had wrought on his party, the Democratic nominee would go into the election with huge advantages. Hillary Clinton was the woman everyone referred to as "the next president of the United States of America." Senator Clinton was not there herself, but she spoke to the room on video, promising that she was in the race, and "in it to win it." Even women voters who had previously not been warm to Clinton—because they felt she was too ambitious or because her husband's presidency had left them discouraged—got caught up in the history-making aura of the moment.

Two of the biggest stars at the luncheon were Amy Klobuchar and Claire McCaskill. The two new senators stood in for Hillary Clinton, absorbed all the love in the room, and gave it back. Klobuchar stole the show when she told a story about her husband that spoke to changing gender roles. McCaskill and Klobuchar had driven to the convention center from the Capitol together, and as they were leaving, Amy saw her husband crossing the street in front of their car. She rolled down the window and asked him where he was headed. As she recounted, "He said, 'Well, I'm here for a Senate spouse event. It's Jim Webb's wife's baby shower.' I thought—this is a great victory for women. Of course, Claire yelled out the window, 'That is the sexiest thing I've ever seen!'"[7]

These two women were heroes not because they had won elections, but because they had proven to be exceptional candidates in states that were very difficult for Democrats. They were senators who had come to Washington in familiar but very different ways. As the state auditor, McCaskill talked a lot about fiscal responsibility. Klobuchar was a prosecutor, and she used that experience to present herself as a tough law-and-order candidate. McCaskill wanted to audit the war, because she felt the nation was spending too much money, and Klobuchar wanted to bring the troops home—particularly the units of the Minnesota National Guard that had been the longest serving of any Guard units in Iraq.

These two women were the reason Emily's List existed.

On June 20, 2007, the Senate began consideration of a bill to increase fuel efficiency in cars. Every one of the new senators was a cosponsor. The official description was "a bill (H.R. 6) to reduce our Nation's dependence on foreign oil by investing in clean, renewable, and alternative energy resources, promoting new emerging energy technologies, developing greater efficiency, and creating a Strategic Energy Efficiency and Renewables Reserve to invest in alternative energy, and for other purposes."[8]

It was an important debate, in part because the price of gas was going up. But Democrats had also pledged to do something about climate change and global warming. Frustrated in their effort to end the war in Iraq, they hoped for better success on this bill.

Amy Klobuchar had an amendment she wanted to make to the proposal, her first important one, and she wanted to see it considered, but she ran into one of the realities of the Senate; one senator objected to her bill and would not let it come to a vote. The senator in question happened to be the ranking Republican on the Energy Committee, James Inhofe of Oklahoma. Klobuchar wanted to talk to Inhofe in person, hoping to persuade him to change his mind, but she was under the clear impression that he was avoiding her.

What Klobuchar proposed was the establishment of a federal carbon registry to measure the level of greenhouse gases being released into the atmosphere. In her mind it would hold companies accountable for carbon emissions while at the same time measuring progress in reducing those emissions. The proposal would have forced companies of a certain size to make public the amount of carbon they pump into the atmosphere each year.

It was a simple proposal, she said, which was why Inhofe—a conservative, pro-business Republican who saw this as a restrictive measure for businesses—was so set against it. As the leading Republican on the Energy Committee, he made it part of his portfolio to make sure that legislation like this never saw the light of day. "He knows if he lets it come to a vote, it'll pass," Klobuchar said. She knew at this point that there was no changing his mind. "I've tried everything; I've been nice; I've been firm. Today I'll not be so nice."[9] She decided to take him on right on the floor of the Senate.

As Klobuchar was trying unsuccessfully to do with Inhofe, senators have to grab people when they can. In order to get things done in the Senate, you need face time with the actual senator, not the staff, even though the institution is so heavily staff-driven and senators are rarely in their offices. Because so many other senators lunch there, the urge to engage in deal making is irresistible.

On this day, Klobuchar had lunch in the members' dining room—a small salad and the sea bass. During lunch, a member of the waitstaff asked her to move her chair out of the way—something that would never happen to a male senator. Klobuchar chatted with Senator Sheldon Whitehouse, who was meeting his daughter Molly for lunch, about a man who was appearing before the Judiciary Committee, about intelligence. Then she and Molly had a long conversation about Yale, where Klobuchar had graduated magna cum laude with a major in political science.

Just after 4:00 P.M., as Klobuchar walked into the Senate chamber, Lamar Alexander, the senior senator from Tennessee, was trashing the proposal to spend $10 billion to develop wind power as a source of energy. "The average utility bill for Tennesseans is $100 a month. This is $2 billion a year. We could just give the money to Tennesseans, 1.7 million households, for a full year. One month's electric bill for 20 million households, that is what we could do for $2 billion," he said.[10]

Klobuchar took off her watch and put it on her assigned desk. She pinned the microphone to the left lapel of her light green suit.

That morning, Harry Reid had established the schedule for the day. It included the energy bill. Time for debates on particular bills is broken up equally between the majority and the minority, by agreement between the two leaders. Klobuchar had informed the clerk that she wanted to speak on the energy bill—using time allotted to the majority—and was given a time to speak. Once she was recognized by the presiding officer, Ben Cardin from Maryland, she went right after Inhofe, who had sent out a letter saying that the amendment would impose new regulations on every business in America. "In his letter, the senior Senator from Oklahoma also said organizations such as the Sierra Club or the Natural Resources Defense Council would be put in charge of third-party verification and have access to confidential business information," Klobuchar said. "This is so inaccurate I do not even know where to begin."[11]

Her cause was already lost. There was no chance of her provision being adopted. Inhofe had enough power to convince Jeff Bingaman, the chairman and leading Democrat on the committee, that there were other, more important provisions to be made than those of this freshman senator. Still, her case had to be argued:

> We have a major challenge confronting us. There are people out there waiting for us to do something about it. There is a scientist out there right now seeing how the sea level is going up. There is another scientist who measures the temperatures and sees how, since the ice age, we have only had a five-degree increase in temperature and just the last century we have seen a one-degree increase, with the EPA estimating a three-degree increase in the next hundred years. There are little kids out there wearing "Save the Penguins" buttons right now. There is a hunter in Hinckley, MN, who sees changes in the wetlands. He is waiting for us to act.[12]

It is striking to note that, in the end, the most powerful weapon a senator has is her voice, and that so often it is employed on behalf of lost causes. During their freshman year, Webb, Tester, and Klobuchar all had to watch as their amendments or provisions died before they even got to the floor of the Senate. As difficult as it is for any senator to get something done in the Senate, for freshmen it's almost impossible. They don't yet have the relationships, the favors to trade, or the chits to call in that longer-serving senators can bring to bear. In the Senate, longevity is an important commodity.

△

One of Amy Klobuchar's most embarrassing moments came in the spring of 2007 as she presided over a morning session of the Senate. A page approached and handed her a note. "Pull up your shirt," the note said. It was signed "Anonymous." She was horrified. "Could you believe that?"[13] She couldn't help telling the story, though, because she is a great storyteller. The next time she presided, Klobuchar received a second note, also signed

"Anonymous." This one read, "Your earrings don't match."[14] When she looked up, Tester was cracking up in the back row.

The truth is that women in the Senate are severely disadvantaged by the fashion choices available to them. No male senator ever goes to the floor of the Senate without a jacket and tie. In order to fit with the tone of the Senate, and in an effort to avoid ostentation, the women compromise on some female version of a man's gray suit. The result is a lot of pantsuits, and various ensembles that require blazers and jackets.

Early in the 2008 presidential campaign, the Senate had been in heated debate about immigration, and when the bill failed, the next debate was about higher education. Hillary Clinton, like her mentor and model in the Senate, Ted Kennedy, was on the Education Committee, and though the Senate had been consumed by rancor over immigration for weeks, the minute it was over, both Clinton and Kennedy were ready to move on to education.

Senator Clinton came to the floor wearing a pantsuit with a jacket over a low-cut round-neck camisole. She spoke for nearly half an hour, clearly establishing herself as an expert on the issue and displaying a passion to the point of obsession. "The college-going rate has been pretty stagnant now for about 20 or 30 years. As the cost of higher education has gone up, it has become even more difficult for young people to work their way through, to afford the increases in tuition and room and board," Clinton said.[15]

But the big story about that moment in the Senate was whether Hillary Clinton was sexing up her presidential campaign by showing a little cleavage on the Senate floor. The *Washington Post* published a story by fashion writer Robin Givhan: "It was startling to see that small acknowledgment of sexuality and femininity peeking out of the conservative—aesthetically speaking—environment of Congress," she wrote. "After all, it wasn't until the early '90s that women were even allowed to wear pants on the Senate floor. It was even more surprising to note that it was coming from Clinton, someone who has been so publicly ambivalent about style, image and the burdens of both."[16] The coverage seemed petty, thin, and in the end curious, because the picture of her outfit didn't seem to reveal any cleavage.

△

Senators' desks are assigned by seniority but also by the desires of the senior members. So, for example, Ted Kennedy sat in the back row of the Senate for his entire career, the same desk his brother Jack used. Klobuchar's was the same desk that Eugene McCarthy, George McGovern, and Barbara Mikulski once sat at. Claire McCaskill sat in a desk that Truman once had used in the Senate, and during the election, she had earned her own reputation as a straight talker in the same vein as her illustrious predecessor. In June 2007, McCaskill went to Baghdad to get a look at how the United States was spending the $2 billion that was gushing out of the treasury each week for the war in Iraq. The former state auditor had been railing about the need for more congressional oversight since she got to Washington. She came back from Baghdad lamenting the "cost-plus" contracts that had enriched so many of the independent contractors doing business with the U.S. government in Iraq. Such contracts pay contractors a profit as a percentage of whatever the project costs. McCaskill said she had eaten in very nice mess halls and wanted to assure her constituents that the troops were eating well at least. But "cost-plus is a dangerous contracting device," she insisted in a conference call with reporters from Kuwait, "because what cost-plus says to someone is, 'The more you spend, the more you make.' And that's a dangerous thing to do around public dollars."

It was already clear at that point that the cost of the war was going to surpass a trillion dollars. "I think that, if there's any conclusions that I can draw about the contracting piece of this," McCaskill said on the same call, "it's that in an effort to succeed in the military mission, there was an abdication of stewardship as it relates to the way that the money was spent, particularly as it relates to some of the contracts, both on reconstruction and in supporting our troops." In other words, we overpaid to win battles that we have not won.

McCaskill's predecessor, Harry Truman, essentially established the model for this kind of congressional investigation during World War II with the Truman Committee, which exposed waste and fraud in military procurement and gave the until then little-known senator a very visible public profile. In an October 2007 press release, McCaskill wrote, "Late into the night when our amendment was finally brought up, miracle of all miracles, it passed without a single 'no' vote. As I said on the floor of the United States Senate that night, 'Harry Truman would be proud.'"[17]

It was obvious that the war wasn't going that well militarily either. McCaskill said that all the troops she met with were proud of their work, but on the question of effectiveness, she was left with a "mixed bag" of reactions. "I think all of them were proud of the job they were doing and that certainly was my message to them, how proud we are of them in Missouri and in America," she said from Kuwait. "But, honestly, there were some that said, 'We need to get out. We're not doing any good over here. We need to get out immediately. We need to all get out.'"

McCaskill directly dismissed efforts by some to overdress the good news in Iraq. "I will tell you that anyone who has come over and spent time talking to the troops and comes home and says, 'They all think what we're doing is great and we need to stay here as long as it takes,' is not honestly talking to the troops," McCaskill said. "There are many of them at this point, especially those, I found, that have been deployed for the second or third time, that are very discouraged and do not believe that we are making meaningful progress in terms of what we're trying to accomplish over here."

Truman once tried to minimize his reputation as a confrontational rabble-rouser by denying the appropriateness of his nickname, "Give 'Em Hell Harry." He said, "I never gave anybody hell! I just told the truth and they thought it was hell."[18] Democrats had been taking heat because the focus had shifted from the war to other issues, like immigration and energy. But Iraq wasn't going away, and party leaders were aware of that. McCaskill said cleaning up the Iraq contracting mess, before and after the war ends, was going to take a long time. "It's going to take a fairly long attention span," she concluded.

"This isn't something that's going to be fixed by one press conference or by one change of command or by one change of one rule or procedure."[19]

Since January, Klobuchar had been going home to Minnesota nearly every weekend, while her husband and daughter stayed in Washington. It is the curse of a modern senator that if you get sent to Washington, you have to make sure that everyone back home understands that you are not "of Washington." To lose touch with the home folks is a reelection liability. So Klobuchar was back in Minnesota frequently throughout the year. But when school was out in the summer, it was easier for the family to be back home together in their two-story house on a modest street in Minneapolis down from the local fire station.

Indeed, in late August that year, Klobuchar took the opportunity to hold a staff retreat at the house for her entire Senate team. People flew in from Washington and from around the state for a debrief and collegial fun. The day got off to a good start, but suddenly, standing in the kitchen preparing some food, her house full of people who worked for her, Klobuchar saw a mouse skitter across the kitchen floor. Like any embarrassed host, she hoped no one else had seen it. One aide, standing on the staircase above the kitchen, caught a glimpse of the critter, and was about to scream. Klobuchar noticed, motioned threateningly that that was a bad idea, and the woman stifled her shriek.

After the event broke up, Klobuchar, who had managed to preserve the secret of the mouse in the kitchen, called the exterminator and had the house treated. She did not have enough cash on hand to pay for the service and borrowed twenty-six dollars from her twelve-year-old daughter Abigail to complete the transaction.

The following week was the Minnesota State Fair, and the senator and her daughter were paying a visit. Trips to the fair had proved to be successful during the campaign the year before. The day began with a visit to the Science Museum of Minnesota in downtown St. Paul. It was the last Saturday in August and it was hot. Klobuchar had just returned from Greenland on a fact-finding trip to see the effect of climate change on some of the world's biggest glaciers. The Science Museum was the perfect place to talk about the trip. The new senator met with a group of school kids to talk about global warming in a second-floor meeting room, with bright, yellow walls and heavy blinds that, when closed, could shut out all the light glancing off the Mississippi River outside.

There was a small contingent of Klobuchar staffers present, including Mark Wilson, who had taken the trip to Greenland with her. But the person introducing Klobuchar that morning was none other than Abigail, who told the kids that she cared about what was happening with climate change, and she hoped they cared, too. And after a little more small talk, Abigail said, "And now, here's my mom."[20]

The senator began by showing some pictures of the trip on an overhead projector. In one she is not wearing her sunglasses and is looking out on a sheer expanse of white.

"The reason I went to Greenland was because I heard there were places where they used to have ice in the front yard and now they are growing potatoes."

Of the next photo she said: "This is a glacier, but it looks like a sheet of ice that you might see on a Minnesota lake where you can go fishing." She described for the group what she ate in Greenland—halibut and reindeer—while looking at a photograph of her group at dinner. "We were trying not to sing the song from *Titanic*," she said.

As her mother talked, Abigail stood at the door of the room like a member of the senior staff, making sure the event came off well. The senator talked about the national carbon registry provision she tried to have adopted as part of the energy bill, and why she failed. "It was kind of a fight for five days," she said, "but I'll win in the end." One of the kids in the audience—who clearly was not interested in the details of Washington politicking—wanted to know how long it had taken her to get to Greenland. "That's a really good question; we went by dogsled," she said, before admitting she had taken a direct flight from Newark, New Jersey.

By this time, the group had grown to about thirty people. Klobuchar pointed to the kids in the front row and said, "They are the reason we need to do something about [global warming]."

On the way out, Abigail wanted to make sure to get some astronaut ice cream, a freeze-dried, vacuum-packed piece of glob that could survive space travel. It was out of this world—and not in a good way. But food would be a central theme for the rest of the day—it was time for the State Fair, and Abigail had some advice about the menu. "It's either fried or on a stick, unless it is fried and on a stick."

The Minnesota State Fairgrounds lie in Falcon Heights between St. Paul and Minneapolis, and the fair always runs for the twelve days leading up to Labor Day. The Minnesota State Fair, Minnesotans always argue, is the largest fair in the country. In 2007, more that 1.6 million people visited it. Klobuchar had always been a regular attendee. If you're in politics, showing up here is an absolute necessity. Minnesotans refer to the event as the "Great Minnesota Get-Together." Amy Klobuchar started working the crowd as soon as she got out of the van. "Hi! Nice to see you," she responded to all the shouts of "Hello, senator" that came her way.

Klobuchar's office was operating a booth at the fair, and the senator had brought a little bit of Washington work back home with her. Even though she'd lost the National Carbon Registry fight to Inhofe's seniority, visitors to the Klobuchar booth were invited to take the Minnesota Energy Challenge and become "carbon busters." The challenge was essentially a quick energy audit to figure out how someone might reduce energy costs and consumption. Her office had put out a press release urging Minnesotans to make "small changes in their homes" and to find "homegrown solutions" to combat the price of gas, which was skyrocketing that summer. "These simple changes can save consumers more than the cost of Fair admission," the press release concluded.[21]

A more immediate challenge facing the senator, however, was trying to locate the actual booth in the massive crowd. More than once, someone had to say: "It's at Judson and Underwood." That intersection also happened to be the location of the famous Snake Zoo, which has been in the same place and run by the same man, Bob Duerr, for forty years.

Klobuchar's booth had the façade of a house so she could stand out in front of it and pretend she was standing on a front porch. Once she had found her booth and after she had been there for a few minutes, an aide set up a microphone. Klobuchar made a short speech reveling in the fair and urging people to find ways to be more energy efficient. Innovation was in a Minnesotan's blood, she insisted: "We are the state that brought you everything from the Post-it note to the pacemaker."[22]

Later, as the crowd grew denser, Al Franken, the former *Saturday Night Live* regular who was campaigning for the U.S. Senate in 2008, appeared on the corner. He was lost and looking for his booth. Someone on a cell phone was shouting the intersection into his ear, but that did not seem to help. Finally a Franken staffer found him and took him to his booth, which was just around the corner from Klobuchar's.

Amy and Abigail set off to see what was out there. Klobuchar wanted to show her guests—reporters and some of her out-of-state staff—the big overgrown vegetables that are popular features of the show. As they waded through the crowds, Abigail looked at her mom and said: "Maybe we should power up with some cheese curds."[23]

State fair cheese curds are something of a religious experience in Minnesota. In essence they are chunks of cheese dredged in a batter and deep-fried in oil, and they taste like chunks of cheese dredged in a batter and deep-fried in oil. There is an ongoing debate about which version of the delicacy is the best, and the consistent front-runner is the one served up at an establishment called the Mouse Trap, where Abigail did decide to power up. Her mom declined. She also passed on the frozen chocolate banana on a stick at the booth next door.

When Klobuchar drifted into the Democratic-Farmer-Labor Party booth, there was a burst of applause. She was greeted as the conquering heroine, the winner of the last big election. As it turned out, Mark Dayton, the man Klobuchar replaced in the Senate, was also in the booth, casually chatting with some young people. They greeted each other and talked briefly. Already the political chatter had turned to the 2008 presidential race. Dayton told me that he did not miss Washington at all, and added that he thought Klobuchar was off to a good start.

Over Dayton's shoulder was a wall with notes posted all over it. At the top there was a sign that read: "Tell us why you're a DFLer." Two funny postings jumped out at me: "Troubles: I've got Pawlenty," a reference to the popular Republican governor Tim Pawlenty. The other said simply: "Because you never hear anyone say, 'There goes a nice piece of elephant.'"

Klobuchar made another speech, along with several other Democrats who were on the 2008 ticket, including Franken, who did a long and complicated star turn on the innards of the national farm bill and why it needed to be improved for Minnesota.

After a visit to the giant pumpkin house, Klobuchar was ready to leave. She had dinner plans and said she would be back at the fair a few more times before it ended. Abigail wanted to stay; there was music she wanted to hear. So she stayed at the booth.

Klobuchar was meeting old law school friends for dinner, just down the street from her house. As they prepared to leave, Abigail reminded her mother that she had helped pay for the exterminator back at the house. "You still owe me twenty-six dollars."[24]

△

Toward the end of 2007, there was a sense that the mood of 2006—which put Democrats in control of the Congress—and the national political conversation would play a huge role in the upcoming 2008 presidential year contests. Al Franken would go on to win the election, defeating the incumbent Norm Coleman—but the election was so close that it took the courts and election officials almost eight months to declare a winner. Nearly 3 million votes were cast in the Minnesota Senate election of 2008, Franken's official margin of victory was 319 votes, and he was not seated until after the next Fourth of July—in 2009.

But back in the summer of 2007, the Democratic nomination for president seemed to be Hillary Clinton's in a walk, and Barack Obama's chances seemed bleak. At the DFL booth at the Minnesota State Fair in August, former senator Mark Dayton was excited about Clinton's prospects. "I used to sit next to her in the Senate, and I think she's going to be a great president."[25] There was a sense that the mood and the politics of the moment had come together to make Hillary Clinton president, that the nomination was hers to lose. And she did lose it. Ironically, the three superstar female politicians of 2006—Pelosi, Klobuchar, and McCaskill—would all choose not to endorse Clinton for president, and all of them, in time, would be strong supporters of Barack Obama.

In 2008, when the nation suddenly got a primer on the ins and outs of the nomination process, with the debate about the role of superdelegates, the pressure was intense on the high-ranking party and elected officials who would ultimately decide the nomination. Klobuchar recalled that she was at the Costco store in Arlington, Virginia, stocking up for a party when a man in line behind her began interrogating her about how she was going to cast her superdelegate vote.

For a long time, Klobuchar refused to commit, saying that she would leave it up to the voters of Minnesota to decide during their primary contest, which was held on February 5. Obama won that contest, but Klobuchar waited until the end of March to make a formal announcement. The decision, she said, was based on what she perceived as Obama's different voice and ability to bring "a new perspective and inspiring a real excitement from the American people."[26]

There was some unspoken expectation among Clinton supporters that female politicians would back Clinton, but Klobuchar said she decided on the endorsement because of her "own independent judgment about [Obama's] abilities."[27]

She, as it turned out, had backed the right horse.

CHAPTER EIGHT
ODD MAN OUT

Bob Corker came to Washington under bittersweet circumstances. There was no denying that he had achieved something remarkable with his election to the U.S. Senate, and that he had done it under very difficult political conditions, for the Republican label was the path to defeat in the fall of 2006 and 2008. Republicans were, at best, only able to hold on to their own seats. Corker's was the solitary victory Republicans had to celebrate on election night 2006, for they lost every other competitive Senate race in the country. Corker's was a seat held, too—he succeeded the Republican majority leader, Bill Frist—but his, unlike the rest, was a high-profile race against a well-known candidate. Tennessee's lieutenant governor, Ron Ramsay, saw the Corker victory as the place where the Democrats were stopped and turned around. "We in the State of Tennessee were the firewall," he said in the spring of 2007.[1]

In addition to being the Republicans' last line of defense, the victory was a personal vindication for Corker: He was going to replace Bill Frist, the man who had beaten him in the Republican primary twelve years earlier, in 1994. Corker, memorably, had gone to work for Bill Frist's reelection the day after he lost the primary to him. Now Bob Corker's patience, his perseverance, his willingness to play by the rules, had been rewarded.

Bill Frist was part of a Republican wave that had, a dozen years later, been turned on its head. In 1994, Republicans had picked up eight seats to take control of the Senate; Democrats, in 2006, had gotten the six they needed. Now Corker was riding the wave in the opposite direction.

In some ways, Bob Corker should have been in a position to be a GOP star. After all, he was the most recent Republican to face the voters on a big stage and win. Theoretically, that should have given him some credibility in the debate about how to defend the Republican brand and resell it to a skeptical electorate. That is partly what had happened on the other side of the fence with Barack Obama in 2005.

In 2004, Democrats lost all of the five open seats they were defending, and they lost their leader, Tom Daschle, for a sixth. There were only two freshmen Democrats that year, Barack Obama and Ken Salazar, who had picked up a GOP-held seat in Colorado. Both of them were sought out by the press, but Obama made more interesting copy, and it was clear that he was thinking about broader themes for the party, and how it should position itself.

"I think that my values are deeply rooted in the progressive tradition, the values of equal opportunity, civil rights, fighting for working families, a foreign policy that is mindful of human rights, a strong belief in civil liberties, wanting to be a good steward for the environment, a sense that the government has an important role to play, that opportunity is open to all people and that the powerful don't trample on the less powerful," Obama said in late 2005. "I share all the aims of a Paul Wellstone or a Ted Kennedy when it comes to the end result. But I'm much more agnostic, much more flexible on how we achieve those ends."[2] A key difference between Obama and Corker was that Democrats in 2005 were out of office and looking for new voices while in 2006 the Republicans still had a president whom they needed to support.

When Corker was asked for advice about the future direction of the party, he was decidedly more mundane in his offerings than the Illinois freshman had been two years before. In 2008, for example, he said, "People want to know, 'Do you understand the issues I care about?' People need to be able to relate to you as a person who could understand issues in their lives. Make sure they understand you are a real person and understand their concerns in a visceral way."[3]

The deep sense of doom that afflicted Republicans in the wake of the 2006 drubbing made it difficult for anyone in the party to look very far ahead, and Corker didn't have the chance to reshape the debate the way Obama had started to do two years earlier. So badly did Republicans feel defeated that when Corker won President Bush didn't call to congratulate him—even though he was the only new Republican senator-elect. Corker was quick to point out that he had nothing but warm relations with the president, but he did note that on election night "he did not have that many people to call."[4]

△

Corker came to the Senate in 2006 after one of the nastiest, most racially charged campaigns of the season. He ran against Congressman Harold Ford, a scion of the powerful black Memphis political dynasty, who had been leading in the polls early in the campaign. Ford was seeking to become the first black senator from the South since Reconstruction. Corker had been thinking and planning for this race for a long time, and came to believe that being a Democrat in the Republican stronghold of Tennessee would be more of a handicap than being black—it was a long shot.

However, the contest in Tennessee became famous for one incendiary ad that apparently helped to sink the Ford campaign. Ford and Corker seemed locked in a dead heat in the polls for most of the campaign. Corker's ads portrayed Ford as a young, pampered Washington insider who was not really from Tennessee, while Ford portrayed Corker as a well-connected moneyman with no interest in the common people.

A couple of weeks before the election, the Republican National Committee ran an ad that made fun of previous reports that Ford had attended a Super Bowl party hosted by *Playboy* in 2005. The ad showed a white woman dressed as a Playboy Bunny saying enticingly that she had met Ford at the party. The ad ended with the woman whispering, "Harold, call me." Some people saw in the ad an effort to play on the history of racial prejudice, and protests rose from Democrats all across the country.

Corker denounced the ad and said it should be taken down. There is an open question about whether it was the RNC ad or the reaction to it from Ford's supporters—who called it racist, attacking Corker as a racist himself, suggesting the voters of Tennessee were susceptible to that kind of race-baiting—that did the greater damage to Ford. In either case, the damage was done, and Corker cruised to victory by 3 percentage points—51 percent to 48 percent. Even though that ad became the signature moment of the race on the national stage, Corker remembered the election fondly, which is not unusual for winners. Still, the grueling nature of campaigns can be deflating for some politicians, but seven months later Corker could say, smiling, "Our campaign was a lot of fun."

Corker not only had a tough general election race, but he earlier had to win a tough primary battle against a group of formidable Republican candidates. He estimated that with all the money spent in the primary and by the candidates and their supporters in the general election, more than $55 million was spent electing the junior senator from Tennessee in 2006. Most of that money was spent on nasty ads on television. The ads against Corker accused him of being a greedy rich businessman who looked out only for people of his economic class. The ads against Ford had a subtext that he was a young, frivolous Washington insider who had gotten ahead on his father's name. Ford's father, Harold Ford Sr., had represented that congressional district for twenty-three years before bequeathing the role to his son.

"Little children could not watch cartoons in the morning on Saturday without seeing a bunch of political ads," Corker quipped.

The national attention, brought largely by Ford's candidacy, changed the whole tone of the race. "People say that going from a primary to a general election is like going from the minor leagues to the major leagues. Well, this was like going from the minor leagues to the World Series, because the whole country was watching," he later told me.

"People all across the country took an interest in this campaign; even people outside our country came here to see what this was all about," he said on election night. "There was a strong headwind working against us, but in the end, the choice belonged to the good people of Tennessee."[5]

In the end, the country was left with a less than favorable impression of the race, because of the *Playboy* ad. Corker explained that he did not believe that the controversy had affected the outcome of the election. He said he was always confident that he would win. Ironically, Corker said that the time he worried most was on election day when he saw how much it was raining. "I thought this is not good, this is not good at all," he told me. After the polls closed and the raw vote numbers started to come in, Corker said he visited his campaign war room at the hotel in Chattanooga, and was unnerved by the slow, incoherent way the numbers were reported. "The Memphis numbers were still out, and it was kind of disconcerting, so I left," he said. Ford was from Memphis, and so the returns from that part of the state were likely going to be more favorable to him than to Corker. "I just went back upstairs and watched the national television coverage. The atmosphere in that room was not that upbeat."

Despite all the attention on the ad and its race-baiting undertones, Corker said the attention hurt his campaign more than it helped, that it depressed his poll numbers for a few days before he was able to bounce back. He said the ad and ones that take a similar tone leave voters with the wrong impression of people in public life—who suddenly find themselves defined by media consultants and opposition research specialists. He was not denying that his campaign did it, too. For that reason, Corker said he felt the need to reintroduce himself to the people of Tennessee after the election. "They know who you are, but what do they think of you? They have gotten to know you in the context of a campaign, and that is not the best way for people to know you. What I want to make sure that happens over the next five years and eight months is that they get to know me."

△

Bob Corker came to a Washington dominated by Democrats, and not just victorious Democrats, but Democrats who were exuberant at the idea of being in power for the first time in a dozen years.

Left to his own devices, Corker went about things in his usual methodical way, only to quickly realize that it would not work. "The Senate is a very different place, okay. I used to wake up every morning and I had this black notebook, like this one," he said, holding up a legal-size tome. "During the campaign, my car was broken into and I lost the one I'd had for years. It was worn out right here from my hands being on it all the time. But for my entire life I have woken up and before I get my first cup of coffee, I look at my black notebook with a list of things I'm going to do . . . as it relates to what I was going to get done that day."

Once in the Senate, however, he had to change the way he did business. He said his need for a notebook was greatly reduced. "I write in this thing once a week, because the Senate is a very metered environment. What I've had to do here is change that 'wake-up' routine and think about the twelve things I was going to get done today. Here the issues and the agenda are set by others—so much of the time we are building toward . . . an opportunity that will arise in the future."

Corker said the way to create opportunities is to "dig really deep on issues, really understanding them so that, hopefully, you become on certain issues, the person, or one of the people, that others come to rely upon."

The first bill he introduced, on April 16, 2007, was one to ban political parties from running ads in campaigns without the consent of the candidate they are trying to help. The bill went nowhere. Political ads and the money that pays for them are the lifeblood of the political system, and the men and women in Congress who have won at the game were in no mood to change those rules. But it was a nice gesture.

For senators who have had power in business or a profession before reaching the Senate, its byways can sometimes be a shock to their system.

Bob Corker, who had been the owner of a huge, multimillion-dollar company, and who had been the mayor of Chattanooga, Tennessee, was one of those people.

"As a mayor you can wake up every day and see tremendous tangible differences in what you're doing. You do miss that ability to create a vision and then put the pieces in place to make it happen," he told me. Corker knew how to make things happen, and it had made him an important and wealthy man. His first financial disclosure form showed that he was worth between $64 million and $236 million—making him easily the richest of the ten new senators elected in 2006. At least half the new group were millionaires "on paper," with Claire McCaskill valued between $13 and $29 million and immediately one of the ten richest members of the Senate. It was noted by the press that the average net worth of the 100 senators was $8.9 million.[6]

People like Bob Corker are used to making decisions and then taking action. That was not what happened when he got to the Senate, and his difficulties were heightened by the fact that he was the only Republican freshman in the 2006 class. Not only was he in the Senate, where progress is often measured in decades, but he was a junior member of the minority party that had no ability to move an agenda. He was a little frustrated, and he would sometimes let it show. "I will say that for the first four weeks of being here I did wonder to myself, 'You mean I campaigned for twenty-five months and two days to do this?'" he said to me as he sat in a small, well-appointed anteroom in his office on the first floor of the Dirksen Senate Office Building.

He said that in some ways it was worse for a lot of his colleagues, who had gotten used to the idea of wielding power. "First of all, you have to remember the only way I've ever served was in the minority. I don't know the difference. We have the public policy luncheon and I look around at my fellow Republicans, some of them have long faces. For me, this is the way it is in the Senate; we're in the minority, and we are not deciding which bills are coming up in the Senate."

△

Bob Corker's expensive suits testified to his wealth; his jackets sometimes seemed overly long as if to compensate for his lack of height. He could be self-conscious, but he was, by and large, incredibly jovial and very approachable in the early days of the term, when all the new senators were stuck in basement offices in the Russell Office Building. Everyone knew when he left at the end of the day because he would announce his departure with a loud "Great work today, everybody!"

Corker said that the basement digs never really bothered him much. "You gotta remember, I'm a guy who started working at thirteen," he said. "When I got out of college, my friends all went and got coat-and-tie jobs, I went and worked in the construction trade on a job site, and got mud all over me every day. I learned how to build a building. I went into business at twenty-five with a pickup truck and eight thousand dollars, and I've never really had a nice office." The office he was in at the time of our interview was a very nice one, and it had once belonged to Conrad Burns—who lost the same night Corker won.

Corker described one of his early meetings with members of the Republican caucus. "I wanted to make sure I did not sit in the wrong place, so I asked where the junior member sat, and Johnny Isakson, the senior Senator from Georgia, said, 'Any seat you sit in is the least senior seat.'"

But as the only new Republican member in 2007, Corker got his pick of the elite committees. He got spots on Energy and Foreign Relations at a time when the country and the Congress were consumed by Iraq. "As the only Republican freshman, I was kind of a novelty," he said.

Even in the United States Senate, which is disproportionately populated by the ambitious and the obsessed, Corker stood out as type A. He ran on the National Mall several times a week and set himself an early goal of visiting all ninety-five Tennessee counties and meeting personally with each of the other ninety-nine senators. It took a while, but he pulled off both, even if it irritated some Democrats who thought the meetings were just political grandstanding.

But Corker was determined that he would learn his way to success in the Senate. "Our view is that knowledge is power in the Senate," said Todd Womack, Corker's chief of staff, in October of the senator's first year. "He feels that he can go deeper on issues."[7] And Corker very quickly came to understand the power of the position, even as a junior member of the minority party. "In the Senate, you can call anybody in the country and they will stop whatever they're doing to give you a briefing," Corker said, "because they feel like they are affecting policy."

Corker took advantage of that perk until he realized that it was not serving him well. "I am on four committees—Energy, Foreign Relations, Small Business, and Aging. I was doing twenty-seven or twenty-eight meetings every week, and I realized I was only hitting the surface issues." Within the first month or so, he pared back on the briefings because he felt like he was spinning his wheels. It is not atypical for freshmen senators to be overwhelmed by all the new issues and information coming at them before they decide what is beneficial and what is not. "What we found ourselves doing was running from meeting to meeting to meeting to meeting. It was difficult to have any substance," he said. "The schedule was driving us instead of vice versa. So what we've been doing since then is having a lot of meetings with people who come in from outside government to really drill down on issues, especially energy, but also on foreign relations. We've been spending a lot of time on the Middle East."

He said he thought the three most important issues he would deal with were health care, energy, and Iraq. But that was not always the focus in the Senate. As he confessed to one group of constituents after a few months in office, "About half of what we do in the Senate is absolutely useless." Corker said that high quotient of pointlessness stemmed from all the time and effort both parties spend trying to outmaneuver each other. "It's like an arms race. We send all these messaging votes, and then they have to send messaging votes. They are a waste of time. We take so many votes that do not matter."

△

Every Tuesday, both parties met separately for what they called policy lunches. "They are more like a locker room," Corker said. "Those lunch meetings place so much emphasis on countering the other side." In terms of policy debates, Corker said he had learned that gaining the respect of more senior members depended as much on what he did not say as what he did say. "What I've learned in those lunch meetings is that you don't want to talk on every single issue," he said. "They respect you if you know what you're talking about."

Corker found those meetings somewhat counterproductive, because they were so party-centric. "I've been with the forty-nine senators that are on my side all the time. We are together all the time. It's unbelievable," he said. "We have a policy lunch on Tuesday, all kinds of breakfast meetings, a steering committee lunch on Wednesday, and there is a Thursday lunch. Where the effort needs to be made on my part is to reach out and meet other Democrats because the Republicans are around each other nonstop. As are the Democrats."

Although he was a solid GOP citizen, Corker quickly established himself as unpredictably independent by occasionally voting against his own party. In the first five months, he voted to raise the minimum wage, which infuriated fiscal conservatives in his party; he voted for an energy bill that the GOP opposed; and he voted for the expansion of the State Children's Health Insurance Program (SCHIP), which many saw as a move toward the establishment of universal health care and which President Bush vetoed. "I'm not going to repeat the company line that I might hear at some policy lunch," he said.

But luckily for the Republicans, Corker was, for the most part, willing to toe the party line, never publicly criticizing President Bush on the important issue of the moment, the war in Iraq, even though he felt that it was being badly managed. Corker told me that his first meeting with the president left him very concerned about the war effort. "I left there feeling a lot worse about our handling of Iraq than when I went," Corker said. "You just did not get the feeling like there was an overall coherence with the plan." Corker went to Iraq twice in 2007, but his concerns about the president hardly ever showed up in his votes. He was concerned and even wavered on occasion, but he was loyal. Corker's public position on Iraq was that it was part of his responsibility to fix it, not necessarily to criticize how it got broken. "I feel like it's not my job to second-guess policy that has been made before [I got here], but to make policy going forward."

Corker found it easier to speak up when he had the opportunity to be supportive, as when President Bush announced that General David Petraeus was putting in place a new counterinsurgency plan that involved closer collaboration with some Iraqi militias. He said he wanted to be careful about how he dealt with Iraq because the consequences were so monumental. So even though he was the only GOP freshman in the Senate when all the Senate was talking about was Iraq, Corker waited for weeks to speak publicly about the situation there. He said he had an information-gathering process in place. He met with Petraeus three times, with Secretary of State Condoleezza Rice five times, and with the president himself twice. Then he went to Iraq for the first time in mid-February.

"Iraq is a huge issue, and before I ever spoke publicly, after becoming a senator, I went to Iraq and met with General Petraeus there. . . . I met with five generals there. I met with Tennessee troops. I met with their national security adviser, their deputy prime minister, our ambassador. And until I did that, I never spoke publicly about what I thought we should be doing in Iraq, and that is how I want to address all of the issues."

In October 2007, Corker went back home to Tennessee, just after the Senate had waged a long war over the expansion of SCHIP. As part of their effort to reform health care, the Democratic Congress had begun by trying to expand health insurance for poor children. It was a tactical maneuver they hoped would force President Bush and congressional Republicans into the politically unpopular position of opposing health care for poor children.

It worked, but Corker was one of the Republicans who joined the Democrats to pass the bill, knowing that it would be unpopular in some parts of his state. He tried to blunt the attacks by some of his conservative constituents by stressing his independent streak: "You are going to wake up sometime in the next five years and three months and see something I did in the Senate and you're going to say, 'I can't believe Corker did that.'"[8]

In Smith County, Tennessee, Corker held a town meeting in a small restaurant and drew a crowd of about fifty people. The City Café had seven booths along the right wall as you walked in and two round tables in the middle of the room. The menu was all comfort food: creamed potatoes, black-eyed peas, turnip greens, macaroni and tomatoes, bacon on a biscuit. After Corker talked about his respect for the troops fighting in Iraq and how honored he felt to be serving the people of Tennessee in the Senate, he had to deal with Ray Preuitt, a retirement-age constituent with a booming voice who had shown up at his town hall meeting and wanted to talk about his vote on SCHIP.

"This is bringing taxpayer-funded health care to middle-class families, and it is one little incremental step," Preuitt said. "The liberals have learned how to get things done. They do it a little bit at a time."[9]

Corker listened sympathetically and then said that he understood the criticism, but that he had to make choices whenever he voted in the Senate, and on this one he chose to be with poor children. "There are all kinds of budget gimmickry going on in Washington, but I'm going to err on the side of low-income families having health care," he said.[10]

Preuitt was not appeased: "I should not be compelled by law to help other people," Preuitt said. Corker did not seem to fundamentally disagree but said, "It's a moral obligation for us to organize health care in a way that every American should have access to private, and I emphasize private, affordable health care."[11] Of course, there seemed no obvious path toward that goal, and so when health care reform came to the floor in 2009, Corker, like all other Republicans in the Senate, voted against it.

△

Corker seemed to relish being out of Washington and back at home. In a small bright room in Lebanon, Tennessee, that same day, Corker told a small crowd, "I like being a U.S. senator, but I don't think there was anything more rewarding that being mayor [of Chattanooga]."[12] Senators, who have been chief executives—of cities, states, or large and successful companies—often chafe at the collaboration and consultation required to get things done in the Senate. Being a senator, though, put him "in a lot of situations that are kind of fun."

Illustrating one of the real privileges of his job—access—Corker said he was invited into the locker room at the University of Tennessee to visit with the football team in 2007 and prayed with the team. "Coach [Phillip] Fulmer asked them to take a knee, so they could look me in the eye," Corker said, indulging in some self-deprecating humor about his stature.

By the time he got to Joe's Place in Woodbury in Cannon County, Corker was tired. He faced similar rounds of questions, but he was closing in on his ninety-five counties and he couldn't stop now. Joe's Place was an old-time country restaurant complete with a liar's table—designated for the tellers of tall tales—and a sign that read "good country cooking like Mama used to make."

Corker promised to help override President Bush's veto of the SCHIP bill but acknowledged privately that the veto would likely stand because there was not the two-thirds majority in each house needed to make the override stick.

Later, driving back to Nashville, Corker took a call from Tennessee governor Phil Bredesen, a Democrat, to chat about a recent win for the state. Corker had managed to leverage a new waiver for TennCare, his state's expanded Medicaid program that used privately owned managed care companies to provide health care to poor Tennesseans.

After many months of negotiations, Corker finally secured the waiver by holding up Bush administration nominees until he got a deal. The waiver meant the preservation of almost $400 million in federal funding for the program over the next three years.

Corker would leverage his experience in business and his occasional willingness to vote with Democrats into influential roles in some of the important legislation; the bailout of the automobile industry a couple of years later was a key example. At the end of a long day in Tennessee, he said, "I like to focus on big things."[13]

Two days later, Corker held a town hall meeting in Madisonville, in Monroe County. It was the ninety-fifth county he had visited. Mission accomplished.

CHAPTER NINE
HARRY REID,
FIRST AMONG EQUALS

In November of 2007, Democrats—in the form of Steve Beshear—won back the governor's mansion in Kentucky and took control of the Virginia Senate for the first time in a decade. President Bush's approval rating stood at 34 percent, and everything seemed to be trending in their direction.

Apart from the big-ticket item of ending the war in Iraq, the Democrats had had a fairly successful session so far. They had raised the minimum wage for the first time in ten years,[1] the budget they passed was all paid for, and they had passed legislation mandating that U.S. troops in Iraq be equipped with armored vehicles to protect against land mine explosions. SCHIP had passed, and the Senate was still trying to override the veto.

On the floor of the Senate on November 6 was the farm bill—a multi-billion-dollar behemoth that was the lifeblood of American agriculture and one of the great government giveaways of all time. This huge pork-laden bill comes up only every five years. It has many protectors because there is so much money in it that everyone gets something—in 2007 it was expected to cost taxpayers $289 billion.

The newest farmer in the Senate, Jon Tester, was the presiding officer when the Senate opened that day, but it was not long before he was on the floor himself, making his case about why this expensive piece of legislation was critical to the nation's future. Tester came to the floor to announce that he had introduced legislation to create a new twenty-four-hour U.S. port of entry on the Canadian border at Port of Wild Horse, Montana. "American trade with Alberta is growing at a rapid rate," he said. "Excluding pipeline shipments, Alberta's exports to the United States have grown 86 percent over the last decade. America's exports to Alberta have increased 75 percent. So it is a good deal in both directions."[2]

But before saying that, he warned the Republicans not to stand in the way of the farm bill. "The farm bill is far too important to play politics. It is a critical issue dealing with this country's food security and dealing with this country's family farmers. As I have said many times before, if we ever lose family farm agriculture in this country, this country will change for the worse—no ifs, ands, or buts about it."[3]

The farm bill would bedevil Congress for several more days, and the man who presided over all the tumult was Harry Reid, the majority leader of the Senate. Majority leaders are often described as the first among equals. Reid's major power was contained in his control of the calendar, meaning nothing came to the floor without his approval. He also got to speak first in the chamber every day.

A few minutes after Tester was done talking, Reid tried to move to the bill. "Mr. President, I ask unanimous consent that amendments to H.R. 2419 be relevant to the bill or to the substitute amendment," Reid said, employing a familiar collection of words that have never been spoken anywhere but inside the chamber of the U.S. Senate. Reid was essentially asking to limit the number of amendments allowed on the bill. Republicans, as expected, were not going to just let that happen. "I object," came the retort from Saxby Chambliss, the junior senator from Georgia. "Objection is heard," announced the presiding officer.

Though he had expected this move, it was still possible to see Reid's hackles rise. He rose to speak:

Mr. President, I hope beyond all hope that we can have a farm bill that will be related to the substance rather than the procedure. It is a good bill. . . . We are trying to finish the work period before Thanksgiving. There are things we have to do. I say to my friends, do people really want an open process on this bill? Do we want to debate the war in Iraq on this bill? Do we want to debate amendments relating to labor issues throughout this country? I have been told those are some of the amendments that are going to be offered on my side. I have no idea what amendments the Republicans will offer, but I have kind of a good idea. I have seen the rule XIVs in the last few weeks and the very mischievous amendments that have nothing to do with the farm bill—political amendments.[4]

Generally senators add amendments to a bill during the committee hearings, when the text of the bill is "marked up" and the provisions are negotiated. Out of the committee comes the version of the bill to be debated on the floor. Rule XIV is a tricky and complicated procedure to bypass the committee process and get the bill or the provision onto the Senate calendar quickly. If Reid opened up the process, he would face a stampede of procedural moves from people on both sides of the house. Reid was feeling the pressure of the calendar, the session was close to an end, most of the appropriations bills were not done, and the Thanksgiving and Christmas recesses loomed large.

Reid pleaded for cooperation by invoking his own childhood:

I also say this of the farm bill: I was listening this morning to public radio as I was doing my exercise. There was one provision that struck me on this bill. Over a billion dollars for fresh fruits and vegetables will go to schools. That may not sound like much to people. I was raised, as everybody knows, in rural Nevada. When I was a boy 9 or 10 years old, the only grocery store in Searchlight burned down. It was never rebuilt. To this day, I like canned asparagus better than fresh asparagus. I love canned peas and canned fruit. The reason is, we never had fresh fruits or vegetables. We didn't have them and could not buy them. We all know fresh fruits and vegetables are better than that heavily salted stuff you get in a can that I am used to eating.[5]

But as November 6 dwindled down, matters grew more contentious, and Harry Reid is nothing if not contentious. Democrats had blocked several of the president's appointees from taking key jobs over the course of the Bush administration—twice John Bolton was not confirmed as ambassador to the United Nations, the second time in November 2006. Bolton eventually served in the job as a recess appointment. Steven G. Bradbury's nomination as acting assistant attorney general was approved by the Judiciary Committee in November 2005, but he could never remove the "acting" from in front of his name because Democrats wouldn't allow his nomination to come to a vote and kept the Senate in nominal session to prevent a recess appointment. Bradbury remained "acting" through the end of the Bush administration.

Reid realized, however, that if the Senate was in recess, Bush could appoint many judicial candidates Democrats found objectionable. If appointed in a recess by the president, they would be able to serve until the end of the next congressional session, which in this case meant the end of the Bush presidency. The recess appointment is a relic of the days when Congress met infrequently and was scattered to the far reaches of the continent. A president couldn't always wait for Congress to return in order to act.

So from November 16, 2007, when it was due to go on a two-week break, Reid made sure that the Senate was never formally in recess by scheduling "pro forma" sessions over the break. That meant that Jim Webb, the Virginian who lived relatively close by, gaveled the Senate into session every day, for several days, and just as quickly adjourned. No recess; no recess appointment.

The farm bill did not pass until December 14, and the final version, reconciled with the House's effort, did not pass out of Congress until four days before Christmas, and even then it was with a veto threat from the president. The story was far from over. By the time it finally passed in May 2008, the bill had ballooned to $307 billion and had enough support to override the presidential veto in June.

Harry Reid—and Jim Webb, for that matter—were always up for a scrap. When they published books weeks apart in 2008, Reid's was called *The Good Fight* and Webb's was called *A Time to Fight*. Reid comes from Nevada, the Battle-Born State, and he will tell you himself that he is not one of those charismatic extroverts who exist in such profusion in Washington. Reid is a cranky Nevadan who defies all the common stereotypes of modern American politics. He's not a backslapper or a fast talker. He doesn't go out on the town late at night throwing his weight around on the social and fund-raising circuits, but he understands power, and he understands the Senate.

"I am not a party guy," he confessed to me, not speaking of Democrats and Republicans. "I'm very . . . ahem . . . how do I say this? I am not a social guy. I try to take care of my family—my wife and five kids and sixteen grandchildren—the best I can and my second family, which is now fifty senators. I consider them my family. I devote my life to my two families; that's what I do. I'm not a golfer, I don't play cards, I don't shoot baskets."[6]

Reid's major public indulgence is an afternoon movie when the Senate is not in session. "I go to the movies every chance I get," he told me in his lavish conference room just off the Senate floor at the north end of the Capitol. A narrow beam of sunlight from the window behind him rested on the right side of his face so that half his face was in light, half in shadow, and for some reason his right eye appeared bluer than his left.

Reid's enthusiasm for the movies may speak to a fantasy life he is unable to indulge in the Senate, but more likely it reveals him for what he is, a man in thrall to the American Dream. Which is why he so often tells stories about where he grew up, and why he loves Woody Guthrie and the Senate. The one thing that movies provide that the Senate does not is an ending, a resolution, whether happy or sad. Whatever happens, the movie is over in two, two-and-a-half hours. Nothing happens in the Senate in two hours.

Maybe two years, or two decades. At one point in our conversation we were interrupted by Ted Kennedy, an example of a senator who has been working on some of the same issues for forty years and who was still hobbling around the Senate as if he would be there forever.

Reid grew up poor, eating his canned asparagus, in a wooden A-frame shack with no plumbing in the Mojave Desert. Before Barack Obama was elected president, an event that he encouraged and worked for, Reid was the most powerful Democrat in Washington, and on some days he still is.

During the fall of 2007, when debate on Iraq, Iran, the farm bill, and the budget was heating up, Reid had managed to see several movies, and would have much preferred to talk about them than the gridlock he was facing in the Senate. He hated *The Bourne Ultimatum*—too violent and too unrealistic. His habit of listening to National Public Radio in the morning led him, on the advice of *Los Angeles Times* movie critic Kenneth Turan, who also reviews movies for NPR's *Morning Edition*, to see *The 3:10 to Yuma*, which he loved. (Gunfights in the desert—what's not to love?) For an instant, the sixty-seven-year-old Reid sounded like a seven-year-old on the winning end of a double-dipped ice cream cone. "That was good," he declared of the remake of the 1957 western.

Kenneth Turan trashed *In the Valley of Elah*, but Reid saw it anyway, and enjoyed it despite the review. "The acting," he said, trailing off rapturously. "Tommy Lee Jones and Susan Sarandon." He emphasized the wrong syllable to come up with SAR-an-don. "I don't know how to pronounce her name," he said, "and then that ugly woman—Charlize Theron, she added a little to it." At this unexpected aside—of what was intended as comedy—Jim Manley, Reid's longtime media aide, burst into fits of laughter.

Reid kept talking, animatedly, in a way that absolutely contradicted the dour, sometimes grumpy, partisan man-o'-war that defined his public persona. He was especially taken by the title of the movie: "Whoever came up with that name," he marveled. But he didn't finish the thought. It was apparently the force of the metaphor that had captured his imagination. "The Valley of Elah," Reid said, "is where David and Goliath fought their battle."

There is no question that the Senate over which he tried to exercise some control had turned into a battlefield, but there seemed to be no one to play the part of David, just Goliaths locked in endless combat with one another. But the idea of overcoming long odds held a special place in Reid's psyche. In his successful second run for the Senate, in 1986, Reid ran television ads in which he depicted himself as a David pitted against a Republican Goliath. Reid had been a two-term congressman, but his opponent, Jim Santini, had represented the entire state in the House for ten years when all of Nevada was just one congressional district.

Of course, in the famous biblical tale, there is no battle at all: Two armies faced off, and for a long time they just shouted insults at each other. Then David, who was, according to the Bible, "but a youth and ruddy, and of a fair countenance," decided to take the fate of the Israelites on his shoulders and take the fight to the Philistines. Defying very long odds, he felled Goliath with "a single shot through the forehead."[7] The moral of the story is that courage can pay great and unexpected dividends in hopelessly dire circumstances.

On the very day we talked, the Senate had conducted three cloture votes—attempts to end debates or quash a filibuster—after the Republicans had killed two Democratic proposals the day before. Reid declared: "Yesterday was a day of real negativity by our colleagues on the other side of the aisle."[8] But in present-day Washington it may be fair to inquire how that day is different from any other day in the Senate, on any side of the aisle.

△

Harry Reid is a converted Mormon who reads a few verses of the Bible each night before bed. In the fall of 2007 he was in the middle of an epic struggle between the ideological ambitions of the Bush administration to remake the world, as defined by the disastrous war in Iraq, and the demands of a weary nation that would largely like to see the war end. Reid was the general leading the antiwar forces into battle. The political struggle to end the Iraq war, and to contain the president, rested more squarely on his shoulders than those of any other single person. The big, and at the time unanswered, question was whether the determined, hard-edged, nonideological, partisan deal maker was up to the job, and whether the institution which he leads was capable of the task before it.

Reid had disciples and detractors in equal measure. "He's a tough guy and he loves legislating," said his friend, a fellow Nevadan, Frank Fahrenkopf, the former chairman of the Republican National Committee and the top lobbyist for the gambling industry. "You're not going to find Harry Reid running for president."[9] But he was not afraid to take a run at the president.

In the spring of 2007, as the debate over the Iraq war grew more heated, Reid declared that the war was lost and that to continue with the president's strategy was folly. He outraged Republicans and sent ripples of anxiety through the Democratic ranks. The remark drew an uncommon fusillade of criticism from the dean of the Washington press corps, David Broder, who characterized Reid as amateurish and embarrassing, and compared him to the lowly regarded attorney general at the time, Alberto Gonzales.

"Here's a Washington political riddle where you fill in the blanks: As Alberto Gonzales is to the Republicans, Blank Blank is to the Democrats— a continuing embarrassment thanks to his amateurish performance," Broder wrote. "If you answered 'Harry Reid' give yourself an A. And join the long list of senators of both parties who are ready for these two springtime exhibitions of ineptitude to end."[10]

Broder went on: "Hailed by his staff as 'a strong leader who speaks his mind in direct fashion,' Reid is assuredly not a man who misses many opportunities to put his foot in his mouth." But if you agreed that the war was lost, Reid was only making sense in his persistent efforts to force the administration's hand and begin a withdrawal.

For his part, Reid was unconcerned by the criticism. "Harry Reid does not care what David Broder thinks," said Jim Manley, the majority leader's communications director.[11] Reid had a reputation among Republicans as being difficult and unpredictable. One GOP staffer went so far as to say that he's crazy.

The Reid-Broder feud would go on and on, oddly enough because, though they are ten years apart in age, they are of the same generation. Broder's beef with Reid is that he does not conduct himself in the manner of the giants of the old-time Senate. For Broder, the confrontation is rooted in nostalgia, a sense of what the Senate used to be. His impression is that Reid does not live up to those expectations. "Maybe I have an idealized view of what a Senate leader ought to be," Broder told *Politico* in November 2009, as the Senate and the country slogged through an intense debate about health care. "But I've seen the Senate when a leader could lift it to those heights."[12] Broder has been at the *Post* since 1966 and has worked in Washington since at least 1955, when he was a reporter at *Congressional Quarterly*. His ideal majority leader is modeled on Robert Taft, Lyndon Johnson, and Mike Mansfield—the dominant personalities who ran the Senate in Broder's younger days.

Harry Reid did not come to Washington until 1983, as a congressman. Reagan was president then, and the partisan wars were in full bloom. Decades later, Reid represented a new breed of leader, and there is nothing nostalgic about the Senate anymore. "He's doing a great job," Ted Kennedy said to me on his way out Reid's office the day of my interview. Kennedy entered the Senate in 1962, decades before Reid, and when he died in 2009, his forty-six-year tenure represented the fourth longest in Senate history. "While the focus has been on the war," Kennedy said, "this leader has kept the Democrats together."

Jon Tester, who had just gotten to Washington, said of Reid: "I think he's deceptively good. I think people underestimate him. He knows the rules really well, and he knows the pieces, and I think he comes across on TV as being meek and kind, but he's tougher than nails. I think he does a great job considering the majority he has to work with."[13]

Democrats emerged from the 2006 election with control of both houses of Congress and with some degree of a mandate to end the war. Slowly they tried to force the president into a corner with legislation that would require him to bring the troops home. As their frustrations mounted, it was Harry Reid who had to manage the Democrats until those failures could be transformed into success, which—in the cultural arithmetic of the Senate—simply meant getting sixty votes to shut down the chatter on the other side, by overcoming the GOP's filibusters.

Asked that fall if the strategy was working as he had hoped, Reid said, "Actually, the strategy I envisioned was walking out and giving a speech and having the Republicans crumble and start voting with us." Witness the famous sense of humor. "It is a very dry sense of humor," concedes his friend Fahrenkopf. "This is not a stand-up comedian kind of guy."[14]

You don't say.

Reid was caught between his limited ability to maneuver in the Senate and the huge expectations of the stridently antiwar voters who had put Democrats back in control of the Congress in November of 2006. In many precincts on the left, the unexpected Democratic gains signaled not just a triumph over the president and his party but an imminent end to the war as well. More often than not, it was up to Harry Reid and his House counterpart, Speaker Nancy Pelosi, to explain why President Bush seemed to have remained in the winning column on the war.

The simple answer, which paled in the face of the rising cost of the war in casualties and dollars, was that in the 110th Congress the Democrats didn't have the votes to do what they wanted. "One thing I have learned over many years," Reid said, "whether it's in politics, in your personal life, business, whatever, is that when the same question is asked, give the same answer, and that's what I do on this." He continued:

> Whether I'm talking to a town hall meeting or some other gathering in Nevada, where I know there are some very conservative people there, or whether I'm talking to very progressive people, I say the same thing— Here's what I say: "People talk about the Democratic majority, and I'm glad I'm the Democratic leader, and the majority leader. But my majority is very slim."

And there it was: A sprawling, expensive, deadly war ground on based on what happened against the genteel backdrop of roll call votes within the pink Tennessee-marbled walls of the Capitol. "I don't have a majority on this," Reid lamented.

Reid must have endured extraordinary stress during the moments of uncertainty when Tim Johnson first took ill soon after the elections. The two-term South Dakota Democrat suffered a brain hemorrhage during a radio interview in the Capitol a few weeks after the election. His absence, short or long or forever, suggested drastic consequences in the Senate. Immediately, there were questions about his ability to work in the Senate, even whether he would survive. That quickly led to the political calculations around the possibility that the Republican governor of the state would appoint a GOP replacement for Johnson, undoing the newly minted 51–49 Democratic majority.

Johnson was absent for nine months; he did not return to the Senate until September 2007. And Joe Lieberman, after being rejected by Connecticut Democratic voters in the spring primary because of his support for the war, had been reelected and remained an avid supporter of the war. He became an Independent.

"So my majority went from fifty-one to fifty to forty-nine," Reid said. "On the war in Iraq, we don't have a majority. Lieberman votes with us on everything except the war in Iraq. He votes with them [the Republicans]. My majority is gone." And that lack left Reid working and hoping for enough Republican support to mount a serious challenge to the president on any issue, not just Iraq.

In his ire at the Republicans, Reid acknowledged the special role the Senate had to play in ending the war. "I'm not saying the Republicans in the House [are responsible], because the Republicans in the House have no control over the war," he said, and that concession targeted the heart of his problems. In the House the majority rules, almost absolutely. In the Senate even the smallest minority—one person—can make life difficult for a majority leader, whose powers are notably informal and notoriously ambiguous. The margins that Reid was playing with were so small that the two political parties were less like David and Goliath than two evenly matched tennis players, with the Democrats getting to serve.

△

Mike Mansfield, the Senate majority leader from 1961 to 1977, a tenure that covered almost all of the last period when America engaged in a protracted war, once said that Everett Dirksen (the Republican minority leader from 1959 to 1969) ran the Senate from the minority leader's chair. Harry Reid, too, understands the powers that minorities wield in the Senate. Reid's own years as minority whip (1999–2001 and 2003–2005) and minority leader (2005–2006) saw him expertly making life difficult for former GOP majority leaders Trent Lott and Bill Frist.

Reid came away with different assessments of each man. Trent Lott, an equally committed deal maker, fares a lot better than Frist, whose meteoric rise to the leadership spot may go down in history as a low point in the Senate's role as a coequal branch of the government. "He was the only majority leader that became majority leader because the president said so," said Reid of Frist. He used the moment to pay a certain amount of homage to his then-nemesis, Minority Leader Mitch McConnell, the crafty and determined Kentucky Republican who made it very difficult for Reid to move on the war. Nothing happens in the Senate without unanimous consent or sixty votes where consent is withheld. Reid must negotiate nearly every move with McConnell. He said he didn't understand McConnell, but he respected him all the same. "His style has taken me a little while to get used to, but that is part of my shortcomings, not his," Reid said sardonically. "He holds things very close to his vest."[15]

McConnell's best quality for Reid was that he was not Bill Frist. "I'll say this about Mitch McConnell, he does have some understanding of the institution, which I appreciate. One reason our relationship is as good as it is, is that I know that he understands the institution. Bill Frist did not." Frist did little to endear himself to Reid when, in a break with Senate tradition, he went to South Dakota in 2004 to campaign against the Democratic leader at the time, Tom Daschle. Reid, according to Daschle, forgives but he never forgets. Bill Frist campaigned against Daschle in South Dakota when they were both party leaders in the Senate. Reid thought this violated the unspoken code between Senate leaders who have to work with each other every day—he never forgave Bill Frist.

△

Harry Reid was born in Searchlight, Nevada, on December 2, 1939. It was a hard place in a hard time. In his autobiography *The Good Fight*, Reid says that by the time he was born, prostitution had replaced mining as the biggest industry in Searchlight. There was a local law saying you couldn't run a whorehouse or serve liquor within so many feet of a school. When one such establishment was found to be violating the law, the local officials moved the school.[16] Reid's mother, Inez, took in laundry for money, and his father, Harry Sr., was a hard-rock miner, digging for gold in the hollowed-out mountains of southeastern Nevada. For the Reids and their four boys, the good life was as elusive as the precious metal that was supposed to be buried beneath the mountains.

The story of Harry Reid's tough upbringing is now a matter of legend: the home without plumbing, the forty-mile hitchhike to high school in Henderson. There is the story of the dentures he bought for his toothless mother with some of the first money he ever made.

At Basic High School in Henderson, Reid would meet two people who would make the daily trek worthwhile. One was Reid's history teacher and boxing coach, Mike O'Callaghan, who would also get him into college, and later even a job on Capitol Hill as a cop when he went to Washington to go to law school. The other person was Landra Gould, the daughter of a local chiropractor, whom Reid managed to impress enough despite the lack of plumbing and other deficits at home. They were married in 1959, two years after they graduated from high school, and they went on to have five children and sixteen grandchildren.

Reid went to college in Utah and became a Mormon and a Democrat. At Utah State University he started a chapter of the college Democrats. Accepted to law school at George Washington University, Reid headed to the District of Columbia with a new baby and went to school by day and worked nights in his job with the U.S. Capitol Police Department.

Reid was elected to the Nevada House at age twenty-eight. Two years later, in 1970, he was elected the state's youngest lieutenant governor. The winner of the governor's race that year, though the two ran independently of each other, was Mike O'Callaghan. In 1972, the tough times, the drinking, and the depression caught up with Reid's father, and he shot himself dead at the age of fifty-eight. Hard times are bred into Reid, and on some level it explains why he loves Woody Guthrie, who chronicled those hard times in song.

"I am a Woody Guthrie junkie. I know more about Woody Guthrie than you can imagine." He was almost embarrassed to say it. "You have no idea how much I know about Woody Guthrie." Okay, so what was his favorite song? "Union Maid," a song Guthrie wrote about the labor movement from a woman's point of view.

Reid ran for the U.S. Senate in 1974 and lost by 624 votes to Paul Laxalt, whom he would succeed twelve years later. He practiced law and lost a race for mayor of Las Vegas in 1976. In 1977, Governor O'Callaghan appointed him chairman of the Nevada Gaming Commission, where Reid faced the Vegas mob. The character of the senator in Martin Scorsese's *Casino* is based in part on Reid. One measure of how successful he was in that job was the bomb his wife Landra found rigged to the gas tank of the family car after she had driven their son back from a Boy Scouts meeting. For a while after that day, the Reids turned on the engine of their car by remote control.

Between 1960 and 1970, the population of Nevada grew by more than 70 percent, but there were still not half a million (489,000) people living there. (When Reid was born, there were fewer than 110,000 people in the state.) By 1980, however, there were 800,000 Nevadans, and the state got a second congressional district. In 1982 Reid became the first person to represent Nevada's 2nd Congressional District. Democrats picked up twenty-seven House seats in that election, and four years later, when Reid went to the Senate, Democrats picked up eight seats and took control of the chamber. The minority leader, Robert Byrd, became the majority leader, and Bob Dole became the minority leader.

△

Reid knew that the groundswell of support for Democrats that put him in the leader's chair in 2007 could turn to frustration and maybe outrage without some sense of progress, but he dismissed charges of ineffectiveness and remained unbowed on the war. "I don't apologize to anyone for what we've been able to accomplish. I've been able, having forty-nine votes, out of one hundred senators, to accomplish a lot. My senators have held together. And they have held together quite well."

"The Republicans in the Senate do not represent the mainstream Republicans throughout the country," Reid said to me. "Philosophically, they think the president [Bush] is doing a great job. They support him on virtually everything he does. They support him on not funding health care, education. They support him on not doing anything about global warming. They support him on all these tax cuts. I just think they are making a big mistake and we are just going to keep pushing."

And Reid appeared ready to go into the 2008 election with the same message as 2006, which was that the highest priority for congressional Republicans was to stick with the president. Democrats had to defend twelve incumbent senators in 2008, while the Republicans had twenty-two seats up for grabs. While doodling at a meeting, Reid said he came up with a list of twelve states where Democrats could mount serious challenges for GOP seats.

"If you could bet on Senate races—I guess some people do, but it's not legal—I think you would bet and say that we are going to win Colorado," Reid told me. (He was right: Mark Udall defeated Bob Schaffer 52 percent to 43 percent.) "I think you would bet and say that we are going to win Virginia; I think you would bet and say we are going to win New Hampshire."

(Right and right: In Virginia, Mark Warner easily beat Jim Gilmore 65 percent to 34 percent, and Jeanne Shaheen beat John Sununu in New Hampshire 52 percent to 45 percent.)

Reid noted the recent talk among Republicans about returning to their core values. "This group . . . thinking that they can go around the next election and talk about tax cuts and tax-and-spend Democrats, that we have to build up our defense and gay rights and abortion: These are not the issues the American people are going to want."

"We are going to fight hard," he pledged. "I just do the best I can."

Reid had listed twelve Democratic possibles among Republican seats in 2008, and the election yielded eight gains: Alaska, Colorado, Minnesota (eventually), New Hampshire, New Mexico, North Carolina, Oregon, and Virginia. The seating of Al Franken from Minnesota in July 2009—after the election there was finally settled—gave Reid his coveted sixty seats.

CHAPTER TEN
HOW NOT TO END A WAR

Gradually, during the early months of 2006, Senate Democrats had been trying to raise the stakes on Iraq. They had never believed in the war, but the mood after 9/11 and their historic political disadvantage on national security issues had come together in late 2003 and compelled them to timidly go along with President George W. Bush's plan for an invasion of Iraq. Though the folly of that move quickly became clear, many of those who had voted to authorize the war had a hard time backing away from their votes. The classic, almost tragic, case was Senator Hillary Clinton, who refused to say for many months during her presidential campaign in 2008 that her vote on Iraq might have been a mistake.

At last, in June 2006, the Senate addressed the issue and voted on a John Kerry–Russ Feingold amendment to redeploy troops out of Iraq by July 2007.[1] "It's not enough just to come to the floor of the U.S. Senate and insist we have to stay the course because otherwise what our troops are doing would be lost or be in vain," Kerry said.[2] Most Democrats declined to support the amendment, which called for redeployment without setting a timetable. The amendment died an ugly death, going down to an 86–13 defeat, with thirty-one of the forty-five Democrats in the Senate at the time voting no.

But ten months later, in April 2007, the world had changed; the Senate passed the supplemental spending bill that included withdrawal deadlines, and the president had to use his veto to stop it. And while the Senate passed this weaker benchmark-laden resolution, some of its members were un-willing to let up on the administration when it came to the war. Prominent among the latter was Jim Webb, who was making a name for himself, and not just on the issue that had prompted the most attention directed toward him, the war in Iraq. In his first year in the Senate, Webb was emerging as a mul-tifaceted legislator and, as a former Republican who had triumphed in a tra-ditionally red state, as a man who might represent a model for Democrats going forward.

Webb was not your typical politician; he was a military man who made his living as a writer. "I consider myself introspective, not introverted," he of-fered as a way to explain the widely held feeling that he may not have the personality to make it in the Senate.[3] He said that while he struggled with the demands of campaigning, sitting in the Senate, making policy, and passing legislation made almost perfect sense for him. "There is nothing that comes more natural to me than leading, and there is nothing that has given me greater pleasure than writing, not the process, but the end result," he said.[4]

At the National Press Club on March 22, 2007, Jim Webb delivered a speech that threaded its way carefully through some difficult political terrain and offered an explicit welcome back to a potentially key cadre of lost voters:

> I believe very strongly that the so-called Reagan Democrats—you can put any label on them you want—but the people who once were the back-bone of the Democratic Party when the Democratic Party truly was the party of working people in this country need to come back. . . . The Dem-ocratic Party needs to focus on the issues, I believe, that I was talking about here—economic fairness, social justice, a strong but reasoned foreign pol-icy, and if they do, you're going to see the people in red state America start gravitating back to the party that takes care of their interests.

Webb never made any secret of his antiwar stance, but neither did he minimize the realities of the situation in Iraq and how difficult it would be for the country to extricate itself from the war on the ground. In his speech, Webb asserted the need for diplomacy to end the war in Iraq, to prevent one with Iran, and to stabilize the Middle East: "Properly balanced, robust diplomacy will enable us to bring greater stability to the region, to remove the American military from Iraq, to increase our ability to defeat the forces of international terrorism and, finally, to focus on the true strategic challenges that face us around the world."[5]

More surprising in the Press Club speech was what Webb had to say about matters beyond the war. The senator talked about walking a picket line during his campaign. Most strikingly, he lamented the country's high incarceration rates, especially those among black men when fully 60 percent of those who don't graduate from high school end up in jail. "This is not something that fits into political campaigns, but I have long been concerned about the staggering prison incarceration rates in the United States, which are the highest in the world," Webb said. He is, as a reminder, the junior senator from the state of Virginia. This issue is not one that was often talked about in the United States, let alone by a senator, let alone by a senator from a southern state that was the last home of the Confederacy, where the law-and-order ethic in politics put it among states with the highest rates of execution in the country. He went on:

> We want to keep bad people off our streets. We want to break the backs of gangs, and we want to cut down on violent behavior. But there is something else going on when we are locking up such a high percentage of our people, marking them at an early age and in many cases eliminating their chances for a productive life as citizens.

Webb described the high incarceration rates as a "trajectory" issue. "It will take years of energy to sort it out, but I am committed to working on a solution that is both responsive to our need for law and order, and fairer to those who become entangled in this system."

Like a latter-day Huey Long, Webb rattled off reams of statistics on the subject of economic fairness, one of his favorite subjects, which he acknowledged he might "spend a little too much time on." Among his points, the top 1 percent of Americans take in 16 percent of national income, double what it was in 1980; corporate profits were at all-time highs while wages and salaries were at all-time lows; corporate officers were making four hundred times the wages of an average worker, and there were 47 million people without health insurance.

"Almost equally important, many leaders are seemingly indifferent to these trends," he said at the National Press Club. "Some even maintain that this growth in income inequality is a form of economic Darwinism, and that it should not be a source of governmental concern." Webb made it clear he's not one of those people. When he first appeared in the Senate, Webb was perceived in some quarters as a signal that the party was veering to the right. After his first months in the chamber, few would have repeated the charge. He was coming off like a new species of Virginia populist. In his speech, he declared:

> It's simply not healthy for a democracy like ours to have such a wide gulf between the rich, the poor and the vast majority of hard-working, productive people in between. I am determined to do everything I can to advance a progressive agenda that addresses the issues surrounding economic fairness and social justice. I believe we can work toward solutions that keep the United States economy strong and engaged in the rest of the world, but which also safeguard the right of workers and the environment.[6]

There was no question that this was unusual, but Webb was the prototypical 2006 Democrat—a new group of individuals who set themselves apart not because they lived up to the usual platitudes about bipartisanship and cooperation, but because they were willing to stand up for what they believed in, even, or especially, when it did not fit the party line. As individual personalities, they seemed to stand out more. With Jim Webb that was especially the case.

In April 2007, Democrats had come up with a series of proposals to try to end the war that became known as the Murtha provisions, named for John Murtha, the chairman of the defense subcommittee of the House Appropriations Committee. The provisions were to be attached to the supplemental appropriations bill for the Pentagon and would have restricted the deployment of troops unless they had adequate manpower, equipment, and training to succeed in combat. The Murtha plan was quickly dubbed the "slow bleed strategy," and opened Democrats to criticism that they were trying to end the war by sacrificing the troops—since the soldiers already involved in the conflict would not receive the backup they needed from new troops who did not meet the requirements according to the Murtha provisions.

Jim Webb had a different idea.

On July 11, the Senate considered a proposal introduced by Webb as an amendment to the 2008 defense authorization bill. It would have required the Pentagon to make home leaves in between deployments at least as long as the deployment itself. Democrats thought this was a winner for them, and one question was why they hadn't thought of it earlier. Well, Webb had. Who was going to vote against troops having more time home with their families? There was no way the Republicans could sustain their opposition to so simple a measure; this was the one that would make them crack and break from the president. For his part, President Bush said he would veto the whole authorization bill if this, or any amendment that mandated how the United States was to prosecute the war, was attached.

Webb came up with the detail of the amendment the hard way. "You start with your war plan," he said to me, sitting in his office in the Russell Office Building. "The war plan tradition is the three-part cycle, and it's rational if you can get there." In this scheme, a soldier, sailor, or marine would divide his fighting life into three equal parts—deployment, leave, and training for redeployment. "When you're on the three-part cycle and you're deployed—even if it is an aircraft carrier—you're going hard, you're going twenty-four hours, then you come back and you have to have your gear refurbished; you have downtime, you have to get your mind right, and ideally you spend the next third of the time getting ready to go again," Webb explained.[7]

When in the spring of 2007 the Pentagon announced that soldiers deployed in Iraq and Afghanistan would have their yearlong deployments extended to fifteen months, with little extra time when they did come home, Webb was incredulous. "I just could not believe it."[8] Defense Secretary Robert Gates called the move necessary: "This decision will ask a lot of our army troops and their families," Gates said, and tried to put a sheen of fairness and transparency on it. He said the extension would render deployment rotations "fair, predictable and sustainable."[9] The home portion between deployments, the dwell time, would be twelve months at home.

Webb was flabbergasted. "When they announced 15–12 I just could not believe it. I called the chief of staff of the army, General Peter Schoonmaker, and said I can't believe you're signing off on that," he later told me. He saw the move as a betrayal: "They are not standing up for the troops; they are not standing for the people for whom they have responsibility." Webb was especially unhappy with the idea that these soldiers volunteered and therefore had somehow forfeited their right to complain. That was a favorite argument of former secretary of defense Donald Rumsfeld.

"Rumsfeld says all the time that he has volunteers; these people volunteered. They know what they were getting into," Webb said. Then, after a beat, he waved his arms and said, "No!" As he refuted Rumsfeld, Webb was not shouting, but he was adamant enough that he didn't have to. "They stepped forward and placed their lives and their well-being into the hands and the judgment of the people who are leading them. It is not politics to say that. It is the truth."[10]

The deployment issues so enraged Webb that he got on the phone to the Pentagon: "My first reaction was to call [Chairman of the Joint Chiefs of Staff] General Casey and say I can't believe you're letting this happen, and quite frankly he punted it," Webb said to me. "He basically said, 'Well, we have to feed the strategy. This is what the strategy is.'"

The Democrats had their own strategy.

△

The debate on the Webb amendment began on July 11 on what was a hot Tuesday morning in Washington, with the longest-serving woman in the Senate, Barbara Mikulski of Maryland, speaking. Freshman Ben Cardin, her Maryland colleague, was presiding.

"We need to care about our troops, and we need to care for our troops. We all say we support our troops. Well, let's support them, all 100 of us, all 100 Senators. Regardless of party and how we voted on the war, let's say we support our troops. Then if we really do support them, let's support the Webb amendment," Mikulski began. She was practically pleading:

> The Webb amendment does support our troops and our families, and the employers of those in the Guard and Reserves. The Webb amendment gives our troops a breather, and if the Pentagon will not do it, Congress needs to do it. I salute the Senator from Virginia. Senator Webb is a freshman Senator, but he is no stranger to war. He is a warrior's warrior, a combat veteran. He also was the Secretary of the Navy. He knows full well the stresses the men and women in our military are facing and their families are facing. . . .
>
> Our current President says that the struggle in Iraq will be long and will require continued sacrifice. Sacrifice from whom? There is no shared sacrifice. The sacrifice is falling on our troops now serving in Iraq and Afghanistan. The sacrifice has been made by those who died in Iraq, by the 85 Marylanders who died in Iraq and Afghanistan. . . .

Twelve members of Iraq's 38-member Parliament no longer attend cabinet meetings. So, one third of the cabinet doesn't show up for meetings. Seventy-five members of the Iraqi Parliament are boycotting to do any work at all, so the very Parliament can't get a quorum. So while the Iraqi Parliament doesn't show up and stays home in its air conditioning, our guys and gals are out there patrolling Baghdad in 115 degree heat with 100 pounds of equipment and body armor. I say to my colleagues, "if we support the troops, support Webb."[11]

Some of the most moving moments in the debate came when senators talked about soldiers from their own state who had died, the calls they had to make to grieving families, funerals they attended. Mikulski's voice is naturally just short of a bellow, but even in the cauterized environment of a Senate debate, it was hard not to hear the emotion in her voice:

Mr. President, you are from Maryland. You know that some of the men and women who died came from our service academies—West Point, the Naval Academy. Some came from renowned schools and universities. Some of our kids came from the school of hard knocks. One, named Kendall Frederick, only had a green card. He died when a bomb hit his convoy when he was driving to get his fingerprints taken so that he could become an American citizen. Thousands of others are wounded. Some say we are micromanaging the war. You know what. I am for micromanaging the war.[12]

Debate in the Senate is often tedious and pointless. But on occasion, senators take the opportunity and find the right issue to give voice to their true feelings and those of the people they represent. War is one of those issues. The back-and-forth on Iraq had been going on long enough that Mikulski must have known she wasn't likely to change anyone's vote, but in the Senate, more than anywhere else, declaring your position and explaining why is often the entire point of the exercise.

Jim Webb was very proud of this amendment; he was serving his purpose, he thought. He was legislating, helping his party, and most of all, he was being true to the men and women fighting the war.

△

Within minutes, John McCain—in his role as the top Republican on the Armed Services Committee—was going to "manage" the bill for the Republicans, to lead the opposition, so to speak. McCain and Webb faced each other on the Senate floor. McCain began.

"This amendment calls for a congressionally mandated fence that would surround every soldier, sailor, airman, and marine and every military unit in the Armed Forces. If their days at home don't equal the days deployed, these soldiers, by law, could not be deployed in support of operations in Iraq or Afghanistan. It is quite a restriction."

There is a righteousness about John McCain that is not uncommon in men of his generation, and particularly military men. With McCain, it is sometimes a short journey from righteousness to self-righteousness. That day, he essentially argued that the Congress was meddling in affairs that were more properly the responsibility of other people, particularly the president:

> The amendment has a presidential waiver provision, which I am sure will be emphasized in the course of this discussion, but it doesn't make the amendment better. Attempts at using it would only lead to endless delays and bickering about whether deployment "meets an operational emergency posing a vital threat to national security interests." Those kinds of decisions should clearly be made by the President of the United States. That is what the Constitution says when it outlines specifically that the President of the United States shall serve as Commander in Chief.

Then McCain went on to remind the world that the power that Congress does have has been misused in the past:

If we don't like what the President—the Commander in Chief—is doing, then we can cut off those appropriations. Sometimes we have done that, much to our dismay in afterthought. For example, I referred earlier—yesterday—to a decision to cut off any military assistance or any kind of assistance to Cambodia, and we watched helplessly as three million people were slaughtered in a genocide of proportions almost unmatched in the 20th century. I say "almost." So I believe this kind of decision should be made by the Commander in Chief.

McCain closed on a point not worthy of a high school debater. There are people who would not want to be home that long, he argued. "I would also again point out that there are men and women who want to go back to Iraq. There are men and women who want to serve again in Afghanistan. There are men and women who feel a sense of urgency and a desire to serve. Would the amendment of the Senator from Virginia preclude them from additional service? I don't know."

Webb took ten seconds to let McCain know that there was a waiver for cases like those he had just mentioned.

By this time, Armed Services Committee chairman Carl Levin had arrived and took eight minutes to respond to McCain. Then, in the fashion of the Senate, it was the Republicans' turn again; McCain turned to his close friend and ally Lindsey Graham, a rhetorical flame-thrower, who once served in a judge advocate general unit in the air force.

"As to the effect of this amendment, whether it is good or bad, I am here to say I think it is a terrible idea. I don't think it is remotely a good idea," Graham began.

The intent of the amendment is to take care of the troops. I don't question anybody's intent or motivation. If you want to take care of the troops, let them win. . . . The last thing in the world we should do, in the name of helping them, is to put 535 people in charge of where they go and how they go—because we are not exactly visionary. I don't think we have risen to the level in this Congress of being able to say we are visionary leaders for this country. I think what we have done is reinforced at every turn that this is about the political moment. Congress is at 20-something percent for a reason. What I can't understand is what the 20 percent see and like.

Then it was Jim Webb's turn to speak. He began to rebut some of Mc-Cain's and Graham's statements: There were no constitutional issues, as McCain had insisted, and this was not about politics, as Graham had "alleged." Webb's word.

Webb does not like McCain; he is suspicious of his position on the war, but the two men agree that the government bungled the war in Vietnam. So Webb took the opportunity to say something nice before launching into his defense of his amendment. "Before I get into the amendment, I wish also to express, again, my admiration for the Senator from Arizona—we have been friends for many years—and my appreciation for his service. I watched his comments yesterday with respect to the end of the time in Southeast Asia. I think he knows I still adamantly support what we attempted to do in Vietnam and I have written about those days with some frequency and clarity over the years. In my view, this is not about the situation in Southeast Asia."

At that point, Democrats knew that they had at least fifty-six of the sixty votes they needed to end the debate. Webb knew from conversations he and Harry Reid had that some Republicans were wavering. Against the odds, he tried to pry them loose: "I would like to emphasize a few points. The first is, this amendment does not represent strategy. It is an amendment that protects the well-being of our troops by setting a bare minimum floor on how they are being used no matter what strategy is in place," he said reasonably.

"Second, the experiences that led some of us to this conclusion did not come from sitting in air-conditioned offices. I would like to point out, as far as I can determine, Senator Chuck Hagel is the only ground combat veteran on the other side of the aisle. He certainly is the only ground combat veteran from Vietnam on the other side of the aisle. He is a lead cosponsor of this amendment."

Note Webb's phrase: "Ground combat veteran." No mention of flyboy John McCain.

At 11:38 A.M. that day, Bob Casey, sitting in the presiding officer's chair, called for the vote: "By unanimous consent, the mandatory quorum call has been waived. The question is, 'Is it the sense of the Senate that debate on amendment No. 2012, offered by the Senator from Virginia, Mr. Webb, shall be brought to a close?' The yeas and nays are mandatory under the rule. The clerk will call the roll."[13]

The alphabetical incantation began: "Mister Akaka, Mister Baucus, Mister Bayh, Mister Biden, Mister Bingaman, Mrs. Boxer, Mister Brown, Mister Byrd, Ms. Cantwell, Mister Cardin, Mister Carper, Mister Casey . . ."

The vote was 56–41, with three senators absent.[14] The cloture motion to come to a vote had failed, and the Webb amendment was dead. Four more votes and the filibuster could be overridden and a vote taken on the amendment itself.

△

Harry Reid pulled all other amendments relating to the war from the floor. But when he took the floor, it was not to address the Iraq debate. Word had reached the Senate that a former first lady, Lady Bird Johnson, had died that morning at the age of ninety-four. Standing at his desk in the well of the Senate, Reid began an extemporaneous eulogy: "Inside this desk is the name Johnson of Texas, majority leader. That, of course, is the signature of Lyndon Johnson, who was majority leader, Vice President of the United States, President of the United States. I have the honor of being able to work from this desk." He continued:

> Lyndon Johnson is a legend from the great State of Texas, the Lone Star State. He was a Member of Congress, U.S. Senator, majority leader, Vice President, and the 36th President of the United States. But just as importantly, for those who know anything about Lyndon Johnson . . . he married a wonderful woman, Lady Bird Johnson. What a name. Lady Bird

Johnson. Anytime you read about Lyndon Johnson, you have to understand the power of his wife. Today, America has lost this great woman.
The greatest asset Lyndon Johnson had was his wife. I join my colleagues
and all Americans in tribute to this great American woman.[15]

The display of outrage over the failure of the Webb amendment came
from Reid's deputy, Majority Whip Dick Durbin of Illinois, who attacked
Minority Leader Mitch McConnell for his part in insisting on a sixty-vote
threshold:

> I would say to the Senator from Kentucky who tried to defend the Presi-
> dent's position, he should go back to his State, as all of us have, and speak
> to the families of the soldiers, understand what they are going through. Of
> course, every family of a soldier overseas is lost in prayer and worry every
> single day about their loved one in battle. But this administration, this
> President sends these soldiers over again and over again without rest, with-
> out retraining, without the equipment they need in battle. That is unac-
> ceptable. That is not a standard we should allow when it comes to our
> defense of America.

Freshman Sherrod Brown kept up the attack: "This is the most disappointing vote in my first six months in the United States Senate. The president and almost three-fourths of Republican senators have again betrayed
our soldiers and our Marines and our veterans. It started back in 2003, when
Senator Menendez and I were in the House, voting against the war but were
in the House fighting for body armor for our troops. The administration
and Republican leaders didn't get proper body armor to our troops then.
They're not taking care of returning soldiers and Marines now."[16]

Despite the impassioned oratory, the president had won, and Democrats were going to take even more heat from their constituents for not being
able to end the war, even though they were up against a politically crippled
president and a Republican Party in decline.

The day after the Webb amendment died, Chuck Hagel introduced a similar amendment that would require army units to spend no more than twelve months in Iraq and marines seven months. It fell short of overcoming a filibuster 52–43.

The Levin-Reed amendment was what happened when you pissed off Harry Reid. By mid-July, the pressure to do something about the war was mounting, and with the defeat of the Webb amendment, Reid was mad. "The war's headed in a dangerous direction. New intelligence assessments show al Qaeda getting stronger. All the while, our overburdened military is being stretched further and further," he said.[17]

Then the Levin-Reed amendment was introduced. Named for its two Democratic sponsors, Carl Levin of Michigan and Rhode Island's Jack Reed, the amendment would have required President George Bush to start bringing home troops within 120 days and complete the pullout by April 30, 2008. Under the bill, an unspecified number of troops could remain behind to conduct a narrow set of missions: counterterrorism, protecting U.S. assets, and training Iraqi security forces. On July 12, 2007, the House passed this resolution in the form of the Responsible Redeployment from Iraq Act.

Harry Reid spoke in favor of the Levin-Reed amendment: "It's clear we need a change of course in the war in Iraq today, not 60 days from now. And this week senators have an opportunity to vote to change the direction of that war in Iraq. The Levin-Reed amendment is the only amendment out there that sets a deadline for our troops being in a different capacity: counter-terrorism, force protection, training the Iraqis. All the rest of the amendments are amendments that give the president discretion, wide-ranging discretion to basically do anything that he wants to do."

And Reid was tired of giving the president discretion. "Last week, the Republican senators blocked two votes on measures to protect our troops. The vote turned out [to be]—Republicans voting to protect the president."

Reid decided that if the Republicans wanted to filibuster the Levin-Reed amendment, literally talk it to death, he would make them do that. He said he would invoke Senate Rule 22 allowing up to thirty hours' debate, during which he would make sure that Republicans would have to block cloture votes he would call so they could maintain their filibuster. In other words, for once, they would actually have to filibuster. Reid was keeping the Senate open all night: "We are going to have votes during the night. We're not going to let everybody go home and have a good night's rest. We feel that this is important enough that we have votes during the night, and we will have some votes. On what? I haven't yet decided, but there will be votes."[18]

A few days later, on July 17, Reid said, "I think it's also important that— we talked a lot about filibusters, but, you know, people have gotten pretty lazy about filibusters around here. They just say, okay, you're going to filibuster? Okay, we'll back off that. That isn't the way it's going to be on Iraq, the most important issue facing the American people."[19]

Tester opened the Senate the following day, leading the Pledge of Allegiance, and he was back in the chair again at 5:00 A.M. Thursday. The early hours did not bother him, he said, since that was when he got up to ride his tractor back in Montana.

Through the night, Reid pushed through votes, each time making absent Republicans come to the chamber. The next morning, the vote on whether to vote on the Levin-Reed amendment itself failed 52–47. After more than thirty votes aimed at slowing or changing the course in Iraq, Senate Democrats resigned themselves to the idea that they did not have the votes to beat the president, and they would continue to fail until they had more Democrats or a different president. Reid and the Democrats were accused by the Republicans, the media, and parts of their own base of pointless political posturing, but they had made the calculation that it was to their advantage to show that they were trying to do something about the war and that the Republicans were the ones preventing that.

For Webb, the real losers were the troops. "They did not enlist for political reasons, or political issues, they enlisted for traditions and love of

country, and that places a burden on the part of the people who are making policy to get it right." That was clearly not happening. "Four years into
this endeavor, it is logical to assume that the leadership is figuring out the
proper balance in terms of how you're using your troops and what the mission is—what you can accomplish. Rather than this constant . . ." His voice
trailed off. "It is nothing short of experimentation—the different so-called
strategies that they have employed."[20]

CHAPTER ELEVEN
WHEN FAILURE
LOOKS LIKE SUCCESS

As the summer wore on, Harry Reid thought he had reason to be hopeful. The fifty-six votes the Webb amendment had gained in July had not included that of Senator Tim Johnson, who was on the road to recovery and appeared now to be another vote Reid could count on. On August 23, 2007, Senator John Warner, a surge opponent, said that he thought five thousand combat troops could come home from Iraq by Christmas. "We simply cannot as a nation stand by and continue to put our troops at continuous risk of loss of life and limb without beginning to take some decisive action," Warner said at a press conference on Capitol Hill.[1]

That same day, the nation's intelligence agencies issued a report on Iraq that depicted the Iraqi government as beset by paralysis and incapable of taking advantage of the help that the United States was providing. The assessment—a National Intelligence Estimate—"casts strong doubts on the viability of the Bush administration strategy in Iraq," Mark Mazetti wrote in the *New York Times*. "It gives a dim prognosis on the likelihood that Iraqi politicians can heal deep sectarian rifts before next spring, when American military commanders have said that a crunch on available troops will require reducing the United States' presence in Iraq."[2]

Warner's call to bring the troops home only added to the pressure the administration was coming under to act on Iraq. He was a highly regarded member of the Armed Services Committee and its former chairman. He had been to Iraq that month with Carl Levin, the current chair of the committee, and Warner said at the time he would rather have the president set the timetable than the Congress.[3] Still, his public critique of the status quo was exactly the kind of signal that congressional Democrats had been looking for—a Republican willing to make principled breaks from the White House on the war. The fact that it was Warner—who might as well be called "the senator from the Pentagon"—only raised their hopes higher.

On August 24, just after he got back from Iraq, Warner appeared on NBC News's *Meet the Press*, sounding for all the world like he was going to vote to bring the troops home. Warner noted that the fifteen-month deployments were placing extreme stresses on military units in Iraq and that the chairman of the Joint Chiefs was worried that they might jeopardize the all-volunteer force. "And, secondly," Warner said, "if America is faced with other contingencies and has to resort to the utilization of our—particularly our ground forces—very quickly, will that contingency be able to be fulfilled by trained and ready troops?"[4]

"What's the answer?" asked Tim Russert, the moderator of the program. "The answer is clearly we have a problem, and we better solve it," said Warner. Later in the program, Russert asked Warner directly if he was close to publicly abandoning the president's position on Iraq. The response was a mini Senate-style oration that managed to answer the question with both a yes and a no.

"If the president does not set a timetable, do you reserve the right to break with him and begin supporting efforts to set a congressional timetable?" Russert wanted to know.

"You know, this president—I know him pretty well, it's been a privilege," Warner said. He told of how Bush had invited him to go to Arlington National Cemetery on Memorial Day for ceremonies honoring the nation's war dead. "My wife and I went up, we drove up in the car with him and drove back. And I sense, as we passed those white crosses . . . he feels, most sincerely, the loss of our forces. No one wants them to come home more than the president of the United States and the first lady, but I'm telling you, he'll have to make that decision. Am I going to suddenly go breaking [with the president]?"

Warner said he was considering it. "I'm going to have to evaluate it and then, as all other senators, we'll have to make our decision as to what we do. I don't say that as a threat, but I say that is an option we all have to consider."[5]

That evening, just before 7:30 P.M., the Associated Press moved a story to all 1,700 of its daily newspaper clients in the United States as well as to the more than five thousand radio and television outlets that subscribe to the AP. The headline: "GOP Senator May Back Dems on Withdrawal."[6]

Hundreds of newspapers carried the story on their front pages the next day.

Warner would later allow on *Meet the Press* that he did not see an easy path for Congress in trying to establish a timetable over the objections of the president. "There is the opportunity for Congress to do it," he said, "but look how they would have to do it—they would have to vote, let's say, some type of troop program taking away from the president, really, his constitutional power to make those decisions. Then that would have to go to the president. He could veto it, then it comes back for 67 votes. I don't think the president will be, in any way, overridden in his veto."[7]

But hope is the pilot light of American politics, always on, waiting to erupt into something bigger. So the Democrats hoped that Warner was with them, if not for a withdrawal timetable, at least on the Webb dwell-time amendment.

Then, just before Labor Day, Warner announced that, after thirty years in the Senate, he would retire at the end of his term in 2009. He had hinted at his decision on *Meet the Press* when Russert asked if he would seek a sixth term. "The Senate requires you to go full bore, six or seven days a week, tremendous energy, go to Iraq, jump in and out of helicopters, get on the cargo planes, no sleep," Warner said. "I've got to assess, at this age, whether it is fair to Virginia to ask for a contract for another six years."⁸ Warner was eighty at the time.

Immediately, it was clear that Democrats would win the seat Warner was vacating. Virginia voters had elected two Democratic governors in succession—in 2001 and 2005—and they had elected Jim Webb in 2006. The state was trending Democratic, and Mark Warner, the popular former governor, who had announced that he would not seek the presidency, quickly got into the race for John Warner's seat.

Warner's retirement raised the hope among Democrats that he would vote with them on an Iraq resolution still further. Senator Warner was now completely free to do as he wanted without making the political calculations that come with a reelection bid.

When Reid opened the Senate in September after the summer recess, he made sure to praise Warner, not just for his years of distinguished service, but for his willingness to work with Democrats. "So many of us appreciate Senator Warner's courage to stand up to a president of his own party—and reach across the aisle—to reach a responsible end to the war," Reid said.⁹

But John Warner would turn out to be the least of Harry Reid's problems.

As Harry Reid looked for a measure that could possibly gain the sixty-vote threshold, critics of the war outside Washington viewed any softening of the demands for a timetable of withdrawal as a backward step. When the Democrats decided they'd be willing to compromise on what had been deadlines for the withdrawal of all combat troops by backing a revised version of the Levin-Reed amendment that lacked a firm date for final withdrawal, a headline in Politico.com summed up the critics' viewpoint: "Democrats Retreat on War End."¹⁰

The problem, of course, was that the Democrats had been elected to end the war. Harry Reid was cast as the master capitulator, and his life was made more difficult by the fact that four members of his caucus were run-

ning for president and felt the need to have a position, a very public position, on every issue.

Two of the candidates, Senators Hillary Clinton and Christopher
Dodd, announced immediately that they would not support any measure
that did not mandate firm withdrawal dates. "No one is backing off of anything," Reid said. His plan all along had been to line up sixty votes in the
Senate that said the president's strategy was wrong. "The American people
understand, and we understand that we need sixty votes, and we will do
everything we can."[11]

All summer, the hubbub was about the reports on the military and political situations in Iraq expected from General David Petraeus, commander
of the multinational force in Iraq, and Ryan Crocker, the U.S. ambassador
in Baghdad. There was growing concern among Democrats that the Petraeus report would be so positive about progress in Iraq that it would leave
them politically wrong-footed in their opposition to the war.

Reid tried to blunt that possibility by drawing attention away from Petraeus and refocusing it on President Bush: "We must remember that the
President's report comes after more than four years of war—after more than
3,700 troops [were] lost and tens of thousands more injured, and after American taxpayers have footed a bill of nearly $500 billion. President Bush will
send General Petraeus to testify. There is not one member of this body who
does not respect General Petraeus. He is a good man and a good soldier.
But the President can't hide behind his generals. This is George Bush's war,
and he is responsible for the mistakes and missteps that leave our troops
mired in a civil war with no end in sight."[12]

△

On September 10, 2007, the day General Petraeus began giving his testimony to Congress on the progress of the war in Iraq, the grassroots liberal
pressure group MoveOn ran an ad in the *New York Times* with the headline
"General Petraeus or General Betray Us?" which said the general was
"cooking the books for the White House."[13] Republicans immediately

seized on the ad as a rallying point and called on Democratic leaders to condemn it.

Then, in his testimony on the military situation, General Petraeus said that "the military objectives of the surge are, in large measure, being met."[14] Noting that the Iraqi Security Forces had continued to grow, develop their capabilities, and shoulder more of the security burden in the country, General Petraeus recommended a gradual reduction in troop levels over the first months of 2008 to reach presurge levels by July of that year. Beyond that point, however, the general was unwilling to predict how quickly force reductions could proceed.

When Petraeus handed in his report, it quickly became clear that all it would do was add to the political theatrics in Washington and the war debate here at home. On September 13, 2007, in a prime-time address to the nation titled "On the Way Forward in Iraq," the president said, "Our military commanders believe we can succeed. Our diplomats believe we can succeed. And for the safety of future generations of Americans, we must succeed."

The president directed remarks to members of the United States Congress: "Let us come together on a policy of strength in the Middle East. I thank you for providing crucial funds and resources for our military. And I ask you to join me in supporting the recommendations General Petraeus has made and the troop levels he has asked for."[15]

But Democrats continued to try to press. "We have put forth a plan to responsibly and rapidly begin a reduction of our troops. Our proposal cannot erase the mistakes of the last four and a half years, but we can chart a better way forward," said Senator Jack Reed, who was designated to deliver the Democratic response.[16]

The following week, as Congress was set to begin consideration of the Department of Defense authorization bill, Harry Reid dismissed the idea of any compromise legislation that would give the president and his Republican supporters an easy out. "We are going to continue to be as aggressive as we have been," he said.[17]

From President Bush, there had been no acknowledgment that Iraq had become a disaster. What emerged from the Petraeus report was a stark and saddening truth that the war in Iraq was not winding down. There were 130,000 troops in Iraq in November 2006, and there would be 130,000 troops in Iraq in November 2008. The week of the Petraeus report, the Pentagon released the names of more American dead. They were twenty-one-year-old Marine Lance Corporal Lance Phillips of Cookeville, Tennessee; Army Corporal Javier Paredes, twenty-four, of San Antonio, Texas; and nineteen-year-old Private First Class Sammie Phillips, of the Kentucky National Guard.

In the fall of 2007, the Iraq war had been reconciled with some rather puny aims—to create "breathing room for political reconciliation," as President Bush put it.[18] But one of the reasons the debate was growing so difficult was that no one in the White House could admit that it was a mistake in the first place.

There was a sense that the political underpinnings of the war had been torn loose. For the voters who had believed the war was going to end when Democrats won control of the Congress, there was a conviction that American elections have consequences. But the war did not end. Now the disappointment was building, and detractors were pointedly asking whether the Democrats had the guts, or even the will, to effectively confront the president. With public pressure mounting, tension rose inside the Democratic caucus. On one side were those who wanted some bold, decisive stroke that left no question about their seriousness about ending the war and willingness to take on the president over it. Most of the presidential contenders were in that camp. On the other side were the reflexive, conscientious legislators, people who understood, often rightly, that as they sat in Washington thousands of miles away from the actual fighting, the tools available to end the war were dull, blunt-force instruments—resolutions, amendments, embarrassing votes foisted on the Republicans, points of orders, motions to end debate—all measures with limited efficacy.

Legislating an end to the war could last longer than the war itself.

On both sides, however, there was a determination to continue trying.

One consequence of this determination was that Harry Reid and his colleagues were prepared to take another shot at the Webb amendment. By the time the amendment came to a vote again in the third week of September, it was called the Webb-Hagel amendment, having attracted the support of the most vocal GOP critic of the war in the Senate, Nebraskan Chuck Hagel. He also served in Vietnam, and he and Webb, often as a slap to the war-hero credibility of John McCain, who was on the other side of all the issues related to Iraq, would describe themselves as the only "ground-combat veterans" of the Vietnam war in the U.S. Senate.

Hagel had once blamed the disastrous results in Iraq on President Bush's lack of personal curiosity, coupled with the fact that he was surrounded by strong-willed, ideological personalities like Vice President Cheney and Defense Secretary Rumsfeld. "He needs to spend some time by himself, thinking," Hagel told me in his office in 2004.[19] It was a conversation memorable for the fact that a senior Republican senator would not say whether he would vote for the Republican president when he stood for reelection that fall.

John Warner was different. He had none of the taint of Hagel's enemy-combatant inexperience with regard to Bush. Because of the respect that he commanded, he was seen as the key to moving GOP votes, and by Reid's count the Democrats really needed only one more vote. Warner, who was once married to the actress Elizabeth Taylor, was one of the grand eminences of the Senate, particularly on military matters. He, like Webb, had been secretary of the navy before he was elected to the Senate. He had been the longtime chairman of the Armed Services Committee, and was always seen as a voice of reason in foreign policy matters, however partisan he was on domestic issues.

In July, Warner had voted for the Webb amendment, giving Democrats hope that with him as an example, they might be able to attract more Republican votes. The analysis was that if Warner could vote for the amendment, then it should not be hard to convince some other moderate Republican to support a measure that gave troops more time at home with their families and away from a war that everyone hated.

Democrats hoped that Warner would provide an exit ramp for other GOP senators looking for cover if they chose to abandon the president and his very unpopular war. One senator who considered voting with the Democrats was Bob Corker, and he told Jim Webb as much.

The amendment was a political document crafted to avoid some of the ideological sniper fire from the White House and war supporters, but there was a human resonance to it that Republicans chose to ignore even as they watched the president grow more and more unpopular because of the war.

"We cannot continue to look at war and the people who fight and die in wars as abstractions, as pawns, as objects," Chuck Hagel said as his amendment was about to go down to defeat. "This, somehow, is framed, always, in policy dynamics. The humanity of this is lost."[20]

But it was not lost on the voters, who would go to the polls in 2008 and punish the Republicans all over again. It offered the Democrats a clear strategy: Tie GOP senators as closely as possible to the president and the war. "I call on the Senate Republicans to not walk lock-step as they have with the president for years in this war," Harry Reid said, urging Republicans to abandon their strategy and trying to open some division between the White House and congressional Republicans.[21]

On September 19, 2007, the Senate voted on the Webb amendment, in its amended form, for a second time and for the second time failed to beat the filibuster (56–44). Warner changed his vote—meaning six rather than seven Republicans supported the measure in September versus July. Of the six Republicans who voted for the measure, two were not up for reelection—Hagel was retiring, and Maine senator Olympia Snowe had just been reelected in 2006; one, Susan Collins of Maine, was reelected; and three of them lost—John Sununu of New Hampshire, Gordon Smith of Oregon, and Norman Coleman of Minnesota.

Bob Corker had been convinced by arguments put forward by Pentagon brass who met with senators to lobby against the measure. "I like Jim Webb," Corker said. "I know he has a lot of first-hand experience. But I don't think you can do this in the middle of a conflict."[22] And for his part, on the Senate floor, Warner told Webb, "I agree with the principles that you've laid down in your amendment, but I regret to say that I've been convinced by those in the professional uniform that they can't do it."[23]

Warner said Petraeus changed his mind. "It is a change of vote for me, I recognize that," he said before the vote, "but I changed that vote only after a lot of very careful and analytical work with the uniformed side of the Department of Defense."[24] Warner's yes vote was counterbalanced by the previously ailing Tim Johnson, who was sick in July and was now back in the Senate. It was yet another example of how fragile the Democrats' numbers were that year. Once again, they were frozen in place. The White House touted the Petraeus report, and President Bush began talking about a strategy that would stress "return on success."[25]

On September 19, the two men who would face each other in the 2008 presidential election were on the floor at the same time. John McCain followed Warner and praised the Virginian for his thoughtful analysis of the current situation and "the wisdom he has acquired since World War II, when he served as a brave marine."

Warner, who served mostly in the navy, interrupted without the usual formalities: "Sailor, you rascal. How could you forget that?"[26]

"Rascal" is a rare word, especially when applied to a seventy-one-year-old man, but the speaker was eighty, both were military men, and this was the United States Senate. McCain made the appropriate apologies. Then he moved to his own opposition to Webb.

"I, in no way, denigrate what Senator Webb is trying to do. It is just that we have an honest difference of opinion, mine based on basically the same facts that have been given to him. He has a different analysis than do I," Mc-Cain said, adding that he believed that there were constitutional prohibitions on Congress making this kind of decision: "I also believe that it is unconstitutional for this body to dictate the tours of duty and the service of the men and women in the military and how that is conducted. I am absolutely convinced, from my reading of history and of the Constitution, that to enact such an amendment would be an encroachment on the authority and responsibility of the Commander in Chief." He added: "I see my friend from Illinois is waiting. I yield the floor."[27]

The senator from Illinois was recognized.

"Mr. President, let me begin by expressing my utmost support for Senator Warner. I am absolutely convinced of his commitment to our troops," Senator Obama began. "I do not think there are many people in this Senate Chamber who understand our military better or care more deeply about our military. So I have the highest regard for him. I have to say I respectfully disagree on this issue and must rise in strong support of the amendment offered by Senator Webb." He went on:

I opposed the war in Iraq from the beginning and have called repeatedly for a responsible end to the foreign policy disaster that this administration has created. Over 3,700 American service men and women have died in this war. Over 27,000 have been seriously wounded. Each month, this misguided war costs us a staggering $10 billion. When all is said and done, it will have cost us at least $1 trillion.[28]

There was no doubt the presidential campaign was in full swing.

In July, the Webb amendment had garnered fifty-six votes in the Senate, a clear majority, but not enough to fend off a GOP filibuster. When it came to the floor again in September, it got fifty-six votes—again. In the two and a half months between the first and second Senate votes, 180 American troops had died in Iraq, but nothing had changed in the Senate, except John Warner's vote.

Reid had thought he was close: "I'd had conversations with Republican senators, one of whom said, 'The biggest mistake I ever made was voting against [the Webb amendment],' and that person voted against it again," the majority leader said to me after the vote, his anger barely contained. "Logically, that does not make a lot of sense. So, I'd assume that I'd had that vote, and I think I did it on the basis that was a rational assumption."[29]

Reid had assumed that John Warner was with him. He was not. "Warner"—and here Reid paused for a long time, obviously digging deep for some Senate decorum to mask his outrage—"was a terrible disappointment. Here was a man who had agreed to cosponsor the amendment, and had voted for it before, and suddenly with a hug from Bush, he decides that he can't cosponsor, nor can he vote for it again. I mean talk about flip-flopping, that's as about as flip-flopping as a fish on the wharf after he gets caught. That's flipping all over."[30]

Harry Reid has an almost spiritual regard for the Senate and deep respect for those who share his views of the place, but clearly John Warner, the Virginia gentleman who came to embody the high-minded seriousness of the place, pissed him off. "I guess he wants to be invited to White House dinners or something," Reid told me after Warner switched his vote. He said he thought Warner's retreat and the flare-up over the MoveOn Petraeus ad cost them on the Webb amendment. "To be very candid with you, I think the Warner situation hurt us, and I also think the MoveOn ad diverted the argument, and I think that hurt us."

The loss on the Webb amendment may have doomed any chance of a bipartisan deal on Iraq. It hardened the lines, and Reid, a consummate deal maker who reveres pragmatism, seemed little interested in reaching out anymore. He turned his thinking to how to make support for the war as politically costly as possible for Republican senators. "I just think they are making a big mistake and we are just going to keep pushing," he vowed. "This is no longer just Bush's war. This is Bush's war and the Republicans in the Senate's war."[31]

To make matters worse for the Democrats, Republican senator John Cornyn of Texas introduced a resolution condemning the MoveOn ad; it passed 72–25 ten days after the ad ran and after the defeat of the Webb-Hagel amendment. Republican senator Gordon Smith, who was in favor of withdrawal timetables, said he though Petraeus's testimony and the ad were instrumental in keeping Republicans in line with the president.

From the left, Harry Reid came under fire for allowing the roll call vote on the Petraeus ad to reach the floor of the Senate. "We are just not dealing with the Senate leadership at all," said a MoveOn spokesman. And the head of the organization, Eli Parisier, said in a statement, "No wonder public approval of Congress is tanking. They're so out of touch with reality that they can find time to condemn an ad but they can't do what most Americans want—vote to end this war."[32]

During the Columbus Day recess, Jim Webb spent some time checking out the small commuter train line that serves northern Virginia, and he visited the National Museum of the Marine Corps, which is near the Quantico Marine Barracks. The museum's collection includes the two flags flown at Iwo Jima that are now part of American lore. Webb is genuinely emotional in this space.

The tour begins with a short film on the history of the U.S. Marines, including all the famous battles: Belleau Wood, Tarawa, Guadalcanal, and Iwo Jima. After the film, Webb walked away from his hosts, slightly ahead into a darkened photo gallery, and removed his glasses. He rubbed his eyes. He was wearing his signature brown suit with a blue tie, and rubber-soled shoes. He looks like a marine pretending to be a senator. The roof of the museum was hung with old aircraft like the de Havilland DH-4 looming over Webb's head at the moment. The exhibit was full of voices of old marines recounting battles or their time in the Corps. But with the war in Iraq raging, there was nothing archival about this for Webb. He mentioned his son Jimmy, who was home safely from Iraq. Webb said he had to come back here with Jimmy. "We have done battlefields all over the world together," he said to me. "I need to come back and do three or four more hours."

It had been almost a year since the momentous election night that had so radically shifted the political landscape in Washington. When Harry Reid opened the Senate on Monday afternoon, November 5, 2007, Jim Webb, one of the stars of that freshman class, was the presiding officer. Reid, as usual, sounded beleaguered by the schedule ahead. "We have a lot to do," he said, "and only two weeks until the Thanksgiving recess [due to start November 19] when we go home to our states and our families."[33]

The fall had not been politically kind to the Democrats, and Webb was the perfect example of their distress. Having waged a valiant, and so far unsuccessful, campaign to short-circuit the administration's war efforts in Iraq, a discouraged Webb now urgently turned his attention to Iran, worried that the administration was thinking of escalating the war and starting some kind of military expedition there.

On November 1, 2007, Webb wrote a letter to the president, signed by thirty Democrats, warning Bush that he did not have the authority to attack Iran without the express approval of the Congress. The concern about an attack on Iran came after the Congress, at the bidding of the White House, approved an amendment, written by Senators Jon Kyl, a Republican from Arizona, and Joseph Lieberman, that declared Iran's Revolutionary Guard a "Specially Designated Global Terrorist" organization. Webb and his cosignatories were concerned that this vote might give the president cover if he chose to attack Iran. Not only had Democrats failed to end the war in Iraq, but they were actually worried that they may not be able to stop the conflict from spreading into other countries in the region.

The Iran vote also brought into sharp focus the reality that a presidential election was on the horizon. Democrats were going to face off with each other. Hillary Clinton signed Webb's letter; Barack Obama did not. Instead, Obama introduced a resolution that would have explicitly required Bush to come before Congress before taking any military action in Iran.

Clinton spokesman Phil Singer used the vote to attack Obama: "If Senator Obama isn't just playing politics and really believes Kyl-Lieberman gave the President a blank check for war, he would have signed the letter today and would have fought to stop the resolution before it came up for a vote. Instead he did nothing, remained silent, and spoke out only after the vote to engage in false attacks against Senator Clinton."[34]

And Obama spokesman Bill Burton said, "Senator Obama admires Senator Webb and his sincere and tireless efforts on this issue. But it will take more than a letter to prevent this administration from using the language contained within the Kyl-Lieberman resolution to justify military action in Iran." And thus was the Democrat-Republican battle of amendments spilling over into the campaign.[35]

△

Right after Thanksgiving, Jim Webb and Jon Tester took a quick trip to Iraq: four days in Baghdad and the outskirts. Webb said he now understood that his son Jimmy had fought a tougher war than even he had imagined. The close quarters of the fighting in Ramadi were very different from the jungle battle Jim Webb had fought in Vietnam. He sighed when he reflected on the fighting going on in Iraq, and the proxy fight going on in the Senate.

After the trip, the two men were sitting together in Tester's office; Webb was drinking a Coke. It was December, and the fight over Iraq was essentially over; the administration had won. Webb had been criticized for being so vocal about his opposition to the war in Iraq without having been there. He dismissed those people as propagandists, but on some level they were winning. Webb said: "They were trying to affect the validity of what I was saying; it was nothing more than gamesmanship from the other side. You cannot go in for two days and come back and claim you can speak politically for the military people who are in Iraq. You can't do it for military people anywhere."

In February 2007, Kyl invited Tester to take a trip with him to Iraq. Tester said he had too much to do and declined. "I went over to Jim and said, 'Are you going,' and he said 'No,' and I said, 'well, when you go I'd like to go with you.'" Webb's response was "Yeah, we'll get out of the green zone and see some stuff." The level of violence in Iraq was sharply up at that time, and while that may not have worried Webb—who had been shot twice in Vietnam—Tester was a little more skeptical and replied, "Well, I don't know."

Clearly the two had become friends, two nontraditional Democrats, elected from red states, who referred to themselves as the Redneck Caucus. "The question was not whether I'd go with Jon Tester," said Webb; "the question was whether we could get [Senator Claire] McCaskill to come. We worked on her, but she didn't want to do it. We wanted the whole Redneck Caucus."

Webb questioned whether these trips were particularly helpful in policy making. "When you see it firsthand, it kind of drives it home and makes me wonder what these other people are seeing."

Tester was struck by something more basic in Iraq—hatred. "Probably what I did not expect, what I saw as we drove the streets of Ramadi, and walked the streets of Ramadi and in the towns southeast of Baghdad, was hatred," he said. "I could say they don't like us, but I think it went beyond that. I guess I should have known, because if the Canadians were driving up and down my street in Big Sandy, I'd be upset too."

Referring to his ancestral home in the southwestern Virginia mountains, Webb said: "If the Iraqis or the Canadians were patrolling Gate City, Virginia, they'd be dead."[36]

▲

Congress worked its way toward the holiday recess. On December 17, 2007, the night before the last day of the session, there was a vote on a supplemental attached to the passage of the Foreign Operations Appropriations bill. Surprisingly, Republicans had gone along with a Democratic effort to reduce the amount of money spent on civilian operations in Iraq.

"On Iraq, a bipartisan majority of Senators consistently supported changing course," Harry Reid said on the last day of the session. "Like the American people, this majority is saddened to say that after nearly five years, nearly 4,000 American lives lost, more than 30,000 wounded, a third of them grievously wounded, and some say as much as $800 billion spent, there appears to be no end in sight for the Iraq war. But last night, I think we showed that even Republicans are losing support for this war. The President asked for $200 billion; they got $70 billion. So even the Republicans understood that the President should not have a blank check."[37]

Saddened, yes, but it was Christmastime after all, and so in the afternoon, the Senate's oldest member, Senator Robert F. Byrd, went to the floor and put these words—injecting a sense of bipartisan comity—into the *Congressional Record* for all posterity:

Everywhere, everywhere, Christmas tonight!

Christmas in lands of the fir-tree and pine,

Christmas in lands of the palm-tree and vine,

Christmas where snow peaks solemn and white,

Christmas where cornfields stand sunny and bright.

Christmas where children are hopeful and gay,

Christmas where old men [like I] are patient and gray,

Christmas, where peace, like a dove in its flight,

Broods o'er brave men in the thick of the fight;

Everywhere, everywhere, Christmas tonight!

For the Christ-child who comes is the Master of all;

No palace too great, no cottage too small.[38]

The Senate adjourned that cold December 18, thereby ending the first session of the 110th Congress. By the end of 2007, 4,370 Americans had been killed in the fighting in Iraq, and nothing, not a court order, not a recount, could bring a single one of them back.

CHAPTER TWELVE
WHEN SUCCESS LOOKS LIKE FAILURE

It was a fair assumption that if the Democrats could not end the war in 2007, there was no chance they could end it in 2008. This was going to be a presidential election year with no incumbent candidate, and no clear heir apparent on either side of the aisle. The election was going to be a scramble, and when actual voting is going on in the country, Washington politics has to take a backseat.

Iowa's caucuses, always first in the nation, were almost not held in 2008. Insistent on being first—and challenged by any number of other states that kept moving up their contest earlier in the process—Iowa at one point toyed with the idea of holding its caucuses in December 2007: out of the election year altogether. Harry Reid's home state of Nevada was one of those that had jockeyed its way up the electoral calendar hoping to have more impact on the nomination's outcome, but wherever and whenever they were held, these primary contests for the Democratic nomination were going to be a gauge of the level of resentment directed at the Bush administration.

Through the first session of the 110th Congress, Reid was upbeat about his party's chances in the upcoming elections. Back in 2007, during the heat of the Iraq debate, Reid had declared that 2008 would be a good year for Democrats. "We're going to pick up Senate seats as a result of this war," he said in April of 2007. "Senator Schumer [who ran the Democrats' campaign committee] has shown me numbers that are compelling and astounding."[1]

A year did nothing to change his mind. At a breakfast with an audience of liberal and progressive writers and bloggers in May 2008, Reid again predicted: "We are going to pick up seats. We've got a very good organization. Schumer, it's the second time he's done that. It's very rare you have anyone do the DSCC twice. We have a consistent crew, we have a very good program, we're raising lots of money."

The game was on.

Reid wanted sixty Democrats in the Senate, but even he was not bold enough to predict that that would happen. "We're competitive, as I speak, in eleven seats, so I hope that we'll pick up a number, a few of them. I'm kind of a cynic about everything that way I'm not disappointed as often. So I think we'll pick up four seats, five seats."[2] It would take awhile, and some unusual maneuvers, but in the end he got nine.

The ignominy of having voters assemble to begin the 2008 election as early as 2007 was avoided, but not by much. The first votes in the 2008 election were cast in Iowa on January 3 of the New Year. On the same day, nominally at least, the Senate opened its second session of the 110th Congress. The Senate cannot go more than four days without being in session without informing both the White House and the House of Representatives and declaring an official recess. The holiday recess was officially over by the third, but the senators decided that nothing should happen until after the State of the Union address, when the president would lay out his agenda. Furthermore, everyone was focused on the beginning of the primary season.

So, on January 3, Senator Mary Landrieu of Louisiana gaveled the Senate to order at four minutes and twenty-six seconds after noon, and immediately announced that the Senate would stand in recess until Monday, January 7, 2008, at 9:00 A.M. It took all of twenty-six seconds. The same thing happened every two days for the next two weeks. On Monday, January 9, the senator presiding was Edward Kennedy of Massachusetts. He was in and out in twenty-nine seconds.

While the Senate was busy not meeting, the 2008 primary season got underway. Barack Obama won the Iowa caucus with 38 percent of voters; former senator John Edwards had 30 percent, and the onetime front-runner Hillary Clinton was third with 29 percent. For the Republicans, former Arkansas governor Mike Huckabee won Iowa. Clinton turned the tables in New Hampshire, beating Obama by two points: 39 percent to 37 percent. That split decision set off a tough five-month battle for the Democratic nomination that gripped the country and almost broke apart the Democratic Party.

The battle between Hillary Clinton, who, if elected, would be the first woman president, and Obama, who, if elected, would be the first black one, could not avoid the melodrama of race and gender story lines. Quickly the contest turned bitter, challenging the core values of the Democratic Party. The base of the party was a coalition of key groups that had been brought together by a history of grievances—racial and gender discrimination and an overall sense of lack of equal access to the American Dream—to fight injustice and unfairness everywhere. But now that coalition was in danger because two of the most powerful core constituencies—blacks and women—saw a chance to redress history by putting one of their own in the White House. Suddenly they were not allies, but adversaries. It did not take long before these two groups would collide.

After Obama won a majority of young women in Iowa, older women in New Hampshire decided there was a different version of American history that could be written into the outcome of the election. So when it came time to vote on January 8, they showed up in droves and the ten-point polling advantage Obama had going into New Hampshire turned into a two-point loss.

But when on January 19, 2008, in just half an hour, thirty thousand citizens in Nevada picked up forms and registered to vote in the Democratic primary, it was clear that something more than race and gender milestones were in play. The fact that the economy was melting down in front of people's eyes had become a major factor—one that could decide the outcome of this election.

In the six trading sessions leading up to January 22, when the Senate did actually open for business for the year, the equity market was in a tailspin. The Dow Industrial Average plunged 806.96 points in those six days, including a 307-point drop on January 17. It is always hard to get anything done in Washington, but there was no question about how much work there was to do. The situation was so dire that the president felt the need to address it publicly on January 18. He tried to be reassuring:

> The economic team reports that our economy has a solid foundation, but that there are areas of real concern. The economy's still creating jobs, though at a reduced pace. Consumer spending is still growing, but the housing market is declining. My advisers and many outside experts expect that our economy will continue to grow over the coming year, but at a slower rate than we have enjoyed for the past few years. And there is a risk of a downturn.[3]

When the Senate finally gaveled itself into session, things were very different from the previous year. The fervor over Iraq had dissipated, and the troubles of the economy moved to center stage. "Last year, the subprime lending issue was not part of our mantra. Now it is in every speech anyone gives in the political world," Harry Reid said. "What are the new and growing challenges? We don't need an economics professor or philosopher to tell us: A walk through a neighborhood most anyplace in this country to see the sea of for sale signs, foreclosures are all over this country. All it takes is a trip to a gas station or even drive by a gas station to see people are paying over $3 a gallon most everyplace in this country."[4]

Reid opened the Senate on January 22 with an explanation of why so many of his fellow Nevadans had suddenly taken an interest in the Democratic Party. "Because we have an economy that is sliding toward recession.

Hundreds of thousands of families are at risk of losing their homes—millions, really, not hundreds of thousands."[5]

The concern about the economy had grown so dire during the break that from his home in Searchlight, Reid had been on the phone constantly with Treasury Secretary Hank Paulson. The first thing on the administration's agenda when Congress returned was a stimulus package.

The agenda had changed.

△

Every new senator must at some point decide how to define his or her own success, and without Iraq as a focal point, the freshmen of the 2006 class had to make a similar adjustment to that of the Senate as a whole. Individually, members of the class were still riding the popularity that put them in office and trying to find a way to serve their constituents and the country differently than they had in 2007.

At the start of the session, the freshmen banded together to tackle another big and important issue: China and its trading practices. The Iowa results in early January had knocked Senator Chris Dodd out of the presidential nomination contest; he was now back in Washington working on many important items before the Senate Banking Committee, of which he was the chairman. More than a year earlier, Dodd had introduced a bill that would allow the United States to challenge Chinese trading practices through the International Monetary Fund and the World Trade Organization.

On January 31, eight of the nine not-so-new Democrats (Independent Bernie Sanders, who voted with the Democrats, included)[6] wrote a letter to Majority Leader Reid asking that he move Chinese trade higher on the legislative agenda:

> We face a host of difficult trade issues with China that require strong action, ranging from currency manipulation and unfair subsidies, to trade law and counterfeit enforcement problems, to imported food and product

safety. These issues are hurting American competitiveness and expose American consumers to unsafe goods.[7]

Another important issue everyone focused on in early 2008 was of course the housing crisis. Amy Klobuchar and Sherrod Brown held a press conference in February to talk about predatory lending and the foreclosure crisis. They met in the ornate, gloomy Mansfield room, with Dick Durbin and Chuck Schumer and a family from Ohio, John and Vicki Glicken, who were facing the loss of their home to foreclosure. John Glicken told the story of buying their first home, and how in only three years what was supposed to be the family's gateway to the American Dream had turned into a nightmare.

In the summer of 2005, the Glickens were contacted by a mortgage broker who sold them on the idea that for the same amount they were paying in rent, they could own a single-family home. The broker recommended an adjustable rate mortgage and told the Glickens that it was structured so that they had to make interest-only payments for the first two years at a fixed interest rate. After that, the interest rate would be adjustable and would reset.

"It was our understanding that when the interest rate became adjustable, our payment would go up if the interest rates went up and would go down if the interest rates went down. We now know that this is not the case," John Glicken said. "We were not told, and did not understand, that after two years the interest rate was guaranteed to go up substantially, and that it could never go down."

The family's payments went up every six months after the mortgage became adjustable, and by February 2008 was double what they had been paying for rent. Then John Glicken lost his job and could not pay the mortgage for a few months. Although Glicken found work and began making payments again, by then it was too late—the bank had already begun foreclosure proceedings against them.

"We have done everything we can to try to save our home. We got second jobs. We've cut all household spending to a minimum, and we filed a chapter 13 bankruptcy to stop foreclosure," Glicken said. "We just keep getting further and further behind. We don't want to lose our home, but the payments keep going up. And we can't afford to pay them."[8]

This is a story that would be told and retold by millions of American families over the next two years. Amy Klobuchar spoke about a family in Minnesota, the Grays. "They were working in the public school," she said. "[They] wanted to buy their first home. They trusted someone, they got the mortgage, and it turned out that it was $1,500 a month when they started out. They were told it would go up a few hundred dollars, and it ended up by 2008 at $3,300 a month."

The Grays got help and saved their homes, but by then almost 9 million American homes were "under water"—namely, the value of these homes was less than the outstanding mortgage. "The people who are victims of this, they need our help," said Klobuchar. "But we have to remember the victims are not just the people in those houses; they're people in the street, they're people in the neighborhood. It is affecting entire communities."[9]

Democrats introduced a series of proposals to keep people in their homes, including a moratorium on foreclosures and a measure to restructure mortgages so that the payments would be more affordable and a measure that would allow bankruptcy judges to adjust the terms of mortgage contracts.

In February, Jon Tester added a measure to an Indian health funding bill to address the epidemic of methamphetamine use on Indian reservations. The amendment was a Sense of the Congress resolution urging Indian tribes to sign law enforcement agreements with the federal government so that they could have more resources and better coordination in combating the epidemic. It was a small step but a sure sign to the people paying attention that Tester was on their side.

Amy Klobuchar wrote and introduced the American Renewable Energy Act (February 2008), to help promote the development of renewable fuels. The bill called for a tax credit for the production of cellulosic alcohol, ethanol produced from plants and grasses, and would have created a new consumer tax credit for the purchase of plug-in hybrid vehicles. The bill also offered tax incentives for investments in renewable fuels like solar and wind energy.

Klobuchar's legislation was coauthored by two other women senators, one Republican, Olympia Snowe, and one Democrat, Maria Cantwell. As with so much else, nothing happened with the bill in 2008, and so Klobuchar introduced it again in 2009.

△

Jim Webb went back to doing battle over an updated version of the G.I. Bill that he had introduced early in his term, to extend to the veterans of the wars in Iraq and Afghanistan the same benefits that had been given to troops returning from the Second World War and Vietnam.

Webb was also thinking about where the country was headed. The bitter primary fight between Obama and Clinton reminded many Democrats, unhappily, of 1968, when the party, as well as the country, came apart over its position on Vietnam. Webb had come to believe that as visceral and as violent as the debates of 1968 had become, at least the country was disputing issues that went to the heart of the nation's problems, something that was not happening in 2008.

"The United States of America in 2008 is a troubled and divided place, in a quieter but, to me, a more deeply disturbing way," he wrote in his book *A Time to Fight*. At least in 1968, Webb argued, we were having an important debate about meaningful issues. "Oddly one of the greatest difficulties today is bringing the problems that most threaten our future out into the open so they can be honestly debated. Issues such as economic fairness, fundamental social justice, the long term strategic direction of the country, and the hardening of American society along class lines rarely make it onto the Senate floor, much less into the arena of national political debate."

Webb believed that the lack of willingness to confront the country's difficult problems, which is precisely the role of the Senate, was eroding something fundamental in the American idea. "It often occurs to me that although the country was in far greater overt turmoil in 1968, the premises on which our society was founded were never really in true doubt. It is actually harder to make that case in 2008."[10]

Making the opposite case with respect to the Senate was especially easy in 2008. In 1885, Woodrow Wilson, long before he became president, wrote a book about Congress called *Congressional Government: A Study in American Politics.* In it he described the purpose of Senate debate as something that "clears its mind, and to some extent the mind of the public with regard to doing the nation's business."[11] That is an unrecognizable aspiration in today's Senate.

In 2008 the Senate took 215 roll call votes, and 43 of them were cloture motions, which means that a full 20 percent of the Senate's work time was spent simply trying to get to an issue that needed to be addressed rather than just addressing it. Of the 42 cloture motions filed by Democrats to stave off the threat of a GOP filibuster, 17, or almost 40 percent, failed.

The irony, of course, was that there seemed to be no relationship between what was happening in the Senate and what was happening in the country. Republicans were in deep trouble politically, due, in large part, to how closely they had aligned themselves with a hugely unpopular president. But their poor showing in 2006, and the prospect of an even worse showing in 2008, was not enough to force them to alter their strategy. Ideology and partisanship drove them to stick with the president.

△

In the late spring of the year, President Bush, starting to grow a little wistful about his time in the White House, told the *Times* of London that he regretted his tone, if not his actions: "I think that in retrospect I could have used a different tone, a different rhetoric," he said.[12] But the regret seemed cosmetic. He remained unapologetic about the ill-considered and unnecessary invasion of Iraq, which had to that point cost more than four thousand American lives, and countless more Iraqi ones.

As a result, Republicans were completely back on their heels. The only danger to Democrats seemed to be whether they could remain united as a party in the face of the bitter primary being waged for the nomination. Obama ran up a series of unexpected wins in unexpected places—Guam, Wyoming, Montana. A primary fight that was supposed to be decided by Super Tuesday, February 5—when more than half of the pledged Democratic delegates were up for grabs and one candidate would be expected to deliver a knockout blow—would drag on into June. And it was increasingly clear by mid-March that there was no way that either side would be able to compile enough elected delegates to officially close the deal without the input of the so-called superdelegates. That meant that a long, messy battle would only grow longer and more contentious.

Obama was winning in a lot of states, but where he did lose, it was in the big states, making it easier for Clinton to argue that he was not capable of closing the deal. The basic outline of her argument to the superdelegates was that, to win the presidency, a Democrat had to be able to win the places that she had won: California, New York, New Mexico, Nevada, Texas, Ohio, and Pennsylvania. Obama's lead was made up of caucus states cobbled together with a bunch of red states that Democrats couldn't win in a general election.

After winning in Texas, Ohio, and Rhode Island on March 4, Clinton told her cheering supporters in Columbus, "You know, they call Ohio a bellwether state. It's a battleground state. It's a state that knows how to pick a president. And no candidate in recent history, Democrat or Republican, has won the White House without winning the Ohio primary."[13]

But Team Obama outhustled and outflanked Clinton. Even though March 4 was one of the worst nights of the campaign, Obama was able to say in San Antonio, before he knew the result, "No matter what happens tonight, we have nearly the same delegate lead as we did this morning, and we are on our way to winning this nomination."[14] Whatever lay ahead with the superdelegates, he was right, of course.

The Democrats in the freshman class of 2006 had tried to keep their campaign promises to their supporters. They had tried to stop the war in Iraq and had tried to do something about the creeping unease about the economy that they had heard as an undercurrent throughout their campaigns. They had even tried to address global warming and other climate change issues. With their swollen majorities in both the House and the Senate, they had tried to challenge the White House, but the executive had either prevailed or delayed action from the other side. Any fair assessment of the previous senatorial class was that they had failed.

In a session that was dominated by national electoral politics, individual senators were judged as representatives of national trends and issues rather than as representatives of their individual states. Jim Webb was high on the list of mentionable candidates for vice president, because the previous two elections were close enough that picking off one Republican state like Virginia would make the difference. Even Jon Tester's win in Montana was still being held up as evidence that a political realignment was taking place in the West and that this change would accrue to the benefit of the Democratic presidential nominee in 2008.

"This realignment has also come about because a new breed of Democrat has ridden into town. Montana provides a prime example," wrote David Horsey of the *Seattle Post-Intelligencer.* "There, voters have elected a Democratic governor, Brian Schweitzer [in 2004], and a new Democratic senator, Jon Tester, who are both ranchers. They don't carry themselves like citified Democrats in Seattle or Los Angeles or Boston. They don't scare their fellow ranchers with wild schemes to lock up the land and tax folks to death. They are genuine Democrats, but they speak with a Western twang and talk about common sense and common ground."[15]

At the congressional election in November 2008, the Democrats won even more seats—even though the wars in Iraq and Afghanistan were still raging and the economy was mired in the worst recession since the Great Depression. The global financial system, having survived the threat of catastrophic collapse, was now in tatters, having been pulled back from what people in Washington liked to call "the abyss." Democrats picked up at least seven more seats in the Senate and twenty-one more in the House

(Minnesota's Senate race was in the balance), meaning that the party had the largest majority margin in the Senate in more than thirty years: fifty-six Democrats to forty-one Republicans. And most stunningly, they won back the White House with the election of Barack Obama, who would become the first sitting senator in almost fifty years to be elected president. The Democrats seemed on the verge of some great destiny.

△

On January 6, 2009, a gray, drizzly day when the 111th Congress began, there was a new Senate class to swear in, and Democrats were jubilant. But even on the day of the swearing in, the newspapers were full of foreshadowing of the trouble ahead—and hints of how quickly success could turn to look like failure. The president-elect had proposed a stimulus package of almost $800 billion to help jump-start the economy. *The Washington Post* carried an article that morning reporting that Republicans were asking to help design the bill. That seemed an unlikely proposition since the GOP was already pointing to the Obama stimulus plan as an example of the president's big-spending tendencies. This was a theme that would last the entire first year of the Obama presidency. The highly touted and devoutly hoped-for "new tone" had failed to take hold in Washington; it had not in 2007 and it would not in 2009.

Vice President Dick Cheney swore in the new senators, and they would now have the chance to try to fulfill the promises made, not just in their own elections, but in Barack Obama's campaign as well. The new Democrats were Mark Begich (Alaska); Mark Udall (Colorado); Jeanne Shaheen (New Hampshire); Tom Udall (New Mexico); Kay Hagan (North Carolina); Jeff Merkley (Oregon); and Mark Warner of Virginia. Two freshmen Republicans had also won open seats: Jim Risch in Idaho and Mike Johanns in Nebraska.

The new Democrats were as hopeful as, maybe more so than, the class that preceded them. After all, in 2007 they began with fifty-one votes, and in 2009, they began with fifty-six—it would later grow to sixty—and control of the White House. Democratic leader Harry Reid had called it a mandate. "I think . . . that there is a wave of hope that swept the country," he had told an interviewer on NPR on election day, "not a mandate for any political party or any ideology, but a mandate to get over those things that divide us and focus on getting things done."[16]

But that was a difficult goal from the outset, in part because the Senate is designed to do less rather than more, and in part because the distractions began almost immediately. Michael Bennet, formerly the superintendent of Denver public schools and now the new senator from Colorado—appointed by the governor to replace Ken Salazar, who was leaving the Senate to become secretary of the interior—was not ready to be sworn in. Governor Bill Ritter had only made the replacement appointment on January 3. When Bennet was finally sworn in on January 21, he became, at forty-four, the youngest sitting senator. The Senate race in Minnesota between Democrat Al Franken and the incumbent Republican Norm Coleman was seemingly in limbo and would drag on for many months. And on the first day of the new Congress, the Democratic Senate refused to seat Roland Burris, the Illinois Democrat chosen to replace Barack Obama. Burris, a former state attorney general, had been appointed to the Obama seat by Governor Rod Blagojevich, who had been indicted and would later be impeached and removed from office.

At exactly noon on January 6, 2009, when Senate terms expire, the Senate chaplain, Barry Black, offered a benediction that was followed by the Pledge of Allegiance. Then Vice President Cheney announced: "The Chair lays before the Senate two certificates of election to fill unexpired terms and the certificates of election of 32 Senators, elected for 6-year terms beginning on January 3, 2009. All certificates, the Chair is advised, are in the form suggested by the Senate or contain all essential elements of the forms suggested by the Senate. If there be no objection, the reading of the above certificates will be waived and they will be printed in the Record."[17]

Joseph Biden, who had been reelected to his seventh term in the Senate, took the oath of office. (He would resign a few days later to take up the job of vice president, allowing his former chief of staff, Ted Kaufman, to be appointed to the seat.) Soon-to-be-confirmed cabinet secretaries Hillary Clinton, the junior senator from New York, and Ken Salazar, from Colorado, sat in the back row of seats looking like a couple of recent high school graduates visiting their old friends.

Tom Udall, the Democrat who had replaced Republican Wayne Allard of New Mexico, sat with his cousin, Mark, the newly elected senator from Colorado. The alphabetical order put them late in the process, but Mark Udall sat bolt upright in his chair when the second group took the oath, and he held his right palm against bright, overheard lights trying to find his family in the third-floor galleries. Democrats were getting ready to do big things. It was going to be their year.

△

Jon Tester got the first presiding shift of the New Year. He climbed to the podium just as Cheney was leaving. The two men whispered quietly and cordially as they passed each other. As he took his seat, Tester began to slightly rearrange the placement of the items on the desk. There was a pen holder for a pair of pens, a box with two grip gravels, two note cards, and a gooseneck microphone that he used to recognize speakers: "the senator from Alaska," or "the senator from Mississippi."

The clerk handed him a note. The first order of business was informing the president and the House of Representatives that the Senate had managed to get a quorum, swear in its new members, and was now in session. Then the moment had come to set a date and time for the counting of the electoral votes that would officially make Barack Obama the winner of the 2008 election. It was just a formality but a part of the Senate's ceremony. The date was set for two days later, and Tester pronounced it done. "Without objection, the concurrent resolution is considered and agreed to," he said.[18]

Harry Reid, using his privileges as leader, spoke first. He began with some history, reminding the Senate that Daniel Webster had laid the cornerstone for the Senate chamber where they were now meeting on July 4,

1851. It was the 150th year the Senate had met in that chamber, and today, Reid said, the Union of the United States was standing firm:

> When Vice President John Breckinridge gaveled the 34th Congress open in this Chamber in 1859, our Republic had a population of one-tenth what it is today. There were just 64 Senators. Each Senator enjoyed a little more leg room, and that is an understatement. Many of these desks we see behind me, and behind the Republican leader, are from the original Senators of this country. They are real old. This Chamber, for 150 years, has served as the primary working space for most Members. The first session held here 150 years ago began as it did today, with the Vice President of the United States administering the oath of office to new Members.[19]

Reid welcomed the nine new senators to "what many have said, and I agree, is the greatest deliberative body the world has ever known—certainly the greatest legislative body." He tried to sum up the challenges ahead in the context of the last Congress:

> It was just two years ago this inaugural day of Congress that we heralded a new majority for Democrats in both the Senate and House of Representatives, but in the Senate that was a very tenuous majority. We began with 51, but [South Dakota senator] Tim Johnson became very ill and the crowded Democratic primary field left us oftentimes short of an outright majority and far short of the 60 votes needed to prevent filibusters and pass legislation. Although we made substantial progress in the 110th Congress, partisanship with divided Government too often ruled the day.[20]

Now, with fifty-six or fifty-seven Democratic votes in hand—and inching toward sixty—Reid believed that he had enough votes to overcome that time of divisiveness.

When Barack Obama took office two weeks later, he had an approval rating in the upper sixties—over 60 percent of Americans approved of the job he was doing as president. People wanted change; Obama promised change. On January 20, 2009, on the West Front of the United States Capitol with his hand on a Bible used by President Abraham Lincoln, Barack Obama took the oath of office falteringly delivered by Chief Justice John G. Roberts after being hired by the American people to deliver on the promise.

On an otherwise quiet morning in late April 2009, news broke that Arlen Specter, the Pennsylvania Republican, would leave the Republican Party and become a Democrat. It seemed the final chapter in the steady decline of the GOP. Specter explained in a public statement:

> I have been a Republican since 1966. I have been working extremely hard for the Party, for its candidates and for the ideals of a Republican Party whose tent is big enough to welcome diverse points of view. While I have been comfortable being a Republican, my party has not defined who I am. I have taken each issue one at a time and have exercised independent judgment to do what I thought was best for Pennsylvania and the nation.[21]

Specter had looked at his team and decided that they had no chance, so he traded himself to the opposition. Republicans were a species under threat, and moderate Republicans like him were on the verge of extinction. Specter concluded that he could not win reelection in 2010 as a Republican, and so he switched parties. While the move made complete political sense, it raised questions about how much a senator's party should matter in transacting the nation's business. The answer today is "completely"—it seems increasingly that in the Senate the only thing that matters is which side you vote on, not the ideas you bring to the table, not the energy you bring to your work, only the side you cast your nays and yeas with.

In his farewell address to the Senate, delivered in December 1996, Paul Simon—who represented Illinois for twelve years from 1985 to 1997—

warned against the corrosive nature of partisanship. "Probably nothing adds to the public cynicism as much as the perceived sense that we are playing political games rather than serving the public need," Simon said.[22] He said the choosing of sides was bad for the country. "Thought leaders should replace cheerleaders." Simon died in 2003, but he would likely not be surprised to know that the problem he diagnosed in 1996 had by 2009 only metastasized into something much worse.

There were accomplishments the Democrats could point to in the first year of the Obama administration. They passed the president's $787 billion stimulus plan (the American Recovery and Reinvestment Act) in February, then spent $350 billion to bail out the banks, and finally appointed and got confirmed Sonia Sotomayor as the first Latina on the Supreme Court. But given the extraordinary run of success they'd had with the voters in 2006 and 2008, the collapse of the Democratic confidence over the course of 2009 was remarkably swift.

President Obama had decided on health care reform as his number one legislative and political priority, and he went to work on it immediately. Ever cognizant of the fact that many presidents before him had tried in vain to pass some kind of national health care legislation, Obama outlined his ambitions for the plan and then left the details to the Congress to work out. This approach was exactly the opposite of the detailed micromanagement that the Clinton administration had so unsuccessfully employed sixteen years earlier, and there was little doubt that some of what was driving the Obama White House was a desire not to repeat past mistakes.

Republicans, having tried unsuccessfully for months to find some line of attack against the Obama administration, suddenly found one in health care. As they attacked, characterizing the Obama plan as socialist, Republicans seemed to suddenly find their voice. At the same time, even as they proceeded with work on health care and other business, it was clear that Democrats were not as confident as they had been just a few months earlier.

They had lost elections in New Jersey and Virginia, the president's poll numbers were down, unemployment was rising, and the Republicans were finally finding their voice.

A serious and wide-ranging debate broke out about whether there should be a government-funded component in the health care proposal. This "public option," said proponents, would give the government leverage in negotiating prescription prices with drug manufacturers. The public option became enemy target number one of Republicans and conservatives who were packing health care town hall meetings to display their outrage but little else.

When even the White House started backing off slightly on health care, in the fall of 2009, Harry Reid wanted to bring a bill to the floor with the public option included. This was hard ball—only the most liberal members of the party were insisting on a public option—and Reid's determination to play tough was surprising, because the public blowback on health care had caused a lot of Democrats to scatter. Democratic senators like Ben Nelson, Mary Landrieu, and Blanche Lincoln were apprehensive that supporting health care—and especially a plan with a public option—would cost them politically with their constituents. For a long time, they hedged their bets.

But then, just after the Fourth of July 2009, Al Franken became a U.S. senator, and he was a Democrat. Reid finally had his sixtieth vote.

△

It should have been predictable that the Democrats' sixty-vote threshold would not be the umbrella solution that so many had expected. The most immediate effect it had was to raise expectations among frustrated Democratic constituencies. With President Obama in the White House, and solid controlling majorities in both the House and the Senate, it became more difficult to blame Republicans for stalling the Democratic agenda.

While having sixty votes gave Reid the flexibility to move important legislation, it also turned every Democratic senator into a kingmaker or a deal breaker. Franken was the fourteenth seat that Democrats had picked up since 2006, a mood swing to match the sixteen-seat gain that made Lyndon Johnson the majority leader in 1958. But majorities in the Senate are hard to manage, and supermajorities are superhard.

△

As the summer of 2009 wore on, the health care debate took on a new frame: the most intrusive government intervention ever versus the creation of a system allowing every American access to affordable, effective health care. The longer that health care reform was not passed, the more the president and his party looked ineffective on the issue, ineffectiveness that would cost them at the polls.

On November 3, 2009, election day in the off-year elections, all the Democrats' dire predictions came true. Democrats lost two gubernatorial races—New Jersey and Virginia. Incumbent New Jersey governor Jon Corzine, facing hugely unfavorable numbers and 56 percent disapproval going into the race, lost to former federal prosecutor Chris Christie. In Virginia, Democrats never seemed to have a prayer. Democratic nominee Creigh Deeds, a state senator, could never rise to the occasion; he was never in the same league as his GOP opponent, Bob McDonnell, and he lost.

These losses were seen as a blow to the Obama White House, and the Democrats' winning streak that had begun in 2006 was over. The president called the losers on election night, and the winners the next day. Jim Webb, watching his state shift back into the Republican column, appealed to the winners to work together with the losers: "I am very familiar with long and divisive campaigns," he said. "I am confident that we can put partisanship aside and work collectively to further the best interests of Virginia and our people."[23]

△

After months of haggling and deal making, the $871 billion health care bill finally came to the Senate floor for a vote on the morning of Christmas Eve, 2009. It was a monumental moment for Democrats.

Ninety-nine of the hundred senators were present for the votes—only Jim Bunning, Republican of Kentucky, did not cast a vote in the final roll call as part of a personal protest—he didn't think the Senate should be working on health care on Christmas Eve—saying he had "family commitments."[24] Senators voted from their seats as opposed to the usual practice of walking toward the clerk's desk as they enter the chamber, with a thumbs-up or a thumbs-down. Because of the importance of the bill, everyone was already in their seats for the vote. Democrats had the sixty votes they needed to end any Republican maneuvers, and they needed each and every one.

The weeks of negotiation had shown just exactly how powerful each senator can be when he or she is needed. Senator Ben Nelson of Nebraska became the poster child for heavy-handed dealing. Nelson got the federal government to pay to expand Nebraska's Medicaid program to all Nebraskans living below 133 percent of the federal poverty level, while other states have to pay a portion of those costs. Vermont's Bernie Sanders cut himself the same deal, but threatened not to vote for the bill.

The voting began at about 7:00 A.M. The first scare for Democrats came when the clerk called on the eighty-nine-year-old senator Robert F. Byrd. "Present" came the response. The chamber fell into a hush. "Present," instead of a "yes," was not a positive vote, and without sixty yes votes the bill would fail. After a few seconds ticked away, Byrd, now having the complete attention of his colleagues and everyone in the gallery, continued: "This is for my friend Ted Kennedy—yes." The sighs of relief came in a chorus.

The two Udall cousins sat with each other as they always do. The 2006 class—Jim Webb, Jon Tester, Claire McCaskill, and Sherrod Brown—huddled together on the right side of the chamber. "We call it the Dog Patch," Webb once said.[25] Amy Klobuchar sat next to Ben Nelson chatting. Missing was Bernie Sanders, who was running late.

Harry Reid had spent months working on this deal, and he had kept the Senate in session until Christmas Eve so he could line up all the yeas, go through the cloture motions, and finally get this vote. When the clerk called his name, "Mr. Reid of Nevada," the majority leader answered: "No." Laughter ensued. He put his head on his lectern in a show of exhaustion and embarrassment, then changed his vote.

At 7:15 A.M., Sanders came walking in from the south side of the chamber. He was greeted with Democratic applause. He voted on the run. "Mr. Sanders of Vermont."

"Yes."

The Democrats had what they had wanted.

Senators started drifting out, offering sound bites to the press on the fly. "[The bill] really fulfills the social contract we have with the American people," Barbara Mikulski told me on her way to the subway. Virginia freshman Mark Warner said he was worried now about the implementation of what had been passed. Warner, who had been governor of Virginia, said to me that Christmas Eve, as we were chatting in the basement of the Capitol, "The thing with legislation is that you pass it and then other people have to implement it, and that is the difference between a governor and a senator."

In the distance, Jon Tester, facing the long trip home to Montana, waved goodbye and drifted down the marble stairs and into a private office in the Capitol. In the two years he'd been in the Senate, things had changed enough that he had gone from being ranked number 100 to number 82.

It was time to go home.

EPILOGUE

September 8, 2009, was a historic day in the U.S. Senate. There was a single roll call vote that day, beginning at 5:31 P.M. As had been the practice in recent times, it was a cloture vote called by the Democratic leadership, one to end debate and head off a Republican filibuster. The underlying proposal itself might not seem worthy of a filibuster—a motion to create a non-profit quasi-governmental agency to promote the United States as a travel destination around the world. But the Republicans were filibustering everything. Cloture was invoked, 79 to 19, and the next day, at 4:47 P.M., the Travel Promotion Act of 2009 was put to a vote.

The bill passed by 79–19, the same margin that it had taken to end debate the day before, and the Corporation for Travel Promotion was established. The votes themselves would not normally have warranted much comment, but they were indeed historic. For the first time in forty-six years—since November of 1962, when Ted Kennedy was elected—the Senate roll call did not include a "Mr. Kennedy." For three years, from January 1965 to the summer of 1968, it had included a "Mr. Kennedy of Massachusetts" and a "Mr. Kennedy of New York," Robert F. Kennedy. Now, in 2009, the call passed from "Mr. Kaufman" to "Mr. Kerry" to "Ms. Klobuchar," and in so doing it signaled that the Senate had passed from one era to another. Ted Kennedy was dead.

Kennedy's death was not a surprise; he had been diagnosed with a cancerous brain tumor in May 2008 after he suffered a seizure and collapsed in Los Angeles. From the beginning the diagnosis was grim, but Kennedy, who had endorsed Barack Obama for president, seemed eager to follow the campaign through to its conclusion. In 2002, when he turned seventy, he had told me in an interview that he was confident that he would see another Democrat elected president in his lifetime. The 2004 presidential election looked promising for a while, with his fellow Bay Stater John Kerry as the nominee, but the election turned to disappointment.

In 2008, Kennedy threw not just his own considerable weight behind Obama, but rounded up the entire Kennedy clan to bestow the family's aura on the young senator from Illinois. Kennedy went out of his way to compare Obama to his assassinated brother-president and brushed aside complaints from the Clinton camp, especially President Bill Clinton, that Obama was not ready for the highest office in the land.

In a speech at American University in Washington in January 2008, flanked by Caroline Kennedy, Representative Patrick J. Kennedy, and the candidate, Ted gave Obama the endorsement of the whole Kennedy dynasty. "There was another time, when another young candidate was running for president and challenging America to cross a new frontier. He faced criticism from the preceding Democratic president, who was widely respected in the party," Kennedy said, referring to his brother Jack and Harry S. Truman. "And John Kennedy replied, 'The world is changing. The old ways will not do. It is time for a new generation of leadership.' So it is with Barack Obama."[1]

Kennedy would live to see Obama elected and Democrats expand their majorities in the Congress, and under these circumstances he was well positioned to lead the fight for Obama's top priority, health care reform. As chairman of the Health, Education, Labor, and Pensions Committee, this would have been his battle to fight. But he was sick, and when he died on August 25, 2009, there was a sense that he was so tied to the issue that his death might even help pass the bill. "I think it's going to help us," Harry Reid told the *Reno Gazette-Journal* with a certain lack of sensitivity. "He's an inspiration for us. That was the issue of his life and he didn't get it done."[2] The question was—could the Democrats pass this most contentious of bills even with their sixty votes?

There seemed to be little reason for Democrats to worry about losing control of the Kennedy seat. The governor of Massachusetts was a Democrat, and this was, after all, the most liberal state in the Union. Governor Deval Patrick appointed a caretaker senator, former chair of the Democratic National Committee Paul Kirk, to hold the seat until a special election to be held on January 19, 2010.

▲

President Obama had set the Senate the difficult task of passing the health care bill, and the Democratic Senate had gone about it diligently. The president knew as well as anyone that trying to get something done in the Senate is a task replete with political peril. He understood that it was much easier to be someone in the Senate than to do something. Remember, it was the very brevity of Obama's Senate tenure that made him such an attractive candidate for president—because a legislative record was not his priority, and as a result he had fewer enemies.

Now the president was demanding something different from those he'd left behind. And in fairness, he was demanding what the Founders envisioned—prudence, courage, and deliberate action—and what the American people said they wanted, a reform of the health care system.

In politics, things change over time and the mood of the country shifts, and often those shifts in mood show up in Senate election results. In Jim Webb's words, a new Senate class tells you what the country was thinking at the time.[3] In the fall of 2009, as the Democrats on both sides of the Capitol worked on health care, there was a growing sense that they were working on the wrong issue. The big national concern about the unemployment rate began to show up in polls and in the president's sinking job approval rating.

The country may have been nominally coming out of a recession, but the job market, where most people make their judgment about the health of the economy, was in the worst doldrums in decades. Jobs were being lost at the rate of hundreds of thousands a month, and in November the unemployment rate hit 10 percent for the first time in twenty-six years. Democrats began to panic, especially after the gubernatorial losses in New Jersey and Virginia on November 3. A flurry of jobs bills began making the rounds on the Hill, and the president held a "jobs summit" at the White House in early December.

Democrats in Congress recognized that the nation's focus had shifted. "Health-care reform is very important, but we need to move dramatically, quickly, and with real conviction to dealing with this economy and jobs," said Dick Durbin in December. "It's the number-one issue across America."[4]

President Obama went to China in November and addressed the home crisis from afar. "Our first job was to get the economy to recover, and we're now seeing that. We've seen economic growth. We anticipate economic growth next quarter as well. I always said that job growth would lag behind economic growth. The question now is how can we accelerate it?"[5] The big worry was that the acceleration was not happening fast enough.

It did not help the Obama administration that Republicans and other conservatives were trashing the health care plan at every opportunity, characterizing it as an expensive, budget-busting government takeover of American health care that was the first step to socialized medicine and socialism itself. And it helped even less that the White House and congressional Democrats did not have an adequate answer to this criticism.

Despite having control of all the levers of government, the Democratic wave that began in 2006 seemed to be cresting, and the downward spiral would begin in the Senate.

In late 2009, the Senate, on the issue of health care at least, seemed to be working the way it was intended—slowly. The Republican minority was living up to its appointed role of keeping the majority from making any rash decisions. If, in fact, health care reform was the result of a rash decision, the Senate system was working perfectly.

Republicans were forcing the Democrats to do it the hard way. The image of the legislative branch squabbling did not look like wise and prudent government, but the whole idea of the Senate is that the longer and harder it is to reach a decision, the better that decision is likely to be. Health care was taking a long time, and in the meantime the country was getting a look at the process, and not liking what they were seeing.

When Massachusetts voters went to the polls in January, the seat that had been solidly in Democratic hands since John F. Kennedy defeated Henry Cabot Lodge Jr. in 1952, was lost. Massachusetts elected a Republican named Scott Brown, and this cheered Republican spirits from coast to coast. The Kennedy seat was in enemy hands, and a lot of the assumptions Democrats made when they had sixty votes in the Senate were no longer operative. Topping the list was health care. The Senate bill needed to be reconciled with the House version before the president could sign it, and with only fifty-nine votes, Democrats were already conceding that the original conception of health care was dead.

Harry Reid was back in the same position he was in in the 110th Congress when he had fifty-one votes. Either he had sixty or he didn't. And now, once again, he didn't. Even President Obama conceded that there was a larger message in the Brown victory: "People are angry, and they're frustrated," he said in an interview with ABC News.[6]

But the realities of the national political environment overrode the importance of the sixty-vote threshold in the Senate. Democrats still had the White House and solid control of both houses of the legislature. If a Democratic president with fifty-nine Democratic votes in the Senate can't move his agenda, a large part of the problem has to lie with the Democrats, no matter how arduous the system or obstructionist the opposition. This is the embodiment of the Stunted Age—even when one side has huge majorities in both houses of Congress, the level of partisanship at play in Washington today still results in absolute gridlock.

The country had chosen the Democrats to lead a reversal in the nation's course after George W. Bush, and they had made some strides and kept some promises, but health care, like the drive to end the war in Iraq two years earlier, seemed destined to fail. Some will argue that repeated failure

is the role that the Senate is designed to fill in our system because those repeated failures pave the way for successes that represent a prudence and a
wisdom sure enough for the successes to survive beyond their own time.
This is the Senate's constitutional role, to instill in the national character the
longer-term view that does not come to us naturally as individuals in our
instant-gratification society.

Admittedly, it is hard to discern those high ideals in the day-to-day
workings of the modern Senate. And the longer view often means the next
election, but the process justifies itself if only by its longevity. In some cases
the only thing you can say to justify the way the Senate operates is that it has
been operating this way for a long time.

As we have seen, every senator comes to the Senate with high expectations and grand ambitions, and Scott Brown was no different. He promised
to kill the president's health care bill by voting no on it, and he warned Republicans that he was not always going to be a reliable party vote. Such is the
optimism of the novice.

In January 2010 there was a general sense among political insiders in
Washington that Scott Brown's election was a prelude to more Democratic
losses to come in the fall. There was an even chance that they would be
wrong. First off, on March 23, 2010, President Obama, in the White House
East Room, signed the Patient Protection and Affordable Care Act into law.
After more than fifteen months of negotiation and almost a century of debate, Obama and the Democrats had rewritten the national rules on health
care. And not even Scott Brown could stop it. It was a stark reminder that
success in American politics, especially in the Senate, demands both patience and stamina.

Sometimes victory does not pay the rewards one would expect. Democrats,
in 2009, controlled the White House and both chambers of Congress. The
margin in the Senate was enough to shut down a filibuster, but somehow
that did not prevent their mood from going sour. They did not absorb the

gubernatorial losses in New Jersey and Virginia well in November 2009. And in 2010, shortly after the Senate returned from the holiday break, two Democratic veterans—Chris Dodd of Connecticut and Byron Dorgan of North Dakota—announced that they would retire at the end of the year, declining to seek reelection.

These retirements were seen as concessions that both men would have had trouble getting reelected, but they were also crucial to important legislation going forward. Dorgan had been put in charge of writing a Democratic jobs bill at a time when jobs were the only political discussion on the table. Dodd, as chairman of the Banking Committee, was the man in charge of rewriting all the financial services legislation that was supposed to fix all problems in the financial sector.

Suddenly they were both gone, and the widely held political assessment was that they were leaving because their party was in trouble, or maybe the departure was a reflection of how much trouble the Democrats were facing in 2010. That said, Dodd's best friend in the Senate was Ted Kennedy, who had just died from complications of a cancerous brain tumor, and Dodd himself had been diagnosed with and treated for prostate cancer in the summer of 2009. He was sixty-five with two young children. It was possible that he wanted to walk away from the Senate for personal reasons. "I'm very proud of the job I've done and the results delivered," Dodd said announcing his retirement. "But none of us is irreplaceable. None of us are indispensable. And those who think otherwise are dangerous."[7] Dorgan was sixty-seven and had been in the Senate eighteen years, which may have been an incentive to leave. But North Dakota is an overwhelmingly Republican state in presidential elections, and that immediately gave rise to the idea that the consequence of his retirement would be a Democratic seat lost.

The sense of doom turned into a real crisis a few weeks later, when Indiana senator Evan Bayh announced his retirement and essentially said that he was leaving because Congress was dysfunctional. "There are many causes for the dysfunction: strident partisanship, unyielding ideology, a corrosive system of campaign financing, gerrymandering of House districts, endless filibusters, holds on executive appointees in the Senate, dwindling social interaction between senators of opposing parties and a caucus system that promotes party unity at the expense of bipartisan consensus," Bayh wrote in the *New York Times*.[8] Bayh's political calling card was his moderation; he was seen in some circles as the kind of politician that can keep his party from going off the deep end. He was a Democrat from a Republican state, and his resignation was marked as a defection, since Democrats would have great difficulty holding on to that seat as well.

Despite the fact that the Democratic retirements were being cast as the actions of desperate people abandoning a sinking ship, by the time Bayh decided to leave in February 2010, the number of veteran Democrats who had announced that they were leaving the Senate after the 2010 election—three—was half the number of Republicans who had already decided not to seek reelection. Florida's Mel Martinez decided to leave after one term, resigning early in the summer of 2009; Sam Brownback of Kansas was gone after two terms, resigning to run for governor. It seemed a safe bet that this seat would remain in GOP hands since Kansas has not elected a Democratic senator since 1932.

Democrats had a better chance in Kentucky, where, after months of public deliberation, Jim Bunning decided to leave, putting an end to one of the more bizarre Senate careers ever. Missouri's Kit Bond, who came to the Senate in 1986 as part of the last Reagan campaign, decided that twenty-four years was enough. Judd Gregg, the New Hampshire Republican, who was ready to leave the Senate to be Obama's commerce secretary before changing his mind, also announced his intention to leave, as did Ohio's George Voinovich, after two terms and twelve years.

So while Republicans and Democrats were defending an equal number of Senate seats in 2010, eighteen, Democrats seemed considerably gloomier about their prospects.

But Bayh is the perfect example of what the Senate can do to your political potential. His father was a senator. Bayh was a young governor whose moderate positions and Midwestern roots made him a potential candidate for president most of his life. He withdrew from the 2008 race for president early because he said he could not win. He may still run for president again, but for some people, once the Senate is no longer the springboard to the White House, the tedium and gridlock of the Upper House are seen for what they are—tedium and gridlock.

△

Perhaps the freshmen of 2006 and 2008, and even of 2010, will go on to greatness; perhaps their names will one day resonate through history like those of Muskie and Hart and McCarthy and Byrd and Kennedy and Webster and Calhoun and Clay. There is a certain temperament that thrives in this environment, in this unique journey that consists in serving the Senate. There are people who enjoy attending committee hearings, negotiating subparagraphs, appropriation bills, and learning the arcane language of the Senate rules. It is not a place without privileges—pages open the doors to the Senate chambers whenever a senator approaches, their water glasses come precisely as they prefer (with or without ice, half full or all the way to the brim), and some elevators in the Capitol and the Senate office buildings are for senators only. But sometimes an outsider is granted access.

I recall one afternoon in 2007 riding the "senators only" elevator with Amy Klobuchar, who proudly mentioned the Minnesota State Fair only to have the senators from Pennsylvania and Michigan, Bob Casey and Debbie Stabenow, claim to have bigger and better fairs in their respective states. Bragging on your state in a reserved elevator is very much the stuff of the Senate.

The freshman class of 2006 will face reelection in 2012, an election year in which their fortunes may be tied to their president's reelection chances. Those from red states or swing states—Tester from Montana, Webb from Virginia, McCaskill from Missouri, Sherrod Brown from Ohio, Klobuchar from Minnesota—all will likely draw serious challengers. But U.S. senators are uniquely positioned to separate themselves from their party and create an identity all their own. It is the power of being identified with an entire state.

Some of the 2006 class, history tells us, will go on to long careers in the Senate, because after one or two terms, incumbents in the Senate are increasingly hard to defeat, absent the kind of deep political disenchantment we saw in 2006 and 2008. Others will succumb to desire for a less frustrating existence and leave after one term or two. What we can be sure of is that some of them, on both sides of the aisle, will run for president. In early 2010, Republicans looking for a challenger to President Obama were already looking to the Senate. Senator John Thune of South Dakota, elected to the Senate in 2004 with Obama, was one of the early favorites. The list was sure to grow longer.

For those who stay, we know that if they succeed, it will take a long time to know what that success looks like because slow is the way of the Senate. All of the individual members of the 2006 class were able to establish themselves as serious players who had sufficiently learned the ways of the Senate to succeed in the long term. Bob Corker, the lone Republican in that class and one of those who was frustrated by the process very early on, had come to appreciate the deliberate and steady pace of the Senate. "You know you don't want it to move too fast. These are big issues that affect not just our country, but the world," Corker told me. "So no, you don't want to move that fast."[9]

Not to worry, it won't.

ACKNOWLEDGMENTS

This book, more than most, is the result of a lot of work by many people whose names do not appear of the cover. At times it took collaboration and patience, at others, progress came as a result of threats and coercion.

I am indebted to Ian Jackman for his exquisite help with the manuscript and Alessandra Bastagli for her patience and determination in getting this project across the finish line.

Of course, none of it would have been possible without the senators, their families, and the members of their staff who gave me access to their work, their lives, and in some cases their homes.

Amy Klobuchar took me to the Minnesota State Fair and changed my eating habits forever. Her husband, John Bessler, and daughter, Abigail, were very helpful in sharing stories about their changing lives as they adjusted to life in Washington.

Jon Tester saved my life—literally, when he rescued me from a blizzard in Big Sky Country. But he also, along with his wife Sharla, allowed me into his home and office to see what "senatoring" is like for a new member, and I am grateful to them for their help and generosity

Jim Webb is a writer and a thinker and was eager to help with the kinds of things a writer needs; for example, the difference between introverted and introspective, and how that might alter one's success in the U.S. Senate.

I thank Bob Corker for his willingness to talk longer than his gut told him to, as well as for his good humor and uncommon grace.

Ben Cardin, Bernie Sanders, Sheldon Whitehouse, Bob Casey, and Harry Reid all made time for me and added invaluable insights to the book.

My agent Jeff Kleinman deserves almost all the credit for the existence of this book and none of the blame for any of its deficiencies. Ivan Held was the best kind of friend always seeing the upside of every situation.

There is a long list of people who helped at crucial moments whom I will never be able to sufficiently thank. You know who you are and what you did. They include:

Linda Kulman, Lynette Clemetson, Ralph Alswang, Stephanie Schriock, Jessica Smith, Todd Womack, Laura Lefler-Herzog, Jim Brown, Jim Manley, Linda Lipsen, Marc Elias, Mary McMahon, Martin Paone, Trish Hoppey, Katherine Miller, Chris Mather, Amy Dacey, Bob Dove, Laura Dove, Dick Baker, Jennifer Luray, Mark Patterson, J. B. Poersch, Gwen Florio, Guadalupe Paz, Kevin O'Brien, Matt McKenna, Semonti Mustaphi Stephens, Linden Zakula, Anna Greenberg, Maria Speiser, Brian Schweitzer, Tod A. Martin, Marlene Samuel, and Allyson Samuel. The crew at the *American Prospect* that allowed me to think out loud about this book for a long time: Mark Schmitt, Mike Tomasky, Harold Meyerson, Phoebe Connelly, and Alexandra Gutierrez. Bernie Hamilton, Mary Ann Akers, Holly Yeager, Natalie Hopkinson, Nick Charles, Donna Cohen, Jeff Rickert, Chuck Enda, Marilyn Enda, Eve Sparberg, Marshall Sparberg.

Finally, to Ilana who has been the source of a very special kind of inspiration. (Are you still stuck on Chapter 8, Daddy?)

And most of all, my eternal gratitude and thanks to Jodi, the love of my life, who endured every bump along the way and without whom I'd be a much lesser person.

Terence Samuel
Washington, D.C.
March 2010

NOTES

AUTHOR'S NOTE

1. Tom Daschle, *Like No Other Time: The 107th Congress and the Two Years That Changed America Forever* (New York: Crown Books, 2003).
2. Ibid., 34.
3. All quotes from Trent Lott come from interviews with the author held in the majority leader's office in 2001, unless otherwise indicated.
4. The Leader's Lecture Series, May 23, 2001. The Leader's Lecture Series was a chance for distinguished former Senate leaders and other Americans to share their insights about the Senate's recent history and long-term practices. The lectures are delivered in the Capitol's historic Old Senate Chamber to an audience of current senators and specially invited guests from the executive branch, the diplomatic corps, the media, and private enterprise.

INTRODUCTION

1. "Obama in Senate: Star Power Minor Role," *New York Times*, March 9, 2008.
2. "A Rising Political Star Adopts a Low-Key Strategy," *Washington Post*, October 17, 2008.
3. "Obama in Senate: Star Power Minor Role," *New York Times*, March 9, 2008.
4. James Madison, *Federalist Papers*, no. 62.
5. Webb, interview by the author in his office, May 2007.
6. Madison, *Federalist Papers*, no. 63.
7. Jim Webb, *A Time to Fight: Reclaiming a Fair and Just America* (New York: Broadway Books, 2009).
8. "The Republican Assault on the Senate," *Time*, October 26, 1970.
9. Doug Willis, "Reagan Endorses U.S. Role in Vietnam, Calling It 'A Noble Cause,'" Associated Press, August 18, 1980.
10. Madison, *Federalist Papers*, no. 62.
11. *Congressional Record*, March 1, 2005.

CHAPTER ONE: ELECTION NIGHT

1. Tester, interview by the author at his home in Big Sandy, Montana, April 2007.
2. All quotes by Sharla Tester are from interviews conducted at the Tester home outside Big Sandy, Montana, April 2007.
3. "He shook my hand, introduced himself and then replied, 'What a piss poor job' we were doing. I replied, 'Have a nice day.'"—firefighter Gabe Templeton, on meeting Senator Conrad Burns. Charles S. Johnson, "Sen. Burns' Comments Detailed in Reports," *Missoulian*, August 1, 2000.
4. Senator Burns apologized to the Montana Equipment Dealers Association for "using a term pertaining to Arabs that I should not have used and which is widely considered offensive." Burns

told the association he "became too emotionally involved" in a February 17 speech to the group on U.S. dependence on foreign oil and called Mideast producers "ragheads." "I regret the use of such an inappropriate term," Burns said in a February 22 letter to association president Brad Griffin. He also apologized to "the people of the Radisson Northern Hotel" in Billings, where the group met, saying he was hoping to speak to the dealers again, "while at the same time choosing my words more carefully." Al Kamen, "Burns's A List: African Americans, Arabs," *Washington Post,* March 12, 1999.

5. "GOP Sen. Conrad Burns apologized Thursday for saying that living with blacks in the nation's capital is 'a hell of a challenge.' Burns said he made the remark in response to a rancher who had asked him, 'Conrad, how can you live back there with all those niggers?' In apologizing Thursday, Burns said he didn't use the racial epithet himself and was sorry he told a story that could suggest he shared the rancher's racist views." "Montana Senator Apologizes for Racial Slur," Associated Press, October 20, 1994.

6. "Last Friday, while speaking at a GOP rally in southwestern Virginia, Allen singled out Sidarth, a Webb volunteer, and called him 'Macaca.' He also said: 'Welcome to America and the real world of Virginia.' The term 'macaca' refers to a genus of monkey and is considered an ethnic slur in some cultures. Allen apologized, saying that he did not know what the word meant and that it was a play on 'Mohawk,' a nickname given to Sidarth by Allen's campaign staff because of his haircut. Allen's campaign has responded to the incident by accusing Webb of tolerating anti-Semitism." Tim Craig and Michael Shear, "Allen Flap May Give a Boost to Webb; Reenergized Va. Democrats Gain Support," *Washington Post,* August 19, 2006.

7. "Minnesota. The Democrats' most vulnerable seat is the one that Mark Dayton is giving up after just one term. The contest to succeed him is likely to become a classic open-seat struggle in which everything from candidate quality to campaign competence, fundraising, and the overall political climate matters. The Republican candidate is Rep. Mark Kennedy, who was first elected in the 6th Congressional District in 2000 after a career in corporate finance; he has been battle-tested by difficult reelection campaigns. The likely Democratic nominee is Hennepin County Attorney Amy Klobuchar, who might face veterinarian Ford Bell in the September primary." Jennifer E. Duffy, "How Many GOP Losses?" *National Journal,* May 6, 2006.

8. Manley, interview by author, Washington, D.C., spring 2007.
9. Katherine Miller, interview by author, Washington, D.C., December 2006.
10. Tester, interview by author at his home in Big Sandy, Montana, April 2007.
11. Ibid.
12. Ibid.
13. McMahon, telephone interview by author, spring 2007.
14. Schweitzer, telephone interview by author, May 2007.
15. Ibid.
16. McMahon, telephone interview by author, spring 2007.
17. Katherine Miller, interview by author, Washington, D.C., December 2006.
18. Schweitzer, telephone interview by author, May 2007.
19. Tester, interview by author, Washington, D.C., spring 2007.
20. NBC News Transcripts, November 8, 2006.

CHAPTER TWO: THE GREAT REVERSES

1. Jim Webb, *A Time to Fight: Reclaiming a Fair and Just America* (New York: Broadway Books, 2009).
2. Thomas E. Mann and Norman J. Ornstein, *The Broken Branch: How Congress Is Failing America and How to Get It Back on Track* (Westport, Conn.: Praeger, 1977).
3. Thomas E. Mann and Norman J. Ornstein, "When Congress Checks Out," *Foreign Affairs,* November/December 2006.
4. Mann and Ornstein, *The Broken Branch.*
5. Interview with the author, Washington, D.C., Spring 2007.
6. Ben Cardin, interview with the author, Washington, D.C., March 28, 2007.
7. "Poll: No Role for Government in Schiavo Case," *ABC News,* March 21, 2005.

8. *Congressional Record,* March 20, 2005.

9. *Congressional Record,* May 24, 2005.

10. The fourteen senators: Republicans Chafee, Collins, DeWine, Graham, McCain, Snowe, and Warner and Democrats Byrd, Inouye, Landrieu, Lieberman, Nelson, Pryor, and Salazar.

11. "Compromised Compromise," *American Prospect,* May 27, 2005.

12. *Will the November Elections Help Mend the Broken Branch?* Transcript, Brookings Institution, Tuesday, October 31, 2006.

13. President Woodrow Wilson, speech to Congress on April 2, 1917.

14. Text of the Act, *Congressional Record.*

15. Text of the Act, *Congressional Record.*

16. President Woodrow Wilson, speech to Congress, April 2, 1917.

17. Ibid.

18. Senate Historical Office, "A Bitter Rejection," *Historical Minute Essays,* November 19, 1919.

19. United Press International, October 25, 1986.

20. Ibid.

21. Tower Commission Report (Report of the President's Special Review Board), February 26, 1987 (Washington, D.C.: U.S. Government Printing Office).

22. "The Battle Over Bork: Senate Liberals Will Try to Block Nominee on Ideological Grounds," *New York Times,* July 5, 1987.

23. *Washington Post,* November 19, 1989.

24. "You start to read Robert Bork that quote. He is in the Grand Hyatt in New York City. He cuts you off. 'You don't have to read me that quote. You think I'm going to forget that quote? That quote's burned into me.' He adds: 'In point of fact, that entire statement had little to do with my whole position on abortion.'" (*Washington Post,* March 10, 1989.)

25. "Reagan's Revolution Ended?" *New York Times,* November 9, 1986.

26. Presidential news conference at the White House, November 8, 2006.

27. Ibid.

28. Anonymous interview with author.

29. Jim Webb, *A Time to Fight,* p. 13.

CHAPTER THREE: ORIENTATION

1. Jon Tester, interview by author, Big Sandy, Montana, April 2007.

2. Bernie Sanders, interview by author, Capitol Hill, spring 2007.

3. Laurie Kellman, "Senate Dems Pick Leaders," Associated Press, November 13, 2006.

4. Bob Casey, interview by author, spring 2007.

5. "'I'm not particularly interested in having a picture of me and George W. Bush on my wall,' Webb said in an interview yesterday in which he confirmed the exchange between him and Bush. 'No offense to the institution of the presidency, and I'm certainly looking forward to working with him and his administration. [But] leaders do some symbolic things to try to convey who they are and what the message is.'" Jim Webb, quoted in the *Washington Post,* November 29, 2006.

6. Robert C. Byrd, interview by author, Capitol, spring 2007.

7. J. B. Poersch, interview by author, Offices of the Democratic Senatorial Campaign Committee, March 2007.

8. News conference, majority leader's conference room, November 13, 2006.

9. Interview with author, April 2007, at his home in Big Sandy, Montana.

10. "Class Struggle: American Workers Have a Chance to Be Heard," *Wall Street Journal,* November 15, 2006.

11. "Newcomers Prepare for the 110th Congress," *Minneapolis Star Tribune,* November 13, 2006.

12. Ibid.

13. The Seventh of March Speech, "A Speech Cost a Senator His Seat," Senate Historical Office, March 7, 1850.

14. Ibid.

15. Amy Klobuchar, interview by author, Capitol Hill, April 9, 2007.

16. Ibid.
17. Josephine Marcotty, "The Life of Amy Klobuchar: Painful Times With Dad Help Create a Drive to Succeed," *Minneapolis Star Tribune,* October 8, 2006.
18. Ibid.
19. Ibid.
20. Amy Klobuchar, *Uncovering the Dome* (Prospect Heights, Ill.: Waveland Press, 1982).
21. Klobuchar interview, Washington, D.C., April 9, 2007.
22. Marcotty, "The Life of Amy Klobuchar."
23. Ibid.
24. Ibid.
25. Ibid.
26. Mark Dayton, "The Blunderer," *Time,* April 14, 2006.
27. Amy Klobuchar, interview by author, Capitol Hill, April 9, 2007.
28. Ibid.
29. Ibid.
30. Ibid.
31. "Newcomers Prepare for the 110th Congress," *Minneapolis Star Tribune.*
32. Ibid.

CHAPTER FOUR: SWEARING IN

1. Text of the oath: Senate Historical Office, Institutional Origins and Development.
2. Author's personal observation.
3. "Smiles, Backslaps, Even a Civility Meeting: For a Day, at Least, Bipartisanship Reigns," *New York Times,* January 5, 2007.
4. Ibid.
5. *Congressional Record,* January 4, 2007, S04.
6. Ibid., S11.
7. Frank Luntz, "Foley: The Final Straw," *Time,* October 7, 2006.
8. Brendan Daly, interview by author, spring 2005.
9. "Jim Webb Takes the Oath as US Senator From Virginia," *Virginia-Pilot,* January 5, 2007.
10. Jim Webb, interview by author, Capitol Hill office, spring 2007.
11. "A Hero's Welcome for Webb in the Senate," *Richmond Times-Dispatch,* January 5, 2007.
12. Webb, interview.
13. Harry Reid, interview, Reid's office, spring 2007.
14. Webb, interview.
15. Jim Manley, interview by author, Washington, D.C., summer 2007.
16. Webb, interview.
17. Manley, interview.
18. Webb, interview.
19. Ibid.
20. *Congressional Record,* January 25, 2007.
21. "Webb Says Bush Took Us to War 'Recklessly,'" CNN, January 24, 2007. Available at www.cnn.com/2007/POLITICS/01/23/sotu.webb . . . /index.html.
22. Brent Budowsky, "State of the Union: Jim Webb for Vice President," *Huffington Post,* January 19, 2007.

CHAPTER FIVE: DEBATE AND RESOLUTION

1. *Congressional Record,* February 1, 2007, S1470.
2. George W. Bush, "What the Congress Can Do for America: Let Them Say of These Next Two Years: We Used Our Time Well," *Wall Street Journal,* January 3, 2007.
3. Jeff Zeleny, "Awaiting Bush's Iraq Plan, Democrats Weigh Replies," *New York Times,* January 4, 2007.

4.   Katrina vanden Heuvel, "The Cost of War in Treasure and Lives," *The Nation,* http://www.then-ation.com/blogs/edcut/157755.

5.   *Congressional Record,* February 1, 2007, S1475.

6.   "Bush Speech Excerpts: The Caucus Blog," *New York Times,* January 27, 2007.

7.   State of the Union address by President Bush, January 23, 2007.

8.   NPR Transcripts, NPR Interview with President Bush, January 29, 2007.

9.   Ibid.

10. *Congressional Record,* February 5, 2007.

11. Martin Paone, interview by the author, Capitol, spring 2007.

12. *Congressional Record,* February 1, 2007, S1469.

13. Interview by the author, in Whitehouse's office, spring 2007.

14. *Congressional Record,* February 1, 2007, S1469.

15. In part, the amendment read: "It is the sense of Congress that—

(1) the Senate disagrees with the 'plan' to augment our forces by 21,500, and urges the President instead to consider all options and alternatives for achieving the strategic goals set forth below;
(2) the Senate believes that the United States should continue vigorous operations in Anbar province, specifically for the purpose of combating an insurgency, including elements associated with the Al Qaeda movement, and denying terrorists a safe haven;
(3) the Senate believes a failed state in Iraq would present a threat to regional and world peace, and the long-term security interests of the United States are best served by an Iraq that can sustain, govern, and defend itself, and serve as an ally in the war against extremists;
(4) the Congress should not take any action that will endanger United States military forces in the field, including the elimination or reduction of funds for troops in the field, as such action with respect to funding would undermine their safety or harm their effectiveness in pursuing their assigned missions . . ."

16. "Embracing Failure," *American Prospect,* February 2, 2007.

17. *Congressional Record,* February 5, 2007.

18. In full, the resolution read: "That—

(1) Congress and the American people will continue to support and protect the members of the United States Armed Forces who are serving or who have served bravely and honorably in Iraq; and
(2) Congress disapproves of the decision of President George W. Bush announced on January 10, 2007, to deploy more than 20,000 additional United States combat troops to Iraq."

19. Whitehouse, interview by author, in his office, May 2007.

20. Ibid.

21. "Leading Democrat Says Party Leaders Must Not Yield on War," *USA Today,* April 12, 2007.

22. From a press conference in the Senate radio TV Gallery in March 2007.

23. Capitol Hill press conference, April 12, 2007.

24. Ibid.

25. "Senate Passes War Spending Bill With Iraq Deadline," *New York Times,* March 29, 2007.

26. Harry Reid, Capitol Hill press conference, March 29, 2007.

27. White House Transcripts, WhiteHouse.Gov, March 29, 2007.

28. Russ Feingold, interview by author at the Capitol, April 13, 2007.

29. Sanders, interview by author, in his office, April 2007.

30. *Congressional Record,* May 1, 2007, 4.

31. Ibid., May 24, 2007, 6840.

32. Ibid., S6822.
33. Cindy Sheehan, "An Open Letter to the Democratic Congress: Why I Am Leaving the Democratic Party," *CounterPunch*, May 28, 2007. It read:

"Dear Democratic Congress,
Hello, my name is Cindy Sheehan and my son Casey Sheehan was killed on April 04, 2004 in Sadr City, Baghdad, Iraq. He was killed when the Republicans still were in control of Congress. Naively, I set off on my tireless campaign calling on Congress to rescind George's authority to wage his war of terror while asking him 'for what noble cause' did Casey and thousands of other have to die. Now, with Democrats in control of Congress, I have lost my optimistic naiveté and have become cynically pessimistic as I see you all caving in to 'Mr. 28%.'"

CHAPTER SIX: MEANWHILE, BACK IN THE STATE

1. In this chapter, unless otherwise noted, all quotes from Jon and Sharla Tester are from interviews at their home in Big Sandy, Montana, in April 2007.
2. Webb, interview by author, Washington, D.C., spring 2007.
3. Tester, interview by author, Washington, D.C., March 2007.
4. Tester, interview by author, Billings, Montana, April 2007.
5. *Congressional Record,* June 19, 2007.
6. Tester, interview by author, Washington, D.C., July, 17, 2007.

CHAPTER SEVEN: WHAT A SENATOR LOOKS LIKE

1. John Bessler, interview by author, Washington, D.C., June 2007.
2. Lee Sheehy, Minnesota Morning, Klobuchar offices, Washington, D.C., June 2007.
3. Amy Klobuchar, interview by author, Washington, D.C., June 2007.
4. Klobuchar, "Senator Mom," Online Chat, *Washington Post,* July 20, 2007.
5. Klobuchar, interview by author, U.S. Capitol, May 20, 2007.
6. Quoted by Klobuchar, ibid.
7. Klobuchar, interview by author, April 16, 2007.
8. *Congressional Record,* June 20, 2007.
9. Klobuchar, interview by author, U.S. Capitol, May 20, 2007.
10. *Congressional Record,* May 20, 2007.
11. Ibid.
12. Ibid.
13. Klobuchar, interview by author, U.S. Capitol, May 20, 2007.
14. Ibid.
15. *Congressional Record,* July 18, 2007.
16. Robin Givhan, "Hillary Clinton's Tentative Dip Into New Neckline Territory," *Washington Post,* July 20, 2007.
17. McCaskill, press release, October 4, 2007, available at mccaskill.senate.gov.
18. David McCullough, *Truman* (New York: Simon & Schuster, 1992), 664.
19. McCaskill, phone interview by Washington reporters, from Kuwait, June 20, 2007.
20. Author present at event Minnesota Science Museum, St. Paul, Minnesota, August 25, 2007.
21. "Sen. Klobuchar Opens State Fair Office," press release, August 24, 2007.
22. Klobuchar and Abigail, interview by author, Minnesota State Fair, August 25, 2007.
23. Ibid.
24. Ibid.
25. Mark Dayton, interview by author, Falcon Heights, Minnesota, August 25, 2007.
26. "Klobuchar Endorses Obama," *Washington Post,* March 31, 2007.
27. Ibid.

CHAPTER EIGHT: ODD MAN OUT

1. *Shelbyville Times-Gazette,* April 16, 2007.
2. Jodi Enda, "Great Expectations," *American Prospect,* January 2006.
3. Jennifer Rubin, "The Man of Nitty Gritty," National Review Online, March 13, 2007.
4. Unless otherwise noted, all quotes from Corker in this chapter are from interviews in his office in Washington, D.C., May 16, 2007.
5. Victory speech by Bob Corker, Corker Election Headquarters, Chattanooga, Tennessee, Federal News Transcripts, November 8, 2006.
6. Jessica Holzer, "Meet Senator Millionaire," Forbes.com, November 20, 2006. Among the other incoming senators, Sheldon Whitehouse's portfolio was worth $4 million to $14 million and Jim Webb's $2.3 million to $6.9 million. Sherrod Brown, Bob Casey, and Bernie Sanders each declared less than $500,000 in assets.
7. Corker, interview by author, Senate Office, October 1, 2007.
8. From town meeting in Tennessee on October 9, 2007.
9. Ibid.
10. From travels with Corker in Tennessee, October 9, 2007.
11. Ibid.
12. Ibid.
13. Ibid.

CHAPTER NINE: HARRY REID, FIRST AMONG EQUALS

1. The minimum wage was introduced under the Fair Labor Standards Act of 1938, beginning at twenty-five cents. In 1997 the wage stood at $5.15; the Fair Minimum Wage Act of 2007 raised the rate first to $5.85, to $6.55 in 2008, and to $7.25 in 2009.
2. *Congressional Record,* November 6, 2007, S13945.
3. Ibid.
4. Ibid.
5. Ibid., S13946.
6. All quotes from Harry Reid come from interviews with the author held in the majority leader's office in November 2007, unless otherwise noted.
7. 1 Sam. 17:42.
8. *Congressional Record,* November 16, 2007.
9. Fahrenkopf, phone interview by author, November 2007.
10. David S. Broder, "The Democrats' Gonzales," *Washington Post,* April 26, 2007.
11. Jim Manley, interview by author, Washington, D.C., spring 2007.
12. Politico.com, November 24, 2009.
13. Tester, interview by author, November 2007.
14. Fahrenkopf, phone interview by author, November 2007.
15. Ibid.
16. Harry Reid, *The Good Fight* (New York: Putnam, 2008).

CHAPTER TEN: HOW NOT TO END A WAR

1. The amendment's purpose: "To require the redeployment of United States Armed Forces from Iraq in order to further a political solution in Iraq, encourage the people of Iraq to provide for their own security, and achieve victory in the war on terror."
2. *Congressional Record,* June 2007.
3. James Webb, interview by author, in his office, April 29, 2007.
4. Ibid.
5. National Press Club transcripts, March 22, 2007.
6. Ibid.

7. Webb, interview by author, in his office, August 1, 2007.
8. Ibid.
9. Ann Scott Tyson and Josh White, "Strained Army Extends Tours to 15 Months," *Washington Post*, April 12, 2007.
10. Webb, interview, August 1, 2007.
11. *Congressional Record*, July 11, 2007.
12. Ibid.
13. Ibid.
14. Seven Republicans voted in favor of the amendment: Chuck Hagel, Olympia Snowe, John Warner, John Sununu, Norm Coleman, Gordon Smith, and Susan Collins.
15. *Congressional Record*, July 11, 2007.
16. Ibid.
17. *Congressional Record*, September 18, 2007.
18. Ibid.
19. *Congressional Record*, July 17, 2007.
20. Webb, interview, August 1, 2007.

CHAPTER ELEVEN: WHEN FAILURE LOOKS LIKE SUCCESS

1. "Warner Calls On Bush to Withdraw Troops," ABCNEWS.com, August 23, 2007.
2. Mark Mazetti, "U.S. Intelligence Offers Grim View of Iraqi Leaders," *New York Times*, August 24, 2007.
3. Transcript, *Meet the Press*, August 26, 2007.
4. Ibid.
5. Ibid.
6. Hope Yen, "GOP Senator May Back Dems on Withdrawal," Associated Press, August 26, 2007.
7. Warner, *Meet the Press* transcripts, August 26, 2007.
8. Ibid.
9. *Congressional Record*, September 4, 2007.
10. John Bresnahan and Martin Kady II, "Democrats Retreat on War End," Politico.com, September 5, 2007.
11. Capitol press conference at the Ohio Clock, July 2007.
12. *Congressional Record*, September 4, 2007.
13. MoveOn.org, *New York Times* ad, September 10, 2007.
14. Transcript of hearings before Senate Arms Services Committee, September 10, 2007.
15. CQ transcripts, "Bush Addresses Petraeus Report," September 19, 2009.
16. CNN transcripts, "Sen. Jack Reed Responds to President Bush's Address on Iraq," September 13, 2007.
17. Federal News Service, press conference with Senate Majority Leader Harry Reid, Senate Radio-TV Gallery, Washington, D.C., September 12, 2007.
18. NPR transcripts, text of President Bush's Speech on Troop Levels, January 10, 2007: "This new strategy will not yield an immediate end to suicide bombings, assassinations, or IED attacks. Our enemies in Iraq will make every effort to ensure that our television screens are filled with images of death and suffering. Yet over time, we can expect to see Iraqi troops chasing down murderers, fewer brazen acts of terror, and growing trust and cooperation from Baghdad's residents. When this happens, daily life will improve, Iraqis will gain confidence in their leaders, and the government will have the breathing space it needs to make progress in other critical areas."
19. Chuck Hagel, interview by author, August 15, 2005.
20. *Congressional Record*, September 19, 2007.
21. Harry Reid, press conference at the Capitol, September 12, 2007.
22. Shailagh Murray and Jonathan Weisman, "Longer Leaves for Troops Blocked," *Washington Post*, September 20, 2007.
23. *Congressional Record*, September 19, 2007.
24. Ibid.

25. Ibid.

26. Ibid.

27. Ibid.

28. Ibid.

29. Harry Reid, interview by author, November 16, 2007.

30. Ibid.

31. Ibid.

32. Greg Sargent, "Reso Condemning MoveOn Passes Overwhelmingly, With Lots of Dems," TalkingPointsMemo.com, September 20, 2007.

33. *Congressional Record,* November 5, 2007.

34. Shailagh Murray, "A New Democratic Split Over Iran," WashingtonPost.com, November 1, 2007.

35. The text of the letter:

Dear President Bush:
We are writing to express serious concerns with the provocative statements and actions stemming from your administration with respect to possible U.S. military action in Iran. These comments are counterproductive and undermine efforts to resolve tensions with Iran through diplomacy.

We wish to emphasize that no congressional authority exists for unilateral military action against Iran. This includes the Senate vote on September 26, 2007 on an amendment to the FY 2008 National Defense Authorization Act. This amendment, expressing the sense of the Senate on Iran, and the recent designation of the Quds Force of the Iranian Revolutionary Guard as a Specially Designated Global Terrorist, should in no way be interpreted as a predicate for the use of military force in Iran.

We stand ready to work with your administration to address the challenges presented by Iran in a manner that safeguards our security interests and promotes a regional diplomatic solution, but we wish to emphasize that offensive military action should not be taken against Iran without the express consent of Congress.

Sincerely,
[signed] Jim Webb, Daniel Akaka, Max Baucus, Barbara Boxer, Sherrod Brown, Robert Byrd, Maria Cantwell, Tom Carper, Robert Casey Jr., Hillary Rodham Clinton, Chris Dodd, Byron Dorgan, Richard Durbin, Dianne Feinstein, Tom Harkin, Tim Johnson, John Kerry, Amy Klobuchar, Herb Kohl, Patrick Leahy, Claire McCaskill, Barbara Mikulski, Patty Murray, Jack Reed, John D. Rockefeller IV, Bernard Sanders, Debbie Stabenow, Jon Tester, Sheldon Whitehouse, Ron Wyden.

36. Jon Tester, interview by author, Washington, D.C., November 2007.

37. *Congressional Record,* December 19, 2007, S15982.

38. Bishop Phillips Brooks, "Everywhere, Everywhere, Christmas Tonight: A Christmas Carol" (1835–1893).

CHAPTER TWELVE: WHEN SUCCESS LOOKS LIKE FAILURE

1. Democratic leadership press conference in the Capitol with reporters, including the author, April 12, 2007.

2. Transcript of the Maria Leavy Breakfast Series, Sen. Harry Reid, May 12, 2008.

3. CNN transcript, "The President Addresses the Market . . . ," January 18, 2008.

4. *Congressional Record,* January 22, 2008.

5. Ibid.

6. Of the nine, Claire McCaskill was not a signatory.

7. Peter Cohn, "Get-Tough-on-China Sentiment Re-Emerges" *Congress Daily,* February 1, 2008.

8. Political Transcript Wire, "Democratic Members of the Senate Hold a News Conference on Foreclosures," February 26, 2008.
9. Ibid.
10. Jim Webb, *A Time to Fight: Reclaiming a Fair and Just America* (New York: Broadway Books, 2008).
11. Woodrow Wilson, *Congressional Government* (Baltimore: Johns Hopkins University Press, 1981).
12. Baldwin and Baker, "President Bush Regrets His Legacy as Man Who Wanted War," TimesOnline, June 11, 2008.
13. Transcript at nytimes.com/2008/03/04/us/politics/04text-clinton.html. For a discussion of how Clinton was wrong, go to washingtonpost.com/fact-checker/2008/03/clinton_stumbles _on_ohio_histo.html.
14. Dan Balz and Jon Cohen, "Clinton Beats Obama in Texas and Ohio; McCain Clinches Republican Nomination," *Washington Post*, March 5, 2008.
15. David Horsey, "How the White House May Be Won—in the West," *Seattle Post-Intelligencer*, January 20, 2008.
16. NPR transcripts, Harry Reid, November 4, 2008.
17. *Congressional Record*, January 6, 2009.
18. Ibid.
19. Ibid.
20. Ibid.
21. Statement released by the office of Senator Arlen Specter, April 28, 2009.
22. Norman J. Ornstein, *Lessons and Legacies: Farewell Addresses From the Senate* (Reading, Mass.: Addison-Wesley, 1997).
23. Evan McMorris-Santoro, "Jim Webb Congratulates McDonnell, Appeals for Bipartisanship," Talking Points Memo, November 3, 2009.
24. David M. Herszenhorn, "Bunning Benches Self on Health Care Votes," *New York Times*, December 24, 2009.
25. Webb, interview by author, in Webb's office, August 2008.

EPILOGUE

1. Jeff Zeleny, "Kennedy Backs Obama With 'Old Politics' Attack," *New York Times*, January 20, 2008.
2. Harry Reid, interview by author, *Reno Gazette-Journal*, August 29, 2009.
3. Harry Reid, interview by author, in Webb's office, Washington, D.C., April 29, 2007.
4. CNN transcripts, December.
5. "Obama: Too Much Debt Could Fuel Double-Dip Recession," November 18, 2009, available at reuters.com/article/idUSN188205120091118.
6. ABC News transcripts, January 19, 2010.
7. Huma Khan, Matthew Jaffe, and David Challen, "Sen. Chris Dodd Announces Retirement From Senate, Will Finish Term," ABCNews.com, January 6, 2010.
8. Evan Bayh, "Why I'm Leaving the Senate," *New York Times*, February 20, 2010.
9. Bob Corker, interview by author, in Corker's office, Washington, D.C., May 16, 2007.

INDEX